Monuments of Central Asia

MONUMENTS OF CENTRAL ASIA

A Guide to the Archaeology, Art and Architecture of Turkestan

Edgar Knobloch

I.B. Tauris *Publishers*

LONDON • NEW YORK

Published in 2001 by I.B.Tauris & Co Ltd
6 Salem Road, London W2 4BU
175 Fifth Avenue, New York NY 10010
www.ibtauris.com

In the United States and Canada distributed by St. Martin's Press
175 Fifth Avenue, New York NY 10010

ISBN 1 86064 590 9

A full CIP record for this book is available from the British Library
A full CIP record for this book is available from the Library of Congress

Library of Congress catalog card: available

Typeset in Garamond by Dexter Haven, London
Printed and bound in Great Britain

CONTENTS

LIST OF MAPS AND PLANS

PREFACE

When I first travelled in Central Asia, in 1959, the Soviet Union was a super-power, Khrushchev's 'virgin lands' campaign was in full swing and Central Asia was a closed country. In most places my friend and I were probably the only foreigners the locals had ever seen. There was no tourism. The local Party organisation had the magic wand. It could find a room in an overcrowded hotel, get a light plane to drop us at a site in the desert, even send a parcel from the local post office. We travelled by public transport, trains and buses, and some-times even by car, courtesy of the almighty Party. The roads were thronged with donkey-carts, horse-wagons, camels and lorries and an occasional bus. Cars were almost non-existent. We slept in local inns, the *mehman-khanas*, in ancient hotels dating from tsarist times or in various establishments destined for the apparatchiks travelling on a *komandirovka* (assignment). The only hotel worth its name was in Tashkent, where we started and finished our journey. We were, of course, closely surveyed. We had to argue constantly about our programme, which was repeatedly altered, scrapped, then allowed to go ahead again. We had to see things we did not want to see and were not allowed to go where we wanted to. But people, although they were sometimes reticent and cagey, were kind and helpful. In museums, we could take artefacts out into the courtyard to photo-graph them. On the other hand, the country police were wary of our cameras, and more than once wanted to confiscate them. There were no markets. Meat was sold in tiny scraps from fly-ridden stalls, but the *plov* (*pilaf*) and kebab sold in the streets tasted delicious.

How things change. In 1997, on my second visit, the Soviet Union was no more, Khrushchev was as good as forgotten, and the Central Asian republics, now independent, were called Uzbekistan, Kazakhstan, Tajikistan, Kirghizstan and Turkmenistan. Frunze was again Bishkek, Stalinabad had metamorphosed into Dushanbe, Leninabad into Khodzhend. Istanbul had replaced Moscow as the main port of entry. Camels had disappeared from the streets, horse-wagons had been converted into cars, and mobile phones were more frequent than donkeys. In offices and banks abacuses sat next to computers. Every village had a lively market, butchers' stalls had refrigerators and meat was sold in decent-sized cuts. In the main cities, Indian companies had built luxury hotels which the local staff still had some difficulties running. Tourists were everywhere. Foreign pilgrims flocked to the holy places and prayed in local mosques. On the other hand, frontiers had sprung up where none had been before, and visas were required at every crossing. Forms, in Cyrillic only, had to be meticulously filled in and checked, only to be stacked away and never looked at again. But in the streets, Cyrillic was in retreat, making way for a Latin alphabet modelled on Turkish.

And the women – tall, leggy girls in fashionable dresses replaced the shapeless things in their hideous *parandzhas,* looking like cloth sacks. The progress of urbanisation was in evidence everywhere.

The famous monuments had been restored and rebuilt, some more skillfully than others. Tilla Kari had acquired a bulbous dome which it never had, the Gur Emir had got back its gleaming interior of shining gold which, perhaps, it had when it was new. Only Khiva was a disaster. Some clever head had had the idea to make it into a museum city. So people had been resettled, rubble removed, crumbling walls restored, peeling tilework replaced. Gone were the camels loaded with brushwood, donkeys, stray cats and mangy dogs. There were workmen in overalls instead of playing children. The bearded old men in their leather boots and quilted *khalats* were gone.

On the Chinese side, Xinjiang is gradually opening up but still suffers much of the 'Soviet disease'. Tourist facilities are few and inefficient, although accommodation is, by and large, acceptable. Movement is, like in the USSR, tightly controlled, but the bland Russian 'nyet' comes here as a polite Chinese promise which never materialises. The Silk Route is fast becoming a popular tourist destination, but its southern branch is still quite difficult to get to. And the crossing of the Karakorum Range into Pakistan is one of the great experiences of our time.

Afghanistan, on the other hand, is an unmitigated tragedy. Since I was there, in 1978, there have been, firstly, three bloody coups d'etat followed by the Russian invasion in 1979, and ten years of guerilla warfare of unsurpassed cruelty. The Russian retreat in 1989 opened the gates to a civil war which is still raging. I can only assume that no archaeological work has been done during that time and hope that the sites and monuments somehow survived the fighting. Tourism was, and is, of course, non-existent and the only foreigners occasionally allowed into the country were a few journalists and aid workers. So, perhaps, the pictures which I took 20 years ago may, in some cases, be the last to show what splendours the country's cultural heritage had to offer.

This book could not have been written without the help of my wife, who was my travelling companion, record-keeper, researcher and, above all, my most persistent and merciless critic.

ACKNOWLEDGEMENTS

The author and publishers wish to express their grateful thanks to copyright owners for the use for the illustrations listed below: Grégoire Frumkin, 'Archaeology in Soviet Central Asia', VII, *Turkmenistan, Central Asian Review* XIV, no 1, 1966 (for Fig. 10); L.I. Rempel, *Arkhitekturnyi ornament Uzbekistana*, Tashkent 1961 (Figs 4–9); Staatliche Museen Preussischer Kulturbesitz, Museum für Indische Kunst, Berlin (Plate 62); S. Flury, 'Le décor épigraphique des monuments de Ghazna', *Syria*, VI, 1925 (Figs 1–3); L. Duprée, *Afghanistan* (Map 10); *The International Merv Project*, University of London (Plan 10); L. Golombek, *The Timurid Shrine at Gazur Gah* (Plan 14); State Hermitage Museum, St Petersburg (Plate 97).

And for Quotations: Hodder and Stoughton Ltd (for extracts from *Tamburlaine the Conqueror* by Hilda Hookham); George Luzac Ltd and the Gibb Memorial Trust (for extracts from *Turkestan down to the Mongol Invasion* by V.V. Barthold); Routledge and Kegan Paul Ltd (for extracts from *Clavijo, Embassy to Tamerlane*, translated by G. Le Strange).

INTRODUCTION

To write a book on Central Asian civilisation without imposing some limits either to the area, to certain periods of history, or to the subject discussed, is an almost unmanageable task.

First, as an area, it had no fixed boundaries. Although its nucleus was what later used to be known as Russian Turkestan, its cultural influence extended at times far beyond its frontiers, to the Volga, the Ganges and the fringes of China. Secondly, its history is one of the most complex and fluid in the world, and yet without a historical introduction any talk of civilisation and art would be meaningless. Not only does this history go back some 2500 years, but the nomads who so often played a key role in it had no written records of their own. Every piece of information about them had to be laboriously compiled from the scattered references in Greek, Arabic, Persian or Chinese writings. Differences in languages and scripts, in calendars, in pronunciation and transliteration make any verification and cross-checking of dates and names extremely difficult and often unreliable.

Four major invasions have altered the cultural pattern of the region: those of the Greeks, the Arabs, the Mongols and the Russians. Most writers select either the Arab or the Mongol invasion as a limit to their work. It has been, therefore, a challenging task to try and sum up the area's development – both the transient and the permanent features – right up to the last of these milestones. It could, and should, give the reader the opportunity to judge for himself the importance of the changes that have occurred in this region during the last hundred years.

Finally, each of the three subjects mentioned in the sub-title – archaeology, art and architecture – is certainly worth a book on its own. But my objective has been to provide the reader who chooses to travel in these parts with a comprehensive guide rather than with an exhaustive and detailed study. I therefore accept in advance any reproof of superficiality and incompleteness.

The first part should give the reader some information – in a very condensed form – about the character of the countries concerned, their history and their pattern of civilisation. I have thought it useful to add a chapter on architecture and architectural decoration and another on sources. The list of these is, of course, far from complete, but I hope that at least the most important works are mentioned.

Sites and monuments, covered in Parts II to IV, can be found, with some exceptions, in oases or irrigated areas on rivers with a permanent flow of water, and along the main trade-routes. It is therefore quite natural that the division into chapters follows this pattern, and a survey of sites from different periods is given under each heading. This may seem cumbersome, but the opposite principle, that is listing sites of the same period regardless of distance and geographical conditions would run, to my mind, into even greater difficulties. Apart from the obvious disadvantage to the traveller, it would be difficult to show the similarity of development of one area in different periods of history; it would not be possible to follow the continuity of certain local traditions in architecture and in ornamentation typical of each oasis or region.

I am not an authority on linguistics, and therefore have preferred to avoid discussion of those problems which fall outside the scope of my work. Although a good deal has been written on this subject, or rather subjects, the complexity of language in this area is such that it needs a specialist to write even a brief note. Wherever manuscripts were part of archaeological finds, I have merely stated the fact and, where possible, just mentioned the languages and scripts in which they were written.

As far as the transcription of names is concerned, whether Arabic, Persian, Turkish, Mongol or Chinese, there is no unity in literature. There are several ways and several conflicting rules. Many of the place-names, for instance, have mixed Persian and Turkish roots, and can be quite legitimately transcribed in two or more different ways. Some of the oriental names had to be taken from Russian, and transcription from the Cyrillic alphabet simply added to the confusion. I have tried therefore to conform, where possible, to current English usage. Where there is no such usage or where there are several, I have had either to follow one of the authorities, or to choose the best way myself – a method which is of course open to criticism.

The transcription of Chinese names presents several problems. Some places are known under various names (Gaochang/Idikut Shahri), others can be transcribed in different ways (Urumchi/ Urumqi/Ürümchi, or even, in Chinese, Wu-lu-mu-chu). Wherever possible, I have used the modern Pinyin transcription. In certain cases, however, I have kept the well established, traditional names (Kashgar rather than Ka-shi etc.).

I have kept the spelling 'dzh' for the ex-Soviet territories in conformity with my sources, whereas I have used 'j' or 'dj' for Afghanistan and Xinjiang. As an exception, I have used 'Tajik' for the whole area.

PART I
THE COUNTRIES

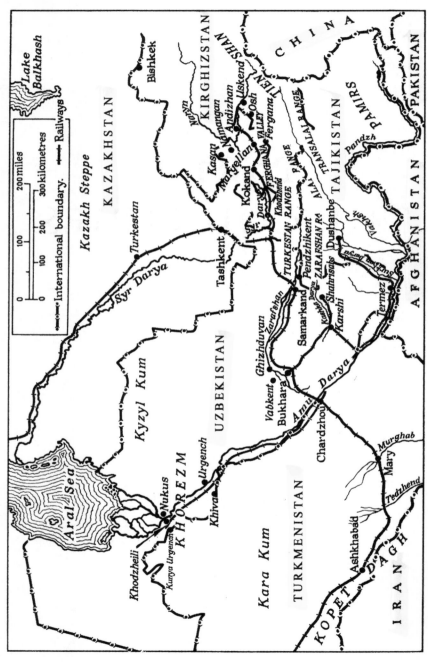

MAP 1 Central Asia

I

LAND AND PEOPLE

THAT PART OF CENTRAL ASIA which is roughly bounded by the rivers Amu Darya and Syr Darya, the Aral Sea and the Tien-Shan mountains, has never been a coherent cultural region. This has been due, on the one hand, to the character of the country – scattered oases separated from one another by steppes and desert which developed more or less independently – and on the other hand, to the fact that this relatively sparsely populated area has been wedged throughout its history between three well-identified cultural entities – Persia, India and China.[1]

Central Asia has been, from ancient times, a melting pot of nations and cultures. Trade, religions, and other cultural currents followed certain routes, and oases and regions, or areas, were stages in the migrations of the nomads. Scythians, Kushans, Huns, various Turkic tribes, Mongols and many other races travelled this way. Central Asia was, moreover, the focal point of influence from Greece, Persia, India and China.

Geographically, the country can be divided into four regions: the steppe in the north, both left and right of the middle Syr Darya; the semi-desert on the lower Syr Darya; the desert, which on the left bank of the Amu Darya is called Kara Kum (the Black Sand), and on the right bank, Kyzyl Kum (the Red Sand), with occasional patches in the Ferghana valley and east of the lower Zarafshan; and the mountains, of which the main chains are the Tien-Shan, the Alai and Transalai, and the Pamirs, with minor ranges along the upper Zarafshan and south of Samarkand.

The climate of Central Asia is continental, with cold, frosty winters and excessive heat in summer. Heavy snowfalls can be expected in the north and east. Occasionally, snow also falls in the west and south, but it never lies for very long. In the Kara Kum region, for instance, there may be snow and frost during the night, but the day which follows will be sunny and hot. The winter itself is short and it is sandwiched between two rather unpleasant rainy periods which transform the entire region into a sea of mud. This is due mainly to the soft and light soil of the oases, the *loess*, which is easily eroded. In mountainous regions, for instance in the Ferghana valley, the hills are eroded into strange, table-shaped formations. Consequently, the rivers carry a lot of earth and sand which form rich alluvial deposits in their lower reaches and lead to frequent changes in their river-beds. This makes navigation and, more particularly, the maintenance of the vital irrigation canals exceptionally difficult. The most interesting season is a short period just after the spring rains (usually the second half of April and early May), when the steppes and the deserts are covered with blossoming plants and bushes. There are, even in the most arid parts of the Kara Kum and the Kyzyl Kum, several kinds of plants which grow from the sand: bushes, and even trees, saxauls, tamarisks, calligonum etc., which exist almost without chlorophyll, have no leaves on their branches, but produce in this period of the year an abundance of tiny blossoms with a very strong scent. The long hot summer is absolutely dry, but in the plains there is a continuous wind which makes the heat bearable.

Agriculture has always depended on artificial irrigation. Water is provided by rivers fed from the glaciers of the Tien-Shan, the Pamirs and the Hindu Kush. The principal crop in the oases is cotton, which has been cultivated here since the Middle Ages. Other classical crops used to be barley, millet and wheat, as well as fine vegetables. The huge melons were justly famous; they were exported, in special brass cauldrons filled with ice, to the court of the caliphs in Baghdad, and to the shahs of Persia, and were rated as the most exquisite delicacy. Under the Soviets, the over-emphasis on the production of cotton has made the country dependent on imports of farm produce, and the remaining production of maize, rice and vegetables does not meet the needs of the local population. Fruit and grapes are usually plentiful, however, and apricots can be seen at an altitude of more than 3500 feet.

Animal husbandry, especially sheep-rearing and cattle-breeding, also has an age-long tradition and still continues on a large, if not very productive, scale. Horse-breeding has declined, but horses and donkeys are still widely used in farm transport. The steppes provide excellent pastures for the herds of cattle and flocks of sheep, many of which are of the famous Karakul, or Astrakhan, breed. They are able to graze on the meagre vegetation on the outskirts of the great deserts. Dairy production seems at present to be very low. Fishing used to be an important industry on the Aral Sea and in the delta of the Amu Darya. Fish and fruit canneries are practically the only significant industry apart from cotton-mills. The wildlife is not very rich, but some rare species of animals such as antelopes, wild asses and giant lizards are kept in natural parks. About a century ago there were still tigers in the reed-jungles of southern Tajikistan, and similar jungles in the deltas of the Amu and Syr Darya are still alive with animals and birds. Giant poisonous tarantula spiders and scorpions are quite numerous.

Civilisation naturally has centred on those rivers with a permanent flow of water. The most important are the Amu Darya (Oxus), in the south, and the Syr Darya (Jaxartes), in the north. Between them, the Zarafshan was once a tributary of the Amu Darya, but now ends in a marshland south-west of Bukhara without reaching its former estuary. Other rivers south of the Amu Darya are the Murghab, which watered the once important oasis of Merv, and the Tedzhend (Tedjend). They both end in the sands of the Kara Kum.

The delta and the lower reaches of the Syr Darya were settled in prehistoric times, and several settlements, mostly Neolithic and Bronze Age, were found and excavated, as were some dating from the ancient period. The Oghuz Turks apparently had their cities here in the tenth and eleventh centuries A.D., of which Yangikent, the present site of Dzhankent-Kala, was perhaps the most important. The next oasis was much further to the east, on the tributary Chirchik, close to the Tien-Shan, where the city of Tashkent was mentioned by Chinese sources in the very early times. There was an important ford at Otrar, where a caravan-route crossed into Transoxania from the north, but the city itself was never resettled after the Mongols destroyed it. Still further east was Khodzhend, the place where Alexander founded his easternmost Alexandria (Eskhate). Upstream from there the settlements were almost continuous along the upper Syr Darya, its tributaries from the south from the Alai glaciers, and also along the Kara Darya, which is one of the sources of the Syr Darya, the other being the Naryn.

The valley of the Zarafshan was always the most heavily populated area of the whole country, in both its lower and upper parts. Samarkand and Bukhara, which alternated as capitals in different periods of history, both lie on the lower Zarafshan. The upper part of the valley constituted the pre-Arab principality of Ushrusana, with the important city of Pendzhikent.

On the Amu Darya, by far the most interesting oasis was around the delta, with the fascinating civilisation of ancient and mediaeval Khorezm. There was a ferry at Chardzhou where a branch of the Silk Route crossed the river. Several minor oases were further upstream; the next large and important oasis was situated where another branch of the Silk Route crossed into Afghanistan. Here was the heart of the ancient Bactria, with the cities of Termez, Balkh (Bactra) and Surkh Kotal. The valleys of the Pandzh (the upper Amu Darya) and its tributaries, the Surkhan Darya, Vakhsh and others, were also densely populated. Settlements existed in the rugged, inaccessible valleys at the foothills of the Pamirs. Here was the semi-legendary kingdom of Badakhshan with its mines of rubies. Settlements could even be found on the high mountain plateau of the Pamirs, where interesting rock-carvings from the Paleolithic period and several locations of Neolithic cave-dwellings were found.

To the Persians, the country was known as Turan, and this still survives in geography as the plain or plateau of Turan. Turan was the country of the Barbarians, Iran was the civilised world. The Arabs, however, referred to it as Mawarannahr – the Land Beyond the River. The river which the Arabs had to cross in their seventh-century conquest was the Amu Darya – Jayhun, as they called it, the Oxus of the ancient Greeks. Mawarannahr is therefore the corresponding term to Transoxiana or Transoxania. Throughout its history this country has been open to the incursions of nomad tribes whose homelands were the steppes and forests of southern Russia, and in particular Siberia. The earliest of them, the Scythians or Saka, were Indo-Europeans; the White Huns, or Hephthalites of the fifth century A.D. were probably of Mongol, or Turco-Mongol, origin. The Turks of the sixth century, the Oghuz or Ghuzz of the tenth century, and the Uzbeks (Ozbegs) of the fifteenth century, all belonged to the same family of South Siberian Turks. The Mongol element is represented by the Kara-Khitai in the twelfth and by Chingiz-Khan's Mongols in the thirteenth century. The Turkic element gradually prevailed over the Iranian in the area. The Samanid Empire in the tenth century was perhaps the last state to be truly Iranian in character. From then on, Persian continued to be the language of the educated class, Persian dialects were spoken by the craftsmen, peasants and the educated class, but the rulers and their soldiers were Turks. It was from these Persian dialects that the present Tajik language developed, the only one in the area which belongs to the Iranian group. Finally, in the second half of the fifteenth century, through the efforts of men like Mir' Ali Shir Nawa'i, poet and politician, the spoken Turkic dialect, the Chagatay (Chaghatay) Turki, was made a literary language. Nawa'i himself wrote both in Chagatay and in Persian, but his work in Chagatay is the landmark which clearly showed the final pre-dominance of the Turkish peoples in what for two thousand years had been the exclusive domain of the Persians. All the other languages spoken in the area are Turkic and belong to the east Turkish group: the Uzbeks, Kazakhs, and Karakalpaks are all Turks. The only representatives of the Mongol family are the Kalmuks.

Ethnically, all these peoples are now mixed, but generally speaking the Tajiks, with their big almond eyes, strong noses, and rich beards present an Indo-Iranian (Persian) type, while the Uzbeks and others may have rather small eyes, flat noses, high cheekbones and thin beards, and show therefore their kinship with the South Siberian or Turkic Family. The Turkmens, now inhabiting the south-western part of Central Asia and the eastern shores of the Caspian, are somewhat different. They are taller, long-headed, and are usually considered as belonging to the south-western group of the Turkic peoples. They are the descendants of the White and Black Sheep Tartars who invaded northern Iran and Transcaspia in the late fourteenth century. Thus, the whole country became known as Turkestan[2] – the Land of the Turks. The Turks live all along the southern border of Siberia, from the Caspian to the eastern parts of the Gobi. The high mountain range of Tien-Shan divides the area, thus separating Western and Chinese (East) Turkestan. The dominant Turkish people on the Chinese side are the Uighurs, but there are smaller groups of Kazakhs, Kirghiz, and others as well. All these peoples are Muslims.

The Tien-Shan has always been inaccessible and inhospitable, but to the north and south are several passes which used to be the only routes by which people from the East and from the West could communicate; the nomads pushing through to the West were forced to use them. The passes are the so-called Dzungarian Gate in the north, the valley of the Ili, the Ferghana valley between the Tien-shan and the Alai, and the valley of Karategin between the Alai and the Transalai. These last two passes were mostly used by the caravans which brought silk from China to Persia and to the Levantine markets. The valley of Karashahr was the favourite gateway for nomadic incursions from the northern steppes into the Gobi plains.

The Silk Route, which, from antiquity, was the most famous trade-route linking China with the Mediterranean world, originated in the Chinese province of Kansu. Its two main branches followed the southern and the northern perimeter of the Tarim Basin, where a belt of oases provided the necessary halts with wells and caravanserais. To name but the principal ones, they were, in the north, Turfan, Karashahr, Kucha, Aksu and Kashgar. In the south, the eastern-most one was Tun-huang, with its Buddhist monastery, then Miran, Charklik, Niya, Keriya, Khotan and Yarkend. From Khotan there was a caravan track across the Karakorum Range into Ladakh and from there to Kashmir. Both main branches met in Kashgar only to split again. One road went due south towards the Kilik and Mintaka passes and from there to Kashmir. This was probably the road taken by Fa Sien in A.D. 399. The modern road uses another pass further east, the Khundjerab, to connect with the Karakorum Highway of Pakistan. In the Pamirs, near the town of Tashkurgan, another branch went west, into the Wakhan valley and down to the Amu Darya. This is supposed to be the road taken by Marco Polo in the thirteenth century. Westwards from Kashgar, the road passed through the Ferghana valley to Samarkand and from there south to Balkh, where it met with the Wakhan route just mentioned. Further destinations on this route were Kabul and India to the south-east and Herat and Persia to the south-west. From Samarkand, the road continued to Bukhara, Merv and into Persia, while yet another branch linked Bukhara with the Volga region via Khorezm.

The Silk Route and the accompanying flow of trade were the main factors in the prosperity of the oases. When trade was disrupted by war or nomadic incursions, the oases suffered and sometimes even perished. Equally, when drought or other catastrophes rendered wells unusable, or when brigands made the route unsafe, trade was diverted to alternative routes and the prosperity of the oases was immediately affected.

Water was, of course, a crucial element in the life of the oases. Thus, when the irrigation network was destroyed, as often happened in wars or nomadic raids, and when the population was reduced to such an extent that it was unable to renew and maintain the network of canals, the soil in the course of time became salty and infertile and the oasis was doomed. The same happened when the trade was diverted for good, for example when, after the voyages of discovery in the fifteenth and sixteenth centuries, maritime trade gradually replaced the overland one and many of the Silk Route oases were abandoned.

As for the population of Xinjiang, a certain part of it is still nomadic. The Kirghiz and the Kazakhs are largely nomads, the Kirghiz grazing mostly in the western part of the country up to the Pamir valleys, the Kazakhs being found mostly in the north, west of Urumchi, in Dzungaria. They both live in transferable *yurts*, of which there are several types. All have a skeleton structure of poles and latticework; they are covered with reed matting, felt or hides; they are all round, but some have a conical roof while others have a rounded, dome-shaped one. An ever increasing part of the population, helped by intensive immigration policy, is of Chinese descent. The Han and Hui, the two main groups, have grown in the last half century or so from around 5 percent to 41 percent of the total population of Xinjiang. However, they stay mostly in towns, whereas the countryside remains peopled predominantly by the Uighurs.

In Afghanistan, the geographical conditions and the ethnic mix are altogether more complicated. The mountain chain of the Hindu Kush divides the country into two unequal halves, the steppe in the north and north-west, deserts in the south and south-east. Fertile areas are mainly the Amu Darya valley, the environs of Kabul and the plain of Jalalabad in the east, as well as some sheltered mountain valleys such as the Panjshir in the east and the Bamiyan valley in the centre. The Herat oasis in the west used to be much larger in earlier times, and the Sistan oases in the south, once highly populated and prosperous, were long ago engulfed by the desert.

The Afghan nation, as it began to emerge at the end of the nineteenth century, is still a vague and at times almost a fictitious concept. Ethnic unity is non-existent and tribal loyalties still largely outweigh national ones.

The tribes of Afghanistan belong to several ethnic groups which, although all Muslim, differ widely in language, customs, dress and, most important, in their way of life.

The main ethnic group are the Pushtun, who live in the east, the south and the south-west. In the north and north-east are the Tajiks, in the north the Uzbeks, and in the centre the Hazara. There are also the Ajmak in the west and north-west and the Persians, mainly in the Herat area. Smaller groups are the Turkomans (Turkmens) in the north-west, the Kirghiz in the Pamirs, and the Baluch in the south. Small scattered communities of Mongols, Hindus, Sikhs and Jews can (or could) also be found. Two interesting groups are the Brahui, of whom some 200,000 live in south-western Afghanistan, and the Nuristanis in the north-east.

The Pushtun, the Tajik, the Persians and the Baluch are of Caucasian stock, while most of the others are Turkic or Mongoloid. The Hazara have typically Mongolian faces and are generally considered to be the descendants of the Mongols of Chingiz-Khan. The Brahui are of Australoid (Indian-Dravidian) stock. The Nuristanis are conspicuous for their Mediterranean features and blond hair.

The two main tribal units of the Pushtun are the Durrani in the west and the Ghilzai in the east of the Pushtun area. An equal number of Pushtun live across the border in the North-West Province of Pakistan.

The two principal languages of Afghanistan, Dari and Pashto, belong to the Iranian family. The second most important family is the Turkic, to which belong the Uzbek, Kirghiz and Turkoman languages. The language of the Brahui is Dravidian. Arabic script with Persian modifications is generally used.

As for religion, the entire population of Afghanistan is Muslim, mainly of the Hanafi Sunni rite. The Parsiwan (Persians) of the Herat area and the Hazara are Shi'ites. The Kafirs in Nuristan were shamanists until fairly recently.

A considerable part of the population, mainly the Pushtun, Baluch and Kirghiz, are nomads or semi-nomads. They live mostly in black goats-hair tents similar to those used in Iran, Syria and Jordan. The tent is usually divided into three parts: in the first, meals are taken and guests received, the second is the women's quarter, and in the third meals are prepared and other domestic work done. The furnishing consists almost exclusively of carpets, blankets and chests in which the family belongings are stored.

Some scholars believe that all Afghan ethnic groups had a nomadic past. However, as agriculture has been practised in the oases since prehistoric times, it must be assumed that the sedentary ancestry of some parts of the population is of a very long standing. It must also be assumed that the bellicose nomads have been the ruling elite of the country for most of the time. This can still be felt in the nomad's contempt for the sedentary farmer and in the higher social status enjoyed by some groups, predominantly nomadic, like the Pushtun, compared with others, like the Tajiks or the Hazara, who have been predominantly sedentary. The Hazara in particular are despised by other groups and are the pariahs of Afghan society.

NOTES ON CHAPTER I
Full details of abbreviations and publications are in the Bibliography

1   Frumkin, G., 'Archaeology in Soviet Central Asia', *CAR* X, p. 341.
2   The term West, or Russian, Turkestan comprises Transoxania, Semirechiye (the so-called Seven River Region, in the north-western foothills of the Tien-Shan) and the eastern Syr Darya province, or the Ferghana valley.

II

OUTLINE OF HISTORY

NORTH OF THE FERTILE BELT of oases and the traditional caravan-routes, the boundless open spaces of Russian, Siberian, and Mongolian steppes constituted another – less marked perhaps, but certainly much older – communication link between East and West. Long before the first caravan set out to exchange the products of one established and settled civilisation for those of another, the nomad herdsmen of the North had been trading in the same way: exchanging products at a leisurely pace and, more important, transferring traditions and skills through the region bounded by the Danube in the West and the Yellow River in the East.

There are indications that already in the Paleolithic Age the Aurignacian culture was spreading into Siberia and from there to northern China. Towards the end of the Neolithic Age, the comb pottery which was developed in central Russia in the middle of the third millennium B.C. had a strong influence on the proto-Chinese pottery of Kansu. The same influence continued throughout the second millennium, and from about 1500 B.C. the Bronze Age developed in western Siberia parallel with the great civilisation of the Danube (the culture of Aunietitz). The Bronze Age came some 300 years later to Minussinsk in central Siberia. China had by then already acquired the technique of working bronze from western Siberia. It was in the Bronze Age that the famous 'animal style' first appeared in the art of the steppes, showing the influence of Assyrian and Babylonian art, which remained a distinct feature of the animal style until the sixth century A.D.

We know little about the bearers of this art – Barbarians, as the Greeks called them – but the few descriptions we have, from Greek, Persian and Chinese sources, are surprisingly identical. According to these descriptions, born out by archaeological discoveries in Russia and Mongolia, it seems that the earliest of them belonged to the Thracian and Kimmerian races of the Indo-European family. Judging by the tombs of central Russia, some time between 1200 and 700 B.C. they were replaced by another tribe of the same family, the Scythians of the Greeks or the Saka of the Persians. Traces of their art are scattered northwards, towards the famous sites of Pazyryk and Minussinsk, all over the Tarim basin, and again eastwards to the Chinese province of Kansu.

With the Scythians this civilisation gradually moved into the Iron Age. The earliest traces of it, found north of the Caucasus, are contemporary with the culture of Hallstadt (900–700 B.C.). The corresponding Siberian sites, Minussinsk and Pazyryk, are again of a later date, about 300–200 B.C. The homelands of the Scythians were probably in the region of Tien-Shan, around Ferghana and Kashgar. The majority of them stayed there, but around 750–700 B.C. some of them moved west, pushing the Kimmerians out of Russia and into Hungary, the Balkans and Asia Minor. Their incursions south into the cultivated land of Persia were the reason for several military campaigns by the Achaemenid kings. Cyrus's last campaign was directed against the Massagetae, Scythians of the Aral Sea region, and led to the establishment of the sixteenth, Khorezmian, *satrapy* of the empire. His successor, Darius I, launched a campaign against the Scythians of Europe and succeeded finally in securing the Persian *limes*, an impenetrable border-zone, against their raids. Turan, south of the Syr Darya, was by then firmly in the hands of the Persian kings and was divided into three *satrapies*: Khorezm, Soghd on the Zarafshan, and Bactria on and south of the middle Oxus.

The Greeks under Alexander arrived here after the collapse of the Achaemenid Empire in 329 B.C. The leader of the Soghdians, Spitamenes, was defeated, and Alexander entered Marakanda, his capital, the Samarkand of today. From here he made contact with the ruler of Khorezm and sent his troops further north and north-east, to the Syr Darya as far as Khodzhend. The Greeks even crossed the river and moved towards Tashkent, fighting the Scythians, but as soon as the Greeks' backs were turned, Spitamenes rebelled and they had to evacuate the whole area and retreat to Bactria. In the spring of 328, Alexander marched on Marakanda again and this time achieved a decisive victory.

The Greeks held Central Asia for some seventy years. Around 250 B.C. Transoxania fell to the Parthians, whose main city was Nisa (Nesa) in present-day Turkmenistan, and who gradually became masters of the whole of Persia, squeezing out the Greek dynasty of the Seleucids. The Greeks, however, were able to hold Bactria for another hundred years, and lost it only when, between 140 and 130 B.C., an invasion by another barbarian people marked the end of Greek domination in this part of the world.

This time the nomads were the Yue-che (Yüe-czi), who, according to one authority (Tolstov), could be the same as the Greater Getae or Massagetae.[1] It was probably a group of tribes, undoubtedly of Indo-European origin, one of which was the Tokhars, who gave their name to Bactria (Tokharistan). The homelands of the Yue-che were pushed further west. They migrated through Kashgar and Ferghana, pushing the local tribes, the Saka, before them. The move then continued southwards, with the Yue-che occupying Soghd and Bactria and the Saka going still further, to southern Afghanistan, then called Sakastan, the present Sistan. Parthia, too, was nearly destroyed by this invasion and two of its Arsacid kings were killed in battles with the Yue-che. Mithridates II, however, contained them and even subordinated Sistan to his rule.

This phenomenon appears again and again throughout the history of the country. The slightest activity at one end of the steppes brings about quite unexpected consequences, continuously subjecting this immense area to migratory movements. Bactria was divided between five clans of the Yue-che, one of whom, the Kushans, founded a powerful dynasty around the beginning of our era. The heyday of the Kushan Empire was the reign of King Kanishka, who ruled over Transoxania, Afghanistan and a considerable part of the Punjab. The date of his accession is disputed and varies between A.D. 78 and 144. The year 128 is generally considered the most probable, although 278 is also suggested by some.[2] The question remains unresolved, however.

It was at this time that the Chinese general Pan-Chao, wresting the Xinjiang oases from the domination of the Huns, arrived in Kashgar, and according to some sources, clashed with a Kushan army sent to give help to the local population in their struggle against the Chinese. The Chinese were victorious, and Kanishka allegedly had to recognise the suzerainty of the Chinese emperor. After the death of Pan-Chao, China was not strong enough to hold these remote areas, and most of the Tarim oases once again came under the suzerainty of the Kushans.

The decline of the Kushan Empire coincides with that of Parthia. In the third century A.D., Soghd and Bactria, but apparently not Khorezm, again became provinces of Persia, this time under the Sasanian dynasty.[3] The rule of the Sasanians had lasted a century and a half when another steppe horde descended upon the eastern provinces. The Hephthalites, or White Huns, of Turco-Mongolian origin, lived in the region of the Altai mountains, and from there they moved into the steppes of western Turkestan. Towards the middle of the fifth century they occupied the area between the Rivers Ili and Talas in the east and the Aral Sea in the west. Then they started moving south, across the Syr Darya, into Transoxania and Bactria. The entire eastern part of the Sasanian Empire fell to them, including the rich and important province of Khorassan.

One of the shahs, Peroz, was killed in battle, but on the whole Persia managed to withstand the pressure.

Within fifty years the Hephthalites became a formidable power. Their move southwards continued, and after replacing the last of the Kushans in Kabul they crossed the passes and invaded India, then ruled by the Gupta dynasty. They established their capital at Sialkot in East Punjab at the beginning of the sixth century, and from there they raided and terrorised India for fifty years. In the second half of the century they disappeared from history. This disappearance was mainly due to the arrival of serious opponents in the northern steppes – the Turks. The Turkish homelands, comprising Mongolia and eastern Siberia, were divided in the mid-sixth century between the eastern and western khanates. The western Turks invaded the territory of the Hephthalites in the Talas region. A simultaneous attack by the Sasanians crushed the Hephthalites, resulting in their final annihilation. The Persians and the Turks shared the Hephthalite possessions. The Turkish khan received Soghd, the shah, Khosroes Anushirvan, received Bactria.

The arrangement was short-lived, for the Turks almost immediately invaded Bactria. The diplomacy of this period shows interesting political manoeuvring between the Turks and the Byzantine emperor, directed against Persia. The Turkish khan, or Yabghu, was obviously well informed about the political and geographical situation. As soon as he touched the Oxus, thus becoming an immediate neighbour of Persia, he approached Constantinople and suggested that all the silk trade with China could now bypass Persia. The emperor, Justin II, was interested in the idea, and sent his envoy, Zemarchos, to the Turks in A.D. 568. This resulted in an alliance which involved Byzantium in a war with Persia (572–91). Several embassies were exchanged between the two allies, but after the death of the khan the alliance broke down and the Turks, although still fighting Persia, invaded Byzantine territories north of the Black Sea and in the Crimea.

Another ephemeral state, the Turkish Empire, disintegrated yet again under the pressure from the East. This time the migration was provoked by the reoccupation of the Tarim oases by the Chinese under Emperor T'ai-tsong of the Tang dynasty. The Chinese advance westward brought them as far as Lake Issyk-kul, where in 714 their army achieved an important victory over the Turkish tribes. Thirty years later, another victory established their possession of this region and of the entire valley of the Ili. This brought the Chinese into direct contact with the Arab forces advancing into this area from the opposite direction.

The first incursions of the Arabs into Transoxania, after the collapse of the Sasanian Empire (642–51), were merely raids conducted with nothing more than plunder as their object. The Khorassan cities Merv and Balkh were used as bases for these raids, and it took another thirty years (until 681) before the Arabs first camped on the other side of the Amu Darya in winter. The first city they actually occupied on the right bank was Termez (689). Meanwhile, the native population of Khorassan rose against the Arabs, and their leader Peroz (Firuz), son of the last Sasanian shah, Yezdegerd III, sought help from the Chinese. After the death of Yezdegerd, Peroz fled to China and was received at the imperial court where he promised to accept Chinese suzerainty in return for military assistance against the Arabs. According to Tolstov, the result was a historical curiosity – Persia was established as a Chinese province (Po-S'), with its capital at Zaranj, near the present border between Persia and Afghanistan, and with the last descendant of the Sasanians as a Chinese viceroy. However, after some consolidation of the caliphate, the Arabs resumed their attacks, and in 667 Peroz was finally defeated. He spent the rest of his life in China.

The permanent domination of the Arabs over the Land Beyond the River is linked with the name of Kutayba ben Muslim. In 705 Kutayba was appointed Viceroy of Khorassan; in 712 he led his army to Khorezm to 'help' the Khorezmshah to crush a rebellion. Skilfully exploiting the rivalries among the local princelings, in the same year he led a campaign against Samarkand, supported by the Khorezmians and the Bukharans. According to Barthold,[4] there were no foreign governors or viceroys in Transoxania after the fall of the Kushans, and the oases therefore developed a strong feeling of independence, but were unable to realise their common interests and thus failed to unite when faced with the threat of foreign domination.

In Bukhara, Samarkand and other places, Kutayba built mosques and forced the inhabitants to evacuate parts of the cities, into which the Arabs then moved. In three years his armies reached Tashkent, occupied Ferghana, and, according to some sources, even crossed into Chinese territory near Kashgar. Kutayba was killed while trying to stir up a revolt against the caliph, and his death in 715 marked the end of the Arab advance. The Syr Darya frontier was soon lost and the Arabs were expelled from Ferghana. In Transoxania they were able to hold only a few fortified towns. It is worth noting that while steppe warfare presented no difficulty to the Arabs, they were far less successful in mountainous regions.

The Turks, mentioned above, were at this time helping the Soghdians against the Arabs. Transoxania, described by the Arabs as 'the Garden of the Commander of the Faithful', was equally important to the Turkish khan, and the Turks and the Arabs contested the domination of the country for more than thirty years. At one stage, the rebellious Soghdians decided to abandon their country, but were intercepted through treason, forced to surrender to the Arabs, and were subsequently massacred.

In 728 the Arabs decided to convert the entire population to Islam. In the general revolt that followed, only Samarkand remained in Arab hands, and it took the Arabs several years to re-establish their hold over the country. The succession in 749 of the Abbasids to the Umayyads as caliphs resulted in a further wave of rebellions aggravated by religious reformists and sectarian movements in both Khorassan and Mawarannahr. The Chinese once again tried to take advantage of the situation, and invaded Ferghana in 748, but were defeated in 751 by the Arab commander Ziyad ben Salih. This was perhaps the decisive event determining which civilisation, the Muslim or the Chinese, would predominate in the country. For a thousand years the Chinese never attempted to penetrate west Turkestan.

In spite of their firm hold on the territory, the Arabs never actually governed Transoxania. Their governor, or viceroy of Khorassan, residing in Merv, was concerned only with military affairs and with collecting tribute from the local rulers. Under the Umayyads there was no policy whatsoever about such borderlands, and naturally every governor was anxious to extract from the province as much money as quickly as he could. In fact, the only decision made about policy during that time was the enforced conversion of the population to Islam, accompanied by tax exemptions for the converts. The Abbasids, on the other hand, sought to create a state where provinces with a Persian or an Arab population enjoyed equal status. Transoxania was, as before, subordinated to Khorassan, but the governors appointed on a hereditary basis from among the local aristocracy, were, as a rule, well acquainted with the situation in the locality, and enjoyed at the same time the confidence of the population. The result was, of course, that the governors acted in their own interests, and their dependence on the caliph rapidly became purely nominal. This was the origin of the powerful local dynasties, the Tahirids in Iraq and later in Khorassan, and the Samanids in Transoxania.

After the defeat of the Chinese, two Turkish kingdoms were formed on the fringes of Transoxania. Semirechiye and the eastern Syr Darya came under the domination of the Karluks (Qarluqs), while the lower reaches of the river became the kingdom of the Oghuz (Ghuzz). Soghd, Ushrusana (upper Zarafshan valley), Ferghana and Khorezm were governed by local rulers who to some extent recognised the suzerainty of the caliph. The Samanids came to power under Caliph Ma'mun, when four brothers were appointed governors of Samarkand, Ferghana, Tashkent and Herat. In the middle of the ninth century they established themselves as hereditary rulers, and in 875 the head of the family obtained the administration of the whole of Transoxania from Caliph Mu'tamid. Detailed information on life in Transoxania under the Samanids is given by Barthold,[5] including government offices, the tax system, trade, postal services etc.

The Samanid dynasty remained in power for about a hundred years, but at the end of the tenth century the country fell into complete confusion, partly due to internal dissent and partly to external pressure from the new rulers of Persia, the Buyids, who acquired a decisive influence over the caliphs of Baghdad. At this critical time a new conqueror approached the northern frontiers of Transoxania and the disintegrating kingdom became his easy prey.

The Turkish dynasty of the Karakhanids established itself in the town of Uzgen (Uzkend), east of Ferghana, on the territory of the Karluks. In the second half of the tenth century the Turks began to press south-west, taking advantage of the situation in Transoxania. A family quarrel among the last Samanids provided a welcome pretext, and in 992 the Turkish khan entered Bukhara almost without opposition. In the confused situation that followed, the Samanids were meanwhile able to restore their possessions; a fresh invasion of the Karakhanids found them in an even weaker position. Hard pressed as they were, they had to apply for assistance to another Turkish ruler, Sabuktagin of Ghazna, in present-day Afghanistan. The result was that the Samanids ceded the entire Syr Darya basin to the Karakhanids and the lands south of the Amu Darya to Sabuktagin, retaining only a greatly reduced territory, centred on Bukhara.

In the year 999, fighting broke out between the Samanid ruler of Bukhara and his nominal vassal, Mahmud of Ghazna, son of Sabuktagin, who at that time ruled Khorassan. Mahmud's victory induced the Karakhanids to renew hostilities, and in October 999 the Karakhanid Governor of Samarkand, Ilak Nasr, entered Bukhara, putting an end to Samanid rule in Transoxania. As Barthold sees it, this was not only the downfall of a famous dynasty but also the end of the domination of the native Aryan (Iranian) element in the country.[6]

The whole area was now divided between two Turkish dynasties, the Ghaznavids in the south and south-west, and the Karakhanids in the centre and north-east. The Turkicisation continued at a rapid pace. The Ghaznavids under Mahmud (998–1030) soon extended their domination as far as Iraq and Khorezm and, on the other side, to Punjab, Multan and Sind. It was under Mahmud that the famous Court Academy of the Khorezmshahs was disbanded and some of the scholars were taken to Ghazna. However, in the eleventh century, another Turkish tribe, the Seljuks, advanced into Transoxania from the lower Syr Darya. They crossed the Amu Darya, entered Khorassan, and changed the whole history of Persia by achieving a decisive victory over the Ghaznavid Sultan Masud (son of Mahmud). Before long they captured Baghdad, and all real power in the caliphate passed into their hands. The Ghaznavids were thus reduced to their possession in Afghanistan and northern India, and the Seljuks, undisputed masters of the enormous land-mass between the Amu Darya and the Mediterranean, soon turned against the Karakhanids of Transoxania. In the second half of the

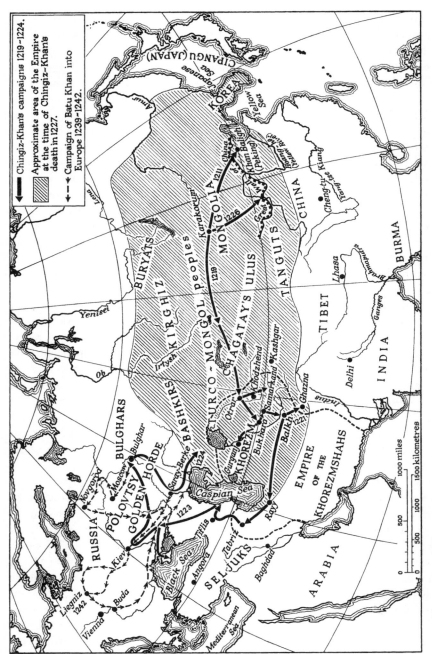

MAP 2 The empire of Chingiz-Khan

Chingiz-Khan's campaigns 1219–1224.

Approximate area of the Empire at the time of Chingiz-Khan's death in 1227.

Campaign of Batu Khan into Europe 1239–1242.

CIPANGU (JAPAN)

Japanese Sea

KOREA

Amur

Khan Baligh (Peking)

Yellow Sea

Yellow River (Yellow R.)

Karakorum

MONGOLIA

1226

1211

Otrar

Great Wall

CHINA

Cheng-tu Kiang

Yang-tse Kiang

1219

BURMA

BURYATS

TURCO – MONGOL Peoples

CHAGATAY'S ULUS

TANGUTS

Lhasa

KIRGHIZ

TIBET

Yenisei

Irtysh

Brahmaputra

Ob

Khodzhend

Kashgar

Ganges

Samarkand

INDIA

Otrar

Delhi

BASHKIRS

KHOREZM

Bukhara

Ghazna

Indus

BULGHARS

Bulghar

Gurganj

Balkh

1221

Moscow

Novgorod

Sarai-Berke

1224

KHOREZM

EMPIRE OF THE KHOREZMSHAHS

RUSSIA

POLOVTSY

GOLDEN HORDE

Caspian Sea

Ray

Kiev

1223

Tiflis

Tabriz

Lieginiz 1242

Black Sea

SEL-JUKS

Boghdad

ARABIA

Buda

Angora

Vienna

Mediterranean Sea

0   500   1000 miles

0   500   1000   1500 kilometres

century, the Karakhanids became vassals of the Seljuk sultans, while other branches of the family continued to rule their fiefs in the east, in Semirechiye and in Kashgaria, until the beginning of the twelfth century.

In the west, the Seljuks continued their conquest of Armenia and Asia Minor. In 1071 they defeated and took prisoner the Byzantine emperor, Romanus Diogenes, and subsequently established the Turkish Sultanate of Rum in present-day Turkey, which, some two centuries later, became the root of the Ottoman Empire. In the east, Sultan Sanjar, the last of the great Seljukids and originally Governor of Khorassan, intervened successfully in the Ghaznavid territories in Afghanistan, Khorezm and the Karakhanid territories in Transoxania, but he was finally defeated and pushed back into Khorassan by a new wave of steppe nomads, the Kara-Khitai. The entire territory of Transoxania fell into the hands of these 'pagans', possibly of Mongol origin. Khorezm revolted and was again subdued by Sanjar, but in another revolt south of the Amu Darya the sultan was taken prisoner. He was released in 1156, but died a year later, his once powerful empire disintegrating completely.

The Kara-Khitai had dominated the region of Beijing for 200 years, and were thus considerably influenced by China. Their offshoots now ruling in Transoxania regarded Islam and the Arabo-Persian civilisation as alien, and quite naturally were inclined to look more towards China. They attempted to introduce some administrative reforms on the Chinese pattern, and it is even possible that their administrative language was Chinese. The Kara-Khitai stayed in Transoxania, either as direct rulers or as overlords of the local Karakhanids, until the beginning of the thirteenth century. The shahs of Khorezm were upholders of the Muslim and Turkish traditions within the country, starkly contrasting with the Mongol, heathen world of the Kara-Khitai so much influenced by China. After the death of Sultan Sanjar, the Khorezmshahs, formerly vassals of the sultan and of the Seljukids, regained their independence and, exploiting the existing power vacuum, quickly expanded their possessions over most of Sanjar's territories.

Between 1207 and 1210 the Kara-Khitai were defeated in two campaigns, and their rule in Transoxania ended. The Khorezmshahs became, for a short while, the most powerful rulers of Islam, but their vast empire was hardly more than a conglomeration of recently conquered provinces and lacked the real backbone of an organised state. This was the situation when, in 1220, they were faced with a much more formidable invasion, of which the Kara-Khitai had been only a vanguard.

The nomadic tribes who lived in the vast steppe area north and north-east of the Gobi desert were a mixture of Turkish, Mongol and Tungus elements. In the twelfth century a slow consolidation process began among them and, somewhat later, the Mongols emerged as a dominating force under their leader, Temuchin, who later became known as Chingiz-Khan. A member of a clan whose pastures were between the Rivers Onon and Kerulen, Chingiz-Khan gradually succeeded in subduing other Mongol clans and neighbouring tribes and was able in 1206 to convene a grand assembly, or *kuriltay*, of all Turco-Mongols, at which he was proclaimed emperor, or Great Khan (*kha-khan*). (See p. 24.) Mongolia thus effectively unified, Chingiz-Khan proceeded immediately to conquer western China, then ruled by the Tanguts. In several campaigns he devastated the country, but he was not able at the time to capture the fortified towns, although he tried, for instance, to divert the Yellow River to flood the town of Ning-hia. Nevertheless, the Tangut king became his vassal, and he turned against the Kin Empire of northern China. The war started in 1211, lasted, with short intervals, until the death of Chingiz-Khan in 1227, and was ended by his successor in 1234. In 1215, Beijing was captured, sacked and burnt down, but the Chinese continued to fight.

In 1218, Chingiz-Khan sent Jebe Noyon, one of his best generals, west against the empire of the Kara-Khitai. In an extremely efficient and disciplined campaign, Jebe took Semirechiye and East Turkestan, and Chingiz-Khan thus became an immediate neighbour of the Khorezmshah. At first, Chingiz-Khan tried to establish commercial and political contacts with the Khorezmians. In the same year, 1218, a caravan consisting entirely of Muslim merchants with a Mongol envoy arrived at Otrar, the Khorezmian border town on the Syr Darya. The Governor of Otrar suspected, rightly or wrongly, that they were spies and put them all to death. Chingiz-Khan claimed indemnity and, receiving none, prepared for war. The Mongol army that collected on the upper Irtysh in the summer of 1219 consisted of between 150,000 and 200,000 men, many fewer than the Khorezmian forces, but with superior discipline and a more coherent and efficient leadership.[7]

The two rivals were of a completely different character. Chingiz-Khan was balanced, cautious, methodical and persevering, while Muhammad was inconsistent, irascible, proud and had little organisational ability. In fact, the first defeat changed this heroic knight into a helpless creature, almost a coward. Of the two, it was the nomad barbarian who had the abilities of a statesman, while the Iranised Turk, emperor of Islam and king of sedentary lands, possessed only the qualities of a knight errant.[8] The Khorezmshah adopted a defensive strategy based on his many fortified towns on the Syr Darya and in Transoxania. He thus divided his forces and, although numerically superior, they were inferior to the Mongols in each combat. Chingiz-Khan left one division to besiege Otrar, commanded by his sons Chagatay and Ogoday, while another under his eldest son Jochi descended along the river, took all the cities in the delta and on the Aral Sea, and finally attacked Khorezm itself. Yet another detachment went upstream to besiege Khodzhend. Chingiz-Khan himself, accompanied by his youngest son Toloy (Tuli), crossed the river with the main army and suddenly, in February 1220, appeared before Bukhara. The garrison tried to break out, but was largely destroyed, and the city then capitulated. The citadel, where the rest of the garrison sought refuge, was taken by assault and the city was then methodically sacked; but there were no executions, apart from some priests who tried to resist the desecration of the holy places.

From Bukhara, Chingiz-Khan proceeded to Samarkand, where he was met by Chagatay and Ogoday, who had meanwhile captured Otrar. The fate of Bukhara was repeated, but this time all inhabitants had to leave the city, and many of them were slaughtered. All who were thought useful, like craftsmen, were deported to Mongolia. The entire Turkish garrison was massacred in spite of the spontaneous capitulation, but this time the priests were spared. When those who were spared were allowed to return there were barely enough of them to occupy a single district.

The strongest resistance was met at the capital, Gurganj (Urgench), which was not taken until April 1221. All inhabitants except some craftsmen were killed and the city was destroyed by flood when the Mongols broke the dam on the Amu Darya. Meanwhile Muhammad abandoned all further attempts at fighting and fled westwards, duly followed by a Mongol detachment commanded by Jebe and Subotay, Chingiz-Khan's best generals. During the entire chase through Khorassan, Persia and Azerbaidzhan, the Mongols met no resistance, and the defenceless population was massacred without pity. At last Muhammad found refuge on an island in the Caspian, where he died of exhaustion in December 1220. Jebe and Subotay continued their raid across Georgia and the Caucasus into Russia where they defeated the army of the Russian princes, on the river Kalka.

In the spring of 1221, Chingiz-Khan crossed the Amu Darya and began the conquest of Khorassan and Afghanistan. In this campaign the cities of Balkh, Merv and Nishapur were completely destroyed and depopulated.

Muhammad's son Jalal ad-Din alone resisted the Mongols. This valiant prince fled first to Ghazna, gathered an army, and fought the Mongols in the mountain passes of Afghanistan. Following the capture of Ghazna, he made his next stand on the River Indus. Jalal ad-Din escaped capture only by jumping into the river on horseback and fully armed. He then fought the Mongols heroically but unsuccessfully for almost ten years in southern Persia, Iraq and Azerbaidzhan. He was killed in 1231 by a Kurdish assassin.

In 1222, Chingiz-Khan left Afghanistan, crossed the Amu Darya back into Transoxania, and began his return journey into Mongolia, arriving in the spring of 1225, almost in his seventieth year. His last campaign was directed against the Tangut kingdom of Si-Hia, but he died in August 1227, before the end of the campaign.

Chingiz-Khan's eldest son, Jochi, had died six months before, thus avoiding a serious breach with his father. Jochi's son Batu inherited his *ulus* (territorial appanage), the western part of the empire, comprising the steppes north of the Aral Sea and west of the River Irtysh, which later was to become the state of the Golden Horde. The *ulus* of Chingiz-Khan's second son, Chagatay, consisted of the former empire of the Kara-Khitai from the Tarim basin in the east to Bukhara and the Amu Darya in the west. In it, Transoxania, with its sedentary population, was considered inferior to the steppe region of Semirechiye, which the Mongols naturally preferred. Big cities like Bukhara, Samarkand and Kashgar were administered by direct representatives of the khan. The heart of the Mongol territories, the region of Onon and Kerulen, became by tradition the appanage of the youngest son, Toloy, while the heir of Chingiz-Khan, his third son Ogoday, received the central-west region, east of Lake Balkash, southern Siberia and western Mongolia.

Ogoday was confirmed as Great Khan by a *kuriltay* in 1229. (See page 22.) It was during his reign that the Mongols began their second wave of expansion with the final conquest of the Kin Empire of northern China, occupation of Korea, and a war against the Sung Empire of southern China which was to last twenty-five years. In the west, most of Persia had gone back to Jalal ad-Din in an unexpected revival of the Khorezmian Empire, and Ogoday was thus faced with the task of reconquering it. A relatively small detachment of some 30,000 men was sufficient to accomplish it and, after the death of Jalal ad-Din in 1231, the Mongols remained masters of that country. From there they proceeded into Georgia, thence into Armenia, later attacking the Seljuk sultanate in Asia Minor. This brought them right to the borders of the Byzantine Empire.

Meanwhile, a nomadic tribe, the Kumans, who fled before the Mongols from the Russian steppes, were given asylum by the Hungarian king, Bela, and allowed to settle in the Danubian plain. The Mongols, however, claimed that the Kumans were their subjects and set out to bring them back and to punish King Bela. This was the beginning of a major campaign in 1239–41, led by Khan Batu, in which Kievan Russia was conquered and the Polish and German knights defeated in Silesia. The Mongols then crossed the Carpathians and defeated the Hungarians on the River Sayo, while King Bela had to seek refuge on one of the Dalmatian islands. Split and Vienna were within reach when, quite suddenly, Ogoday died in faraway Mongolia and all Mongol commanders were summoned back for a *kuriltay* to elect a new khan.

Christian civilisation thus narrowly escaped annihilation. European monarchs gradually recovered from the shock, and within a few years dispatched several missions to the Mongols to obtain information about these 'infernal invaders'. By far the most important is the report by the papal envoy John de Piano (or Plano) Carpini, *Historia Mongalorum*. Between 1245 and 1247 he travelled to Karakorum and was present at the election and enthronement of Ogoday's son, Guyuk, as Great Khan. Another report of importance is that of a Franciscan monk of Flemish origin, William of Rubruck, who travelled to the same place ten years later on behalf of the French king, Saint Louis. He was well received by Great Khan Mangu (Mongke), who succeeded Guyuk in 1248. Each of those remarkable travellers chose a different route, but neither travelled through Transoxania. Carpini went from Lyons to Kiev and from there to the lower Volga, across the Kipchak steppe to the River Talas, and via the Tien-Shan passes to Mongolia. Rubruck started his journey from a Genoese colony in the Crimea and joined the same route as Carpini on the lower Volga. He returned along the western coast of the Caspian, through Transcaucasia and eastern Turkey to Syria.

Guyuk Khan died under mysterious circumstances in 1248. The accession of Mangu, the son of Toloy, was possibly something of a family coup, by which the members of the Ogoday clan were deprived of power and all male descendants of Ogoday were killed. For this Mangu relied heavily on the sympathy, if not active help, of Batu, who, as the eldest member of the clan of Jochi, enjoyed considerable authority. Under Mangu, Batu was in fact an independent ruler in his western *ulus*, and it is in this area that we must seek the origins of the later state or khanate of the Golden Horde.

To Persia Mangu dispatched his brother Hulagu to replace the military governors. Hulagu, who arrived in 1256, first exterminated the dreaded sect of the Assassins and thus pacified the country. He then carried the conquest further west, attacking what remained of the caliphate of Baghdad. The city was sacked and destroyed in 1258, and the last caliph killed, and the Mongols, after the fall of Aleppo, Damascus and other Syrian cities, turned their attack on Egypt. This presented extreme difficulty and the Mamluk sultans succeeded in pushing the Mongols back and reconquered Syria.

In Transoxania and Semirechiye the ruling house of Chagatay was far too weak and divided to achieve any such independence as their cousins on the Volga. In the fighting which broke out between the Chagatayids and the Jochids, the latter lost Khorezm, which once again became part of Transoxania. But the geographical character of the region favoured decentralised rule, and each oasis was soon governed by a semi-independent princeling nominally subject to the khan, who in turn recognised the sovereignty of the Great Khan in Karakorum.

It was in the East that the Mongol expansion still continued. Khubilay, Mangu's younger brother who became Great Khan in 1260, continued the war against the Sungs, whom he finally defeated in 1279. Engaged in a protracted struggle against a pretender from the Ogoday clan, the khan transferred his capital to Beijing. A new city was built there for him, called Khanbaligh (Khan's City), where Khubilay later received Marco Polo. Two expeditions by Khubilay against Japan failed, but in the south the Mongols entered Burma, conquered Indo-China, and even penetrated as far as Java. The descendants of Khubilay, the Chinese Mongols of the Yuan dynasty, ruled China for a hundred years, to be succeeded in 1370 by the Ming dynasty.

Returning to Transoxania, we find the nomad overlords camping with their herds outside the cities and in the steppes, and collecting tribute from the sedentary peasants, craftsmen and merchants. A long period of peace and security under Mongol domination soon brought a revival of trade. The ancient caravan-routes were used again, cities and villages were resettled, wells and cara-vanserais in the deserts were rebuilt. The Muslim advisers to the khan retained the Persian system of administration and taxation, and the country, in spite of the terrible massacres and continuing heavy taxes, once again became generally more prosperous. Some of the oases, however, never revived. This was due mainly to diversions of the trade-routes and also to the state of the irrigation network. In places now bypassed by the trade, there was neither manpower nor money enough to maintain the canals. On the other hand, where the dykes had been completely destroyed and the land was allowed to lie fallow for too long, the soil was likely to become so salty and so covered by sand that recultivation would become impossible; this, in turn, could be a reason why the trade sought a different route.

The revival, of course, was anything but a quick process. For example, in the 1330s, Ibn Battuta found Balkh, destroyed by Chingiz-Khan, still an utter ruin and uninhabited. When another traveller, Clavijo, passed through in 1404, it was again 'a very large city'. Merv, the 'Pearl of the East' of pre-Mongol time, never regained its importance. Here, typically, the great trade-route was diverted: the caravans were taking a more southerly course across the fringes of the Kara Kum desert, and the small town of Mary in present-day Turkmenistan is hardly reminiscent of the former splendours of Merv.

In the mid-fourteenth century, Samarkand was probably the busiest and most important city in Transoxania. The route across the Kara Kum via Merv being cut, the caravans were either diverted south of Samarkand to Termez and Balkh, or west from Bukhara to Gurganj and on to the lower Volga. This latter route, however, was overshadowed in Mongol times by the so-called northern route, which led from the River Talas to Tashkent and Otrar and then followed the Syr Darya down to the delta and continued east of the Aral Sea to Gurganj. For some time this route carried the main East-West traffic, and in consequence the oases on the lower Zarafshan, like Bukhara, were reduced to a secondary role. The redirection of this traffic and of the caravan-trade back to Samarkand and Bukhara was perhaps the main reason for Timur's repeated campaigns against Khorezm, and for his systematic destruction of Gurganj.

Timur the Lame, or Tamerlane, became ruler of Samarkand and of the whole Mawarannahr (Transoxania) in 1370 after a victory over his former friend and ally Emir Husayn. He was born in 1336 in the small town of Kesh in the Kashka Darya valley south of Samarkand. His father was a minor chief of the Turkicised Mongol clan, the Barlas, who came to Transoxania with the Chagatayids. (See Plate 1.)

The original Chagatay *ulus* was by then split between Semirechiye, or the region of the Talas and the Ili – to be known as Moghulistan – which was in the hands of the descendants of Chagatay, and Transoxania, which was more than anything else a loose grouping of semi-independent fiefs ruled by various clans and families, partly Turkish and partly Mongol, few of whom could claim any Chingizkhanid descent. The rulers of Semirechiye considered themselves legitimate heirs of Chagatay and repeatedly invaded Transoxania in an attempt to reunite the *ulus*. Husayn, who ruled Balkh, and Timur, who married his sister, together defended the country against such raids. To match the claims of legitimacy, they themselves appointed a puppet khan of the Chagatayid family, and ruled in his name. Their association came to an end when Timur besieged Husayn in Balkh, defeated him, and thus became the sole master of Transoxania. In the thirty years of continuous campaigning that followed, Timur succeeded in eliminating virtually every rival, real or potential. Moghulistan and Khorezm were the first targets. Khorassan and Persia, with all lands once ruled by Hulagu, followed. The Volga state of the Golden Horde, ruled by Timur's arch-enemy, Tokhtamish, was defeated in two campaigns and became so weak as never to recover. Timur's army came within a stone's throw of Moscow, and his victories over Tokhtamish made it possible for the Russian principalities to reassert themselves and, later, to unite and throw off the Mongol yoke.

Economically, the Volga region ceased to be a major trade centre, and this, together with the destruction of Khorezm, helped Timur accomplish his aim to bring all the lucrative East-West trade back to Transoxania. A campaign to India, which extended his possessions to the Ganges, added to Timur's grand design and made Samarkand an imperial city and a major cultural and trade centre. Having acquired the lands of the Persian Mongols as far west as Syria, Mesopotamia and Azerbaidzhan, Timur found himself a direct neighbour of the Turkish sultanate in Asia Minor, now in the hands of the Ottoman Turks. The power of these Turks was rapidly growing. They had already established a considerable hold in the Balkan peninsula, defeated the Serbs in 1388 and the Crusaders in 1396, and were threatening the very existence of Constantinople.

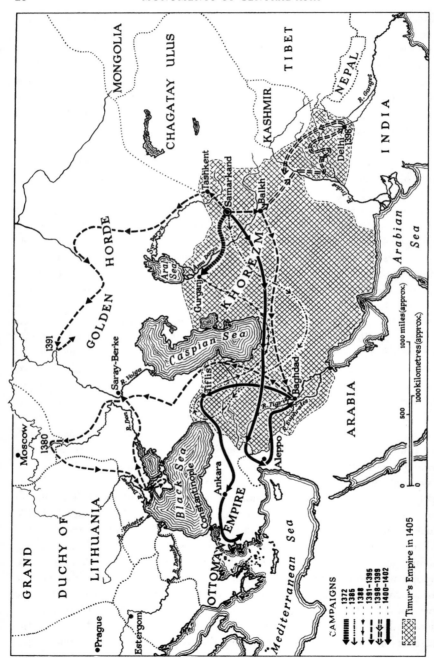

MAP 3 The empire of Timur (Tamerlane)

The emergence of a rival on their eastern flank provided a welcome relief for the hard-pressed Byzantine Empire. European diplomacy was quick to respond. After the first contacts made by the Genoese and Venetian merchants and the Greek Emperor of Trebizond, the king of Castile sent two embassies to Timur. The first was present when Timur crushed and took prisoner the Turkish sultan Bayezid the Thunderbolt, at Angora in 1402. The second, led by Ruy González de Clavijo, followed the victorious army to Samarkand, where they witnessed not only the monumental celebrations of victory, but also the preparations for the last campaign, against the Ming Emperor of China. In February 1405, at the very beginning of the campaign, the Conqueror died, aged seventy.

Almost immediately after his death, the enormous, unconsolidated empire collapsed. Warring factions formed around Timur's sons and relatives fought each other for power, while governors of distant provinces were quick to proclaim themselves independent. Within a few years the empire shrank to its very core: Khorassan and Afghanistan were ruled from Herat by Timur's youngest (fourth) son, Shah Rukh. In Transoxania, Shah Rukh's son Mirza Ulugh-beg, residing in Samarkand, ruled as his viceroy, with some other fiefs in the hands of other members of the family. The long reign of Shah Rukh and Ulugh-beg (1407–47 and 1449 respectively) was a period of stability and prosperity. However, with the assassination of Ulugh-beg in 1449 by his own son, the process of disintegration continued. In the second half of the century, the western territories gradually fell into the hands of the Turkmen tribes, the White Sheep and the Black Sheep Tartars, while in the east the nomad Uzbek khans were able to arbitrate between the Timurid princelings.

In the late 1450s, Timur's great-grandson Abu Said attempted to restore the empire once again, but after some initial success he was defeated by the Turkmens, captured, and put to death in 1469. After his death the only significant Timurid principality was Khorassan, which, under Sultan Husayn Baykara in Herat, enjoyed a period of unrivalled prosperity and cultural progress (1469–1506).

In Transoxania, history was marked by the growing influence of the Uzbeks, who were now firmly entrenched along the whole Syr Darya, from the Aral Sea to Ferghana. At the end of the century, a young Timurid prince, Babur, had to abandon his fief in Ferghana and flee to India, where later he became the founder of the famous Moghul dynasty (he died in 1530).

In 1500 the situation in Transoxania was ripe for Uzbek intervention. Their khan, Muhammad Sheybani, a Chingizkhanid from the house of Jochi, crossed the Syr Darya, occupied Bukhara and Samarkand, and proclaimed himself ruler of Transoxania. His capital was to be Bukhara, and as soon as he consolidated his power, he pushed further south. In 1507, he entered Herat, thus completing the victory of the house of Chingiz-Khan over that of Tamerlane.

In the second half of the fifteenth century, several important events took place that exerted a profound and in a way permanent influence on the history of Central Asia in the century to follow. The fall of Constantinople and the end of the Byzantine Empire not only made the Ottoman Turks a world power; it was also the beginning of the end of all Venetian and Genoese trading-posts in the Black Sea area, Transcaucasia, western Persia, and subsequently in the Levant. Coupled with the destruction of the northern trade-route, this meant that all East-West trade had to pass through Turkey. This in itself provided a powerful incentive for the West European countries to seek new ways of circumventing this Turkish monopoly, and indeed was a driving force behind the Portuguese and Spanish seafaring explorations of that time. The discovery of a maritime route to India, with a further link, also by sea, to China, led to a considerable transfer of trade from land to sea. Sea transport was becoming more economical, in view of the increasing cost of land transportation due to Turkish tolls and duties, and the safety of maritime transport was being greatly improved by progress in ship-building and navigation. But alongside these encouraging developments, security on land deteriorated when strong and centralised powers disappeared both from Transoxania and from Xinjiang. None of the petty local rulers was able to guarantee the security of the caravans, and the cost of armed escort contributed heavily to the increased cost of land transport. This is why Central Asian oases began to lose their main source of revenue, and the most important factor in their economy.

Tamerlane's concept of bringing, by force if necessary, all trade to Samarkand proved on the whole disastrous. The Uzbek Empire, as created in the early sixteenth century, had no economic viability in itself, nor was any one of the Uzbek khans capable of stimulating it. There was not enough work for craftsmen and not enough money to maintain irrigation. The cultivated areas shrank and the revenue of the state dwindled even more. This in turn proved a strain on the khan's finances and resulted, on the one hand, in the debasement of coinage and, on the other, in increased taxes and labour duties.

In the north-west, the Golden Horde, seriously weakened by Timur's blows, was faced with the growing power of Russian princes. Its border regions, the Crimea and Kazan, became independent under local dynasties, thus giving the Russians, namely the able Grand Duke Ivan III, the opportunity to play them off against the khan and further weaken his authority. Finally, in 1480, Ivan ceased completely to pay tribute to the Golden Horde, and a campaign by the Crimean khan in 1502 provided the death blow. Saray, the capital on the Volga, was sacked, and the Golden Horde ceased to exist. Its territory was divided among three khanates: Crimea, Kazan and Astrakhan. Crimea soon fell under the suzerainty of the Turks, and in the eighteenth century it passed over to the

Russians, and was finally annexed by them in 1783. Kazan was stormed by Tsar Ivan the Terrible in 1552; Astrakhan suffered the same fate four years later. Under the same tsar the Russian advance continued eastwards across the Urals and into Siberia. Here a branch of the Sheybani family ruled the Siberian khanate, which resisted the Cossacks for twenty years, until the last khan, Kutchum, was killed in 1600.

For almost a century Bukhara was ruled by the Sheybani dynasty. (Sheyban was a grandson of Chingiz-Khan and a younger brother of Batu.) Muhammad Sheybani succeeded in bringing under his control the whole of western Turkestan, and also Khorassan, but was defeated and killed in 1510 when he challenged the new Persian dynasty, the Safavids. The Uzbeks had to retreat behind the Syr Darya, and for the time being Babur, allied to the Persians, managed to restore Timurid power in Transoxania. But two years later the Uzbeks returned and reoccupied the country as far as the Amu Darya, which henceforth remained the frontier between Iran and Turan, as it had been a thousand years before in the time of the Sasanians. Sheybanid rule then continued uninterrupted until 1599, with Samarkand and Bukhara alternating as capitals. Tashkent belonged to one branch of the family, the head of another branch established himself as an independent ruler in Khorezm, where he founded what became known as the khanate of Khiva; here the Sheybanids continued to rule until 1920. In the eighteenth century, yet another branch of the family wrested Ferghana from the local rulers and founded the khanate of Kokand, staying in power until 1876.

In Transoxania or, as it was known then, the khanate of Bukhara, the Sheybanids were succeeded by their relatives the Astrakhanids. This dynasty ruled over Bukhara until 1785 and Ferghana until about 1700, when the khanate of Kokand was formed. One notable event of this period came in 1740. The Persian conqueror Nadir Shah invaded the country and, being the first to use artillery in these parts, easily defeated the Uzbeks.

The three khanates, Bukhara, Khiva and Kokand, formed the political pattern of the region throughout the eighteenth and well into the nineteenth centuries. This was an uneventful period in the life of the khanates, brought to an end by the mounting pressure from the Russians upon all three.

With the Russian Empire consolidated under Peter the Great and Catherine the Great, Central Asia naturally became the target of Russian colonial expansion. Russian goods appeared on Central Asian bazaars and the old northern route from the Volga to the lower Amu Darya was partly revived. The traders were followed by soldiers and, as early as the 1830s, the khanate of Khiva was the target of an abortive Russian expedition. At the same time, the Russians established a bridgehead on the east coast of the Caspian, in Turkmenistan, and from there pushed eastwards along the Kopet-Dagh mountains. Here, of course, they came rather close to Afghan territory on the left bank of the Amu Darya. Afghanistan was by then regarded by the British as a stepping-stone to India, and the Russian advance caused some anxiety. Meanwhile the Russians, pushing south from Siberia, established themselves on the Syr Darya, and the three khanates became a contested area between the two great powers. This was when Alexander Burnes visited Bukhara, and two British emissaries, Stoddart and Connolly, were executed here in 1842.

In the north, the Russians captured Tashkent in 1865 and created the Governorate-General of Turkestan in 1867. In 1868, they took Samarkand, and the Emir of Bukhara accepted the suzerainty of the tsar. Kokand was taken three years later, Khiva two years after that. In 1876, the Khan of Kokand was deposed and Ferghana incorporated into the governorate. The conquest of the whole area was completed by the defeat of the Turkmens in 1881 and the occupation of the Merv oasis in 1884; the Amu Darya was, once again, recognised as a dividing-line between the two interested powers – Russia and Britain. In 1916, there was a brief but violent uprising when the Russian authorities tried to impose conscription on the population, which had hitherto been exempted. The Emir of Bukhara and the Khan of Khiva were driven out in January and September 1920 respectively. The so-called 'People's Republic of Khorezm' and 'People's Republic of Bukhara' were proclaimed, nominally independent at this time. They were in fact under close Soviet control and were incorporated into the USSR in 1923 and 1924 respectively.

According to the Soviet nationalities policy the whole area of Central Asia was divided in 1924 into five Soviet Socialist Republics, with the Karakalpak Autonomous Region as part of the Uzbek SSR. After the collapse of the Soviet Union, in 1991, all five Republics became independent, allied, more or less nominally, with Russia as members of the CIS (Commonwealth of Independent States). The most (if not the only) visible sign of continuing Russian influence is the right of the Russian army to guard the external frontiers of the Commonwealth.

NOTES ON CHAPTER II
Full details of abbreviations and publications are in the Bibliography

1   Others, however, hold different views: see *Abstracts of Papers...*, Dushanbe, 1968
2   See, for instance, E.V. Zeymal, in *Abstracts of Papers...*
3   On problems of Kushan chronology, see several contributions in *Abstracts of Papers...*
4   Barthold, *Turkestan Down to the Mongol Invasion*, p. 182.
5   Barthold, *Turkestan*, p. 226.
6   Barthold, *Turkestan*, p. 268.
7   *The Secret History of the Mongols* admits that the Muslims of Khorezm were indeed a fifth column working for Chingiz-Khan, and after the conquest of the country those who remained were rewarded with high administrative offices alongside Mongol officials.
8   Grousset, *L'Empire des steppes*, p. 297.

III

CIVILISATION

WE MAY, FOR THE PURPOSE of this chapter, forgo the earliest stages of civilisation – the hunters and fishermen of the so-called Kelteminar culture and, later on, the first farmers and stock-breeders of the Tabagayah culture, as they were christened by Tolstov. The real diversification began much later, some time in the Achaemenid period, with the development of trade and the origins of the towns. Yet the roots of a basic duality between the nomad and the sedentary ways of life existed here from the earliest times – indeed, from the first introduction of farming techniques in the naturally fertile areas of the country. Farming, according to one theory, began at the mouths of the rivers where regular silt provided for natural irrigation; it meant the beginning of sedentary life. The transformation of the nomad into a farmer led to the building of more or less permanent homes, villages and marketplaces which, when trade began to flow along established caravan-routes, gradually grew into towns and cities. It also meant the transformation of the primitive economy producing solely for domestic consumption into a more elaborate one, producing specialised goods for the market. This, of course, is not a special feature of Central Asian evolution. It has happened elsewhere in very much the same pattern, but Central Asia has added one particular feature: the mixing, for centuries and in fact until very recent times, of two different civilisations, existing alongside each other without ever amalgamating completely.

Sedentary civilisations flourished in the oases, which became in some periods cultural centres of world importance. But they were surrounded by vast stretches of steppe and desert, by empty spaces where the nomads continued to live their primitive lives as hunters and stock-breeders. Of course, the luxuries of the cities and the riches of the villages, with abundant food, lush greenery and an apparently easy and safe life, represented a permanent lure for the warlike horsemen of the steppes. There was not, and there could not be, real peace between these two social formations, and what is equally important, there was not a fixed frontier, a clear-cut dividing-line, which could separate them. Every now and then the nomads would join forces and, feeling strong enough, invade the settled areas. They rarely had the strength to break the defences, but, as a rule, the irrigation network suffered and those villages in border areas frequently had to be abandoned. To pacify the nomads, or to defeat them once and for all, was impossible. The empty space could not be conquered simply because it was empty. Only very strong empires succeeded in establishing a safe *limes* between the nomad lands and their own territories. Even this tended to break up as soon as the central power weakened.

More dangerous still were the migrations to which the nomads were periodically susceptible. They were usually provoked by distant causes – wars or droughts – which pushed one nomad people or tribe out of its grazing grounds and against its neighbours, thus creating a chain reaction which resulted, perhaps a generation later, in overwhelming pressure being brought to bear on the settled lands. In such cases 'civilisation' gave way and the 'barbarians' took over. However, nomads, once overlords, have never preserved their way of life very long. Gradually they have learned to appreciate the advantages of their subjects' life and, after a time, have become absorbed, and ceased their nomadic way of life.

One thing should be made clear: the nomads, in spite of being called 'barbarians', possessed a distinct civilisation of their own. It was different, certainly more primitive in many ways, but it had a clearly defined pattern. Their social organisation, laws, discipline, and above all their military skill, both tactical and strategic, led them to some spectacular successes and sometimes, as in the time of Chingiz-Khan, they showed signs of real statesmanship and an ability to organise vast empires efficiently. However, they never possessed a capacity to develop this civilisation. In spite of their mobility, or perhaps because of it, their civilisation was always static. The lack of permanent homes never encouraged the nomads to create things of a permanent nature. This prevented them from exploiting the achievements and experiences of the previous generations, forcing them to learn all the basic skills again and again from the very beginning. Apart from the simplest personal belongings, they never developed a sense of property. There was very little to own, therefore practical communism was natural and easy and there was no individualism; discipline was the accepted way of life. Because there was nothing to own and nothing to accumulate, there was also no inducement towards progress. The skills of the nomads were exclusively physical, not intellectual. Their spiritual ambitions never reached beyond primitive shamanism, and when they needed a script for administering their empires they had, like the Mongols, to borrow it from their subjects.

Having no individual land possession, the organisation of nomadic life – and taxation – could not be based on land ownership or fiefs. The only effective way

of assessment was by heads, which implied an organisation by units, similar to
that of modern armies, with chiefs being, quite naturally, military commanders
at the same time. Grousset quotes the Chinese historian Sseu-ma Tsien, who
describes the organisation of the Huns in the third century B.C. as follows:

> The Khan, or the Son of Heaven, had two viceroys, one on the left and one on
> the right hand. The one on the left was his successor designate. Each one of these
> two had again a 'king' (Ku-li), on his right and left, each 'king' had two generals,
> and so on, down to the commanders of a thousand, of a hundred and of ten men.
> The whole organisation was that of an army and indicated also the position of
> each unit in the field. The general orientation was taken facing south.[1]

The same system may be found with all the nomads down to Chingiz-Khan's
Mongols 1500 years later, and could still be traced in the organisation of Timur's
army at the end of the fourteenth century.

In the field of art, the lack of permanent dwellings again restricted the activities
of the nomads. There was no architecture, monumental art, painting or sculpture.
Yet there existed some astonishing creative forces in this field directed towards
decorative art. The main items which could be decorated were clothes, arms and
harnesses, with possibly a few luxury objects, like goblets or caskets. Jewellery
(gold and silverware), and to a lesser extent weaving and embroidery, were therefore the principal outlets for their creative talent. The 'animal style' of the
Scythians, which incorporated some elements of Assyrian and early Persian art,
represented a highly stylised artistic expression which can well be compared with
that of the European nomads, the Vikings. The naturalism of that ancient art
becomes transformed and stylised for purely decorative purposes. Grousset[2] sees
a double current in the 'aesthetics of the steppes': the naturalistic, with roots in
Assyrian and Achaemenid, as well as Greek, art; and the decorative, which twists
and transforms the naturalistic for exclusively ornamental purpose.

From the third century B.C., the animal motifs of the Scythians were replaced
by the geometrical and floral motifs, equally stylised, of the Sarmatians. This
art was then transmitted, through the intermediary of the great metallurgical
centres of Siberia (Pazyryk, Minussinsk and Katanda) to the Hunnic tribes of
Mongolia, eastern Siberia and northern China. The art of these Huns was just
one branch of the stylised animal art of the steppes, which in southern Russia
showed Greek, Assyrian and Iranian influences and in the Far East, when it came
into contact with Chinese aesthetics, exerted an influence on Chinese art. Steppe
art influenced Chinese art, and Chinese aesthetics in their turn influenced the
art of the nomads.

The question which side of this enormous migration-belt of art is more
ancient, the European-Middle Eastern or the Chinese-Far Eastern, has occupied
experts for decades. The stream might have gone equally well eastwards or

westwards, or indeed simultaneously both ways. However, excavations at Ngan-yang, Chinese capital of the Shang dynasty between 1300 and 1028 B.C., have yielded some bronze objects decorated in animal style which are considerably older than similar objects found in Siberia, and would therefore suggest that, after all, the stylised animal art, or art of the steppes, had its origin in China.[3]

The mobile character of nomad civilisation also poses considerable problems to archaeologists. Practically the only sites where the nomads left any traces of their way of life are their tombs, or *kurgans* as they are called in Siberia. These are usually situated at isolated spots, with hardly any connection between them and no superimposed layers. This makes identification and dating extremely difficult.

We do not know exactly when the great trade-routes between Persia, India and China were opened, but we can assume that in the time of Alexander there were several towns in Central Asia where these routes intersected or divided. The routes must therefore have been in use for some time. From pre-Alexandrian times the following cities are known and have been partly excavated: Giaur-Kala (site of Merv); Kalaly Gyr and Kiuzeli Gyr in Khorezm; Bactra (the site of Balkh, the castle of which is now known as the Bala Hissar); ancient Samarkand; and Shurabashat in eastern Ferghana.

The Greek period added to this list Termez and Kei-Kobad Shah in southern Tajikistan, Ay-Khanum on the Afghan side of the Amu Darya, and Dzhanbas-Kala and Koy-Krylgan-Kala in Khorezm, as well as several other settlements, including Nisa in southern Turkmenistan. We know next to nothing about the social structure of these towns, nor about the changes caused by the century-and-a-half of Greek domination. But in the arts, the impact of the Greeks was very strong, and survived their political decline by several hundred years. In ornament, the Graeco-Bactrian motifs can be more frequently found in the south, in the Amu Darya and Zarafshan valleys, than in the north, in the regions of Tashkent and Ferghana. On the other hand, ornamental motifs of steppe art are more frequent here than in the south, doubtless because the nomads were much closer and their influence was much stronger in these fringe areas of sedentary civilisation. The Graeco-Bactrian art was an amalgam of Greek and local elements which, after the end of Greek domination, was subject to an increased Indian-Buddhist influence. This was the so-called style or art of Gandhara, which flourished under the Kushan Empire. Some writers (Schlumberger, for instance) even speak of Kushan style or Kushan art. This art developed on two different patterns: a religious one designed for temples and religious rites, and a secular one, dynastic, as Schlumberger calls it, designed for the embellishment of royal palaces and homes of noblemen.

In Central Asia, the most thoroughly explored site from the Kushan period is undoubtedly Toprak-Kala in Khorezm. From what Tolstov tells us, it seems that in the preceding period people lived in large tribal families or clans, in huge collective houses of several hundred rooms, all centred around the temple. These long houses can still be found at Toprak-Kala, but the focal point is no longer the temple but a royal palace. In a contemporary settlement, Ayaz-Kala, the system of collective houses had already been abandoned, and each peasant family was living in its own modest house. The settlement was protected by a strong fortress. This, concludes Tolstov, demonstrated the disintegration of the clan system into individual slave-owning families, and a small class of powerful, landowning aristocrats. At the same time, the state system becomes more centralised, the fortifications are taken care of by the central government and not by the town or village, as before. The royal palace dwarfs the temple at Toprak-Kala, as a symbol of the new centralised power; similarly, the fortress of Ayaz-Kala represents the efforts of this power to protect, and to rule, its subjects. This centralisation – if it can be proved for other areas as well – did not survive the decline of the Kushan Empire. In the following centuries the local princelings gained more independence, and some of the provincial courts became lively centres of art. Also, monumental art ceased to be the privilege of the palace and spread into the dwellings of local aristocrats and rich burghers.

When the Sasanians established themselves in Persia, they did not exercise much authority over these outer fringes of their empire. Besides, the invasion of the White Huns, or Hephthalites, and later that of the Turks, provided a sort of barrier against too much influence from Persia. (See Plate 2.) Behind this barrier, the local, Soghdian, art flourished, and reached its peak just before the Arab invasion. The excavations of Varakhsha and Pendzhikent, as well as of the oases in Xinjiang, reveal a surprisingly sophisticated society: prosperous, educated and tolerant beyond expectation. Ethnically, the Soghdians belonged to the Iranian family and their language was related to Persian. Their religion, as far as we can tell, was a synthesis of many creeds and currents, incorporating elements of Zoroastrianism, Manichaeism, Buddhism and Christianity, together with Greek and Indian mythology. Trade with China was entirely in their hands, and their outposts and settlements were scattered practically all over Chinese Turkestan.

The Soghdian civilisation, crushed by the Arabs and the Chinese alike, survived for several centuries in the fringe region of Semirechiye. Here the Soghdian colony at Balasagun still existed in the twelfth century, and Indo-Buddhist, Sino-Buddhist and Central Asian traditions were all equally represented in its art.[4] Soghdian art, although basically of Iranian character, reveals the same synthesis as Soghdian religion. The stuccoes of Varakhsha, the frescoes of Pendzhikent, and the cave-temples of Chinese Turkestan show an amazing variety of motifs coupled with a supreme mastery of techniques and a formally brilliant presentation. The decentralisation of power is reflected particularly in the *kushk* (fortified palace),

1. Head of Timur.
Reconstruction by
Gerasimov

2. Hephthalite statuette.
Samarkand Museum

3. ABOVE. Hauli, fortified country house, Khorezm

4. BELOW. Toprak Kala, Khorezm. The palace

5. Toprak Kala, Khorezm. Excavations

6. Khiva (general view with minaret Kalta Minar)

7. Friday Mosque, Khiva

8. Minaret Khoja Islam, Khiva

9. Minaret of Kutluq Timur, Kunya Urgench

10. Mausoleum of
Fakhr-ud Din Razi,
Kunya Urgench

11. BELOW. Mausoleum
of Sultan Tekesh, Kunya
Urgench (detail)

which was often nothing more than a fortified country house. In the following centuries, the *kushk* lost its defensive role, but the architectural elements remained, becoming stylised and decorative. The whole building developed into an interesting feature of local architecture which is still to be found, for instance, among the country houses in Khorezm – the so-called *hauli*. (See p. 91 and Plate 3.)

The arrival of the Arabs at the beginning of the eighth century brought about a complete reversal. The enforced introduction of Islam marked an end to the religious and artistic tolerance of Soghdian society. Islam at that stage was a warlike and intolerant creed. Every means was used to eradicate existing creeds and convert the 'infidel' population to Islam. Economically, the Arab domination meant an enforced diversion of all trade towards the heartland of the caliphate, interruption, at least for the time being, of contacts with China, and an increase of Persian influence. In the field of the arts, Islam was quick to suppress all traditional modes of expression. Human, animal and even floral motifs in pottery and metalware, as well as in painting and sculpture, were suppressed and replaced by the only acceptable decoration – the geometrical pattern, the arabesque, combined with the equally geometrical Kufic script. We should bear in mind that at this early stage of their expansion the Arabs were still nomads, and their culture was therefore subject to the same restrictions and limitations as that of the steppe peoples. Their nomadic way of life probably provided the background for their inclination towards flat ornamental decor and the religious interdict of all figurative art.

This rigid regime did not last very long. Persia soon began to exercise an influence on the Arab rulers, who underwent the same transformation as all other barbarian invaders in civilised lands. They became gradually imbued and absorbed by the high and sophisticated culture of their subjects. Stylised *islimi* (floral motifs) became common in ornament, and the rigid Kufic was soon replaced by the more flexible and decorative Naskhi, and later Thulth. Animals and birds and occasionally even a human figure, reappeared in the arts, but on the whole monumental sculpture and painting were dead for ever. Architecture received a powerful stimulus with the new need for religious buildings: mosques, minarets, *madrasas* and mausoleums. Pope's words about Iran apply equally well to Central Asia: 'New religious and secular buildings were continuously required and they had to be created out of local materials, techniques and styles'.[5]

The living conditions of the masses in the tenth century were fairly good. Contemporary sources quoted by Barthold[6] mention the possibility that the inhabitants of industrial townships could buy their own land with the approval and assistance of the government. Others give an impressive list of goods supplied by various towns in Transoxania, where it may well be assumed that the inhabitants had everything in abundance and were not dependent on imports from other lands. Industry was undoubtedly developed under Chinese influence, of which the famous rag-paper of Samarkand is good evidence. It was long assumed that this paper was a local invention, but later research has shown that the Chinese manufactured rag-paper several centuries before its production started in Samarkand. Of the products of Transoxania, the greatest reputation was enjoyed by the silk and cotton fabrics of the Zarafshan valley, and the metal articles of Ferghana, especially arms. The development of a metal industry in Ferghana was promoted by the coal-mines in the Isfara district.

Trade with the nomads was always of great importance. Large numbers of cattle and pack animals were obtained from them, as well as hides, furs and slaves. Trade with the settled peoples was indispensable for the nomads, because it provided them with clothing and grain, among other things. The Khorezmians, for instance, founded their prosperity exclusively on their trade with the Turks, and became chief representatives of the merchant class through-out the country, especially in Khorassan. They could be found in considerable numbers in every city of Khorassan, distinguishable from the local inhabitants by the high fur caps which are still worn in present-day Khorezm. The develop-ment of material prosperity was accompanied, as is usual, by that of intellectual pursuits. Almost every teacher at that time could number some Khorezmians among his disciples. This stands in direct relation to the high level of learning in Khorezm itself, particularly in Kath and Gurganj, at the end of the tenth and beginning of the eleventh centuries.

The period of rule of the Turkish Karakhanid dynasty was without doubt a period of cultural retrogression for Transoxania. In spite of the good intentions of individual rulers, the view that the kingdom formed the personal property of the khan's family – and the system of appanages resulting from this view, with its inevitable quarrels – must have been followed by the decay of agriculture, commerce and industry no less than intellectual culture.

In the first two centuries of the second millennium, the Turks became the ruling class – a position developed from their role as palace guards of earlier times – and they were able to impose their taste on the artists. The Persian influence was already weakening when it received a decisive blow from the Mongol invasion. Although after the invasion trade links with China were resumed fairly rapidly, there was no substantial increase of Chinese influence in the arts, and, on the whole, artistic activity was reduced to next to nothing. In the 150 years that followed the invasion, very little was built, and the quality of all works originated in that period remains far behind those of the preceding one. Before the time of Chingiz-Khan the Mongols had no written documents. On adopting the Uighur alphabet, they used it first of all for the codification of their national opinions and customs, as sanctioned by the khan. The observance of these rules was binding on everyone, including the khan himself. Thus arose the Great Yasa or Code of Law of Chingiz-Khan. Along with this, the Mongols borrowed from the Chinese the custom of writing down the sayings of the khans and publishing them after their death. These maxims were called by the Turkish word *bilik* (knowledge). The *biliks* of Chingiz-Khan were studied and taught. In China, on one occasion, the question of the succession to the throne was settled in favour of that candidate who displayed the most thorough knowledge of these *biliks*. Evidently, the *Little Red Book* of Chairman Mao had worthy predecessors.

It was only with the reign of Timur (Tamerlane) that a renaissance began. This was sparked off by Timur's methodical – and frequently forcible – habit of collecting artists and craftsmen in all conquered territories, and concentrating them in his capital city, Samarkand. It was a mixture of styles and currents, most of them imported from as far as Syria, Iraq, the Caucasus and India. With the Persian influence again predominant, Timur's hectic building resulted in some spectacular achievements in architecture, ornament and decorative art. The period of his successors, Shah Rukh in Herat and Ulugh-beg in Samarkand, was less spectacular perhaps, but more balanced and stable. This period marked the beginning of almost a century of prosperity, progress and creativity on a large scale.

Timur's empire did not differ widely from all those that had preceded it. Central Asia had always been their pivot, and Timur, a native of this region, continued the traditions of despotism, conquest and plunder, as well as the deeply established cultural traditions of the country. While Grousset[7] finds in Timur a long-range Machiavellism, 'a hypocrisy identified with the purpose of the State', others see in him simply a descendant of that nomad stock which cultivated the military arts inherited from Chingiz-Khan.

> He was above all master of the military techniques developed by Chingiz-Khan. His hordes of elite Tatar troops were the basis of his power. Timur was not limited in his choice of weapons; he used every weapon in the military and diplomatic armoury of the day. He never missed an opportunity to exploit the weakness of the adversary, intrigue and alliance served his purposes. The seeds of victory were sown before an engagement by his agents who moved amongst the ranks of the enemy, and were reaped later on the battlefield.[8]

Was he really 'a Napoleon with the soul of a Fouché, or a Philip II descendant of Attila'? He was without doubt a brave soldier, an experienced commander, and at the same time a friend of artists and writers, and he could 'enjoy Persian poetry like a Shirazi'.[9] His empire was culturally Turco-Persian, Turco-Chingizkhanid in constitution, with a Mongol-Arab discipline in politics and religion. His campaigns had no pre-established order, but all preparations were meticulously checked and all contingencies were provided for. Geographical continuity was of little value to him. Aggressive, mobile tactics suited him best because mobility and surprise were his chief assets, as they were of Chingiz-Khan.

Like Chingiz-Khan, Timur was the dominant figure of his age. When Chingiz-Khan disappeared, his empire continued to exist in spite of his often mediocre successors. Timur's empire, with all his gifted epigoni, often with a touch of genius, like Shah Rukh, Ulugh-beg or Husayn Baykara, disappeared almost immediately, and shrank to the size of his native Transoxania and Khorassan. But the contribution of the Timurid renaissance, in the century that followed his death, surpasses the narrow limits of these two countries. Samarkand became a centre of scholarship and science which had no equal in the Muslim world until the heyday of Ottoman Istanbul. Herat became the home of the brilliant school of Persian miniaturists, while Bukhara under the Uzbeks lived off the Timurid heritage for almost three centuries.

Little can be said about the development of society and the arts under the Uzbek khans. The 300 years of their rule were marked by growing isolation, intolerance and artistic sterility. The stagnant economy relied on old-fashioned means of production, including slave-labour, and provided no stimuli for improved relations with neighbouring countries. Of these only Persia under the Safavid shahs had a cultural significance, but she was far too occupied with her wars against Turkey to pay any attention to events on her eastern borders.

So it happened that the only interesting moment was the surprising artistic renaissance in nineteenth-century Khiva, which, of all places, might have been considered the most isolated and backward region. But the reopening of the northern trade-route and growing trade with Russia provided the material basis, while internal conditions in Persia, less favourable at that time, probably persuaded some groups of artists and craftsmen to seek work in that remote oasis. Generally speaking, the quality of the tilework, wood-carving, and masonry of Khiva is not outstanding, but some very interesting elements of local tradition were used both in the architecture and in the ornament. Above all, it is the harmony of the whole city precinct, complete with walls, gates, palaces, mosques etc. which survived almost intact, that, until the unfortunate restoration attempt, made Khiva unique among the cities of Central Asia.

NOTES ON CHAPTER III
Full details of abbreviations and publications are in the Bibliography

1   Grousset, *L'Empire des steppes*, p. 54.
2   Grousset, *L'Empire des steppes*, p. 43.
3   Grousset, *L'Empire des steppes*, p. 643.
4   Rempel, *Arkhitekturnyi ornament Uzbekistana*, p. 507.
5   Pope, *Persian Architecture*, p. 78.
6   Barthold, *Turkestan*, p. 234.
7   Grousset, *L'Empire des steppes*, p. 492.
8   Hookham, *Tamburlaine the Conqueror*, p. 6.
9   Grousset, *L'Empire des steppes*, p. 492.

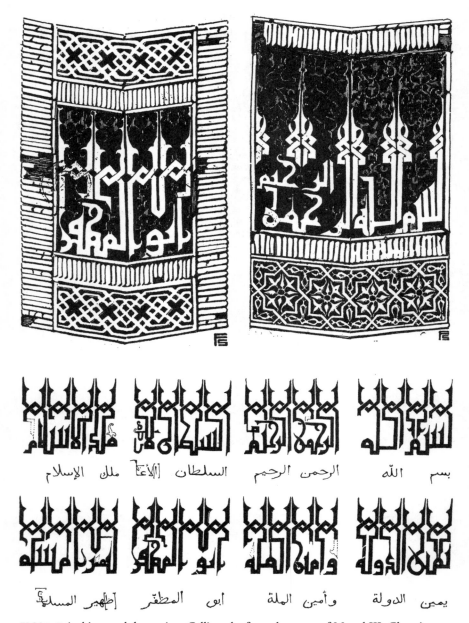

FIGS 1–3 Architectural decoration. Calligraphy from the tower of Mesud III, Ghazni, Afghanistan (after Flury)

IV

ARCHITECTURE AND ARCHITECTURAL DECORATION

IRANIAN AND BUDDHIST

IT MAY BE ASSUMED that the eastern Iranian provinces in the Achaemenid period were administered from some kind of urban centres, and it may be equally assumed that these towns and their monumental buildings, temples, palaces, gates etc. were, at least to some extent, built on Iranian models. Another school of architecture which began to penetrate into the area with the expansion of Buddhism was Indian. With some admixture of Greek elements in the Seleucid and Bactrian periods, a composite style emerged in which Iranian and Buddhist influences coexisted and alternated to a varying degree until the arrival of Islam.

In general terms, the earliest towns were most probably built according to two basic considerations, security and the supply of water, to which trade may be added as the third. The citadel was always built on a strategically suitable place and, if no such place was available, the terrain was conveniently altered, an artificial mound was raised, a river arm was diverted etc. The architecture of the citadel had to correspond to the requirements of defence and to the contemporary technique of warfare, and had to be constantly kept up-to-date with it, which led to frequent reconstructions and even relocations. Gates and walls were other architectural elements with defence purposes, and the gates in particular had an important place in monumental architecture and decoration. The layout of the streets and squares was conditioned, in most cases, by the position of the gates and by the system of water conduits, which had to follow the shape of the terrain. The main surface canals were usually lined with streets and converged in, or led to, a water tank or pool, around which a square formed. The supply of water often dictated the location of the town itself, within easy reach of a stream with permanent water.

The bridge is another ancient type of building though not necessarily part of a town. The *maydan* was originally not a marketplace but merely an open space located within or outside the walls where military parades and training could take place; it was also used for cattle, horse and camel markets, and caravans could discharge their goods here etc. The town's commercial activity centred on the bazaar, which combined manufacture and trading, and more often than not took place in one or more ordinary streets. In later periods bazaar buildings were constructed, such as the vaulted structures covering street crossings which still exist in Bukhara and other Central Asian towns. Gardens were another creation of urban design, though the earliest formal gardens that have come down to us date from the late Timurid period only.

Taking the Achaemenid town of Pasargadae as an example, a town of that period may have developed from a military camp surrounded by a wall. Within its precinct, amid parks and gardens, were palaces and temples. The town gate may have been adorned with statues. The main part of the palace was the audience chamber. Its roof was carried by columns and pilasters with decorative capitals and bases. The temple consisted of a cube-shaped structure, the cella, raised on a terrace and accessible by a monumental staircase. According to Ghirshman,[1] the Persian art of Pasargadae was already a composite art, with Assyrian, Hittite, Babylonian and Egyptian elements.

The terrace of Masjid-i Suleiman, near Ahwaz, somewhat older than Pasargadae, was part of a defensive enclosure surrounded by a wall with buttresses and recesses, built of huge stones without mortar. It was accessible by five staircases. On it, a triple *iwan* was probably the audience room of a princely dwelling. The terraces of Masjid-i Suleiman, of Bard-i Nishundah and of Pasargadae all pre-date that of Persepolis.

The town of Susa, built by Darius on Elamite foundations, consisted of a citadel on the acropolis, a palace and a throne-room, or *apadana*, on a neighbouring mound, and of the city proper which was separated from it by a broad avenue. The whole complex was surrounded by a strong wall of unbaked bricks, with projecting towers, and was protected by a moat.[2]

The palace still showed a strong Babylonian influence. 'The plan consisted of interior courts which opened on to the rooms and living quarters; these again were surrounded by long corridors that permitted the guards to watch every movement. The walls of unbaked bricks were also decorated in Babylonian style.'[3] 'The throne room itself, known as the *apadana*, was a hall, the roof of which was supported by six rows of six columns nearly 65 feet in height, surmounted by capitals with protomes of bulls; on the north, east and west the hall was surrounded by three peristyles of twelve columns... It was approached by three wide stairways... Some of the capitals were simple imposts... in others the protomes rested on volutes.'[4]

The *apadana* of Darius at Persepolis was built on the same principles; his palace there was built of unbaked bricks, with door and window frames of stone, surmounted by Egyptian lintels.

The Greek influence probably reached the Iranian plateau some time in the mid-fifth century B.C. It became much more obvious in the period following the Greek invasion. Ghirshman distinguishes three categories of art under the Seleucids: Iranian, Graeco-Iranian and Hellenistic.[5] The temple retained its classical Iranian shape, although in some structures (Istakhr, Kangovar) Greek motifs can be found in the decoration of capitals and, to some extent, in the general plan of the buildings. Statues are the main manifestation of Hellenistic art, although it is difficult to determine to what extent they were used as architectural decoration. In urban design the Greek contribution was the *agora*, a city square designed as an integral part of the town centre.

The early Buddhist architecture was characterised by three main structures, the *stupa*, the temple and the monastery (*vihara*). The *stupa*, which originated probably in the time of Asoka (third century B.C.), was originally a commemorative mound containing holy relics. The mound was of earth or rubble, with a brick surface, and was surrounded by a wooden fence. Primarily a religious structure, the *stupa* was a monument for every purpose. There were funerary *stupas*, *stupas* as reliquaries or cenotaphs, memorial *stupas* etc. In the course of time, the mound developed into a square base surmounted by a hemispherical cupola. On top of it was a square railing, or box-like structure, called *harmika*, from which rose a shaft of metal or wood supporting a number of umbrellas, usually seven, symbolising the stages of heaven.

The whole structure stood either in a courtyard or on a terrace, to permit ritual circumambulation. The terrace itself was sometimes raised, with one or more monumental staircases leading to it. The umbrellas were often painted gold and carried bells, so that the edifice could be seen and heard from afar. Franz[6] sees in the simple tumulus *stupa* a continuation of the Bactrian heritage going back to the nomad *kurgans*, or tumulus graves, whereas the combination of a square base and a round or cylindrical superstructure contains both Hellenistic and Iranian elements. The earliest *stupas* with a square base, which were the Hellenistic transformation of the Indian *stupa*, were found in Taxila-Sirkap. They date from the end of the first century B.C., at which time, after the end of the Maurya Empire, Greek influence increased considerably. In later periods the structure became more sophisticated. The *stupas* were composed of square and cylindrical parts in various combinations; an octagonal part was exceptional. The base was often star or cross-shaped, raised on several superimposed terraces. The cupola rested on a high and richly decorated drum. The main *stupa* was surrounded by a number of small votive *stupas*. The building material was usually brick or stone, in Kushan times often the so-called diaper masonry, which consisted of thin layers of schist or slate interspersed with large blocks of differently coloured stone. Inside, the *stupa* was filled with earth or rubble, except for a small chamber containing the relic. Brick-built *stupas* seem to be the earliest, with no decoration. The later ones, built of schist or a mixture of schist and brick, often had pilasters with decorative capitals. The architectural decoration was fairly simple: false columns with capitals, cornices, false arches etc. The main decoration, however, were sculptures. Traces of colossal statues, 16–26 feet high, have been found on several sites. Large statues stood in niches either at the base or in the walls surrounding the courtyard. Smaller sculptures were ranged in several rows or tiers on all sides of the base. Paintings were sometimes used to decorate the niches or the flat surfaces between them.

The earliest Buddhist temples may have been circular. To the round sanctum a rectangular assembly hall was added and the two together formed what K. Fischer calls Apsidenhalle (hall with apse).[7] The cella, round or square, harbouring a statue, and the hall became the basic form of the temple. To it belonged a terrace, open or covered. In subsequent periods the terraces became more numerous, staircases were added and the roof was raised into a tower.

The general feature of the *vihara*, or monastery, was a fortress-like structure reminiscent of the Greek and Syrian fort (*hydreuma*). It was square for the most part, with or without towers and with a surrounding wall. The rooms or cells backed onto the wall on the inside. There was one or more courtyards and a principal *stupa* with a number of smaller *stupas* either in front of it or surrounding it. The entrance was always opposite the main *stupa*. The whole complex did not always face the same way. It seems that the direction the main *stupa* was facing was set with regard to a certain position of the sun.[8]

Originally, the *vihara* was a secular building, but often the *stupa* was incorporated into it to give it a sacred character. Sometimes the *stupa* occupied a separate courtyard connected with the *vihara* by a corridor. Some *viharas* were excavated in the rock-side, making a fairly complex troglodyte dwelling like the famous rock monasteries of Haibak, Bamiyan and Foladi, or Kyzyl and Kumtura in Xinjiang.

It is interesting that the cave viharas often imitated in rock certain features of Indian wooden architecture, for example the so-called lantern ceiling, which consisted of wooden beams put across the angles of a square, state by stage, until the square was filled.[9] Imitations of the Persian domed cupola and the squinch can be found in later caves. The open-air monastery of the later period used the Persian principles of the four-*iwan* court, domed ceilings, barrel-vaulted corridors etc.

The Indian Buddhist influence radiated from the great Buddhist centres in the province of Gandhara – now the northern Punjab – and by mixing with the Graeco-Bactrian and later Roman elements produced an art which became known as the art of Gandhara. This art had both a religious and a secular, or dynastic, side; it reached its peak under the Kushan Empire with its capital in Begram, or Kapisa, just north of Kabul, and dominated the area from the first century A.D. until the invasion of the Hephthalites in the fifth century.

It was characterised mainly by the representation of the Buddha in human form. Previously, these representations had only been symbolic. Some scholars saw in the Gandharan Buddha an orientalised version of the Greek Apollo.[10] The Gandharan sculptures mostly represented scenes from the life of the Buddha and the legends connected with it. Apart from purely symbolic images, they contained four main groups of subjects. The Buddhas were all treated in the traditional way, with idealised faces, no facial expression and perfectly balanced features. The bodhisattvas, although equally idealised, show a strong Greek influence and often even imitate Greek models, such as Aphrodite, Alexander or Homer. The donators and soldiers were evidently inspired by real people and reflect different ethnic types, dresses, hairstyles and arms. The demons, on the contrary, were grotesque, anthropomorphic or zoomorphic creatures, not unlike their counterpart in European Romanesque art.

The material was schist, stucco or moulded clay. No paintings in the Gandharan style have been found, and no buildings from that period have survived either, except for some foundations and remnants of walls uncovered on archaeological sites.

With the weakening of Greek tradition, the Gandharan style gradually changed. The Iranian element, never totally absent, became more important as the influence of Sasanian Persia increased in the area. Thus the frescoes of Bamiyan show Buddhist figures clad in Iranian costumes, wearing Iranian adornments and weapons, and in some cases even with distinctly Persian facial features.

Archaeological discoveries on both sides of the Oxus, as well as Italian excavations in the Swat valley in north-west Pakistan, tend to accentuate the regional diversities of Graeco-Bactrian art and its relations with the art of Gandhara, Mathura and also Parthian art. This led D. Schlumberger to coin the term Graeco-Iranian or Kushan art, of which the art of Bactria, Gandhara and Mathura would be only regional aspects.[11]

The later period of the art of Gandhara is sometimes called Indo-Afghan.[12] Politically, it coincided with the rule of the so-called Kidara-Kushans, who came to the Punjab from Bactria at the end of the fourth century A.D. Its main characteristic is the use of terracotta and stucco in sculpture, whereas the older school used almost exclusively stone. The best examples are the sculptures of Mohra Moradu and Jaulian at Taxila.

In the Kushano-Sasanian period some new architectural elements emerged and some of the older ones appeared in a new guise.

In town design, some Parthian towns in the west were laid out in the circular form which, according to some authorities, went back to an old urban tradition in Western Asia and perhaps to the form of Assyrian military camps.[13] The inner city of Balkh was laid out in this form, and in Khorezm the site of Koy-Krylgan-Kala was also circular. In domestic architecture, some houses were no doubt built around a courtyard, a form derived from Mesopotamia, as found in Dura Europos and elsewhere. In others, the *iwan*, mentioned already, developed into a triple chamber with the central part usually somewhat larger than the wings. The Achaemenid cella still survived in the Parthian temple, but it was now separated from the exterior by an ambulatory, while the external staircase was now built into the wall and led up to the roof, where the sacred fire burned.[14]

The material was rubble and pebbles with mortar, rather than stone. The decoration consisted of stone sculpture, moulded stucco and frescoes. The motifs, apart from some geometrical ornaments showing Assyrian traditions, were acanthus leaves, musicians, divinities and royal personages. The Kushan palace of Toprak-Kala in Khorezm (third to fourth centuries A.D.) was probably decorated in a similar style. The buildings of Old Nisa show some affinities with Toprak-Kala and Surkh Kotal.[15]

The Sasanians revived the rectangular town shape based on Greek models, with two main streets bisecting the rectangle and meeting at right angles in the centre. The town of Bishapur is the best preserved example of this type. The invention of the arch which first appeared in the Parthian period, had a profound effect on earlier architectural forms. Thus the *iwan* was transformed into a vaulted archway, with relief decoration covering all the walls and executed mainly in stucco, but it still retained its function as a reception hall.

The introduction of the cupola, or dome, which was the logical consequence of the arch, entirely transformed the whole concept of roofing. The problem, how to put a circular dome on a square base, led to the invention of the squinch which was to become one of the basic features of Iranian architecture. The first squinches probably appeared in the late second or early third century and can still be seen in the ruins of the palace at Firuzabad.[16]

The palace of Shapur I at Bishapur shows, perhaps for the first time, the four-*iwan* courtyard on a cruciform plan, another basic feature of Iranian architecture. (It is sometimes argued that the great hall of the Bishapur palace was covered with a dome, but this cannot be taken for certain.) Round towers, perhaps an influence of Rome, appear at Bishapur and Taxila,[17] and found a widespread use as minarets in the Islamic period.

The Sasanian temple, as described by Ghirshman[18] consisted of the traditional cella enclosed by four corridors. In Firuzabad, there was a tower, on top of which a fire was lit during the ceremonies. These ceremonies centred around pavilions open on all four sides, with four pillars supporting four arches surmounted by a dome. The decoration of Sasanian palaces was in stucco, fresco painting and, later, in stone. Mosaic pavements were found in Bishapur.

In Soghd, a one-time Achaemenid province beyond the Oxus, which reverted to the Sasanians for a century and a half, between the fall of the Kushan Empire and the invasion of the Hephthalites – elements of Iranian architecture and art appear heavily mixed with Indian Buddhist and, to some extent, nomadic influences. Thus the Soghdian *kushk*, or fortified country house or palace, was probably not much different in design from its Parthian or Sasanian counterpart, but its decoration would be considerably different in style, as the frescoes of Balalyk-Tepe, Varakhsha, Pendzhikent and Afrasiyab have shown.

Some other examples of the composite character of the Kushan Empire – which included Soghd, Khorezm, Bactria and other provinces – are given by Frumkin:[19] the Indian-style Kara-Tepe, with Iranian sculptures and Hellenistic features, was Buddhist; Khalchayan, with its Hellenistic sculptures and wall-paintings, was not. The Kushan Toprak-Kala was a huge Khorezmian castle, the temple of which was neither Buddhist nor apparently devoted to any of the major religions, but probably connected with dynastic worship. Liyavandak (Bukhara) showed Hellenistic features, but there is no reason to believe that it was Buddhist. The same applies to Afrasiyab and Tali-Barzu. Whereas a small building of Surkh-Kotal was a Buddhist shrine, the main shrine was presumably devoted to dynastic worship.

The influence of Buddhism was weakened but not eliminated by the Hephthalite conquest. The decline of Buddhist art, however, as manifested by the sites ranging from Bamiyan to Tepe Sardar, is obvious. Colossal-sized statues replaced sophistication of form and attention to detail. Static postures, crude composition and cheap materials confirm the picture of general decadence.

With the disintegration of the Hephthalite Empire, the Iranian influence became stronger, in particular where the local princelings fell under the suzerainty of the Sasanians. It was, however, less pronounced south of the Oxus than north of it. Secular works of art such as the Soghdian frescoes of Pendzhikent, Varakhsha or Balalyk-Tepe, or secular buildings of the *kushk* type, have no counterpart on Afghan territory. The rock paintings of Dokhtar-i Nushirwan remain an isolated manifestation of the Iranian spirit in a country which was still dominated by Buddhist traditions.

The Buddhist sites of Ak-Beshim and Adzhina-Tepe, in the Chu and Vakhsh valley, respectively, which seemed to thrive until the seventh or eighth centuries, indicate that Buddhism was very much alive north of the Oxus, even under the Turks who succeeded the Hephthalites in the sixth century. The evidence of

Bamiyan, the greatest Buddhist centre, is inconclusive, but it seems that it remained Buddhist until the ninth century, and perhaps even later.[20]

It may be concluded, therefore, that although weak and artistically decadent, Buddhism survived in the eastern parts of Afghanistan and Transoxiana until the arrival of the Arabs. Considering the Hindu (Brahmin) presence in eastern Afghanistan, as documented by the excavations at Khair Khane, eastern Afghanistan was not properly secured for Islam until the end of the ninth, or more probably the tenth, century.[21] The rest of the country, Khorassan and Sistan, were already Islamised in the seventh century.

EARLY ISLAMIC

The Iranian architectural principles, such as the *apadana*, the *iwan*, the arch and the dome, were all, one way or another, incorporated in early Muslim architecture (though there is no agreement as to the extent and the timing of these developments).

The towns after the arrival of Islam retained most of their characteristics from the previous period. There was the fortified citadel with its palace, prison and military quarters. The commercial activities and the homes of the wealthy were concentrated in the *shahristan* (medina) which was surrounded by a wall. Outside lay the outer suburbs (*rabads*) where most of the people had their homes, gardens, orchards etc. Sometimes the *rabads* were also protected by a second belt of walls.

The Arab *hypostyle* mosque, for example, may have been a simple imitation of the Prophet's house; but it also may have been inspired by the *apadana*.[22] It had a flat roof supported by rows of columns or arcades, arranged either perpendicularly or parallel to the *kibla* wall.

The other type, the four-*iwan* mosque, may have had its origin in the fire temple which, as we have seen, was a square building with four wide arches covered by a dome, to which sometimes *hypostyle* halls were added.[23] In the Seljuk period this structure was combined with the four-*iwan* courtyard already known from Iranian palaces since Bishapur. One *iwan* was in the middle of each side of the rectangular courtyard. The *iwan* opposite the entrance, which was usually rather shallow, opened into the domed chamber in front of the *mihrab*.

There is, however, no uniformity of views about the original position or function of the *iwan*. Thus Vogt-Göknil[24] argues persuasively that in ancient Iran the *iwan* as an audience hall was oriented towards the outside (to the facade) and not into the courtyard. An analogy in Christian architecture would be the crossing of the transept, a sort of 'throne-room' of Christ. In the mosque, its function was that of a threshold, *lieu de passage*, analogous with the portal of a cathedral. In a *madrasa* it served as an auditorium, while in a caravanserai it was used as a common-room by the travellers. Its function as an entrance, or entrance hall, came as late as the Safavid period (sixteenth century). Earlier, the entrance was behind the *iwan*, any one of the four, but most frequently behind the northern one. The same author also maintains that the concept dominating the design of the facades and the *iwans* was that of the courtyard, and not the interior arrangement of the mosque. The courtyard was more important than the *mihrab* room.

As against the sobriety and simplicity of the North African mosques (for example Ibn Tulun), the Persian mosque displayed an undeniable quest for beauty and grandeur.

However, large congregational mosques were not the only places of worship. Small sanctuaries destined for private devotion no doubt existed alongside, and the fact that we know little about them may be due simply to the fact that they were built of lighter and cheaper material and did not survive. Some mosques of that kind, with wooden ceilings, columns and wooden arcades on the outside, still exist, dating from the sixteenth century or later (for example the Masjid-i Baland in Bukhara), and there is nothing to suggest that this was a late Islamic innovation.

Other religious buildings constructed on the same principles as the mosque were the *madrasa* and the *khaniga* (*khangah*). The former was a religious college, the latter more a kind of monastery destined for meditation. In a *madrasa*, the arcades surrounding the courtyard were transformed into one or two-storey buildings housing lecture rooms and living quarters for teachers and students. The model for such a courtyard lined with cells may have been taken from Buddhist monasteries.

The caravanserais, particularly those built in open country, were often built like fortresses, with protective towers in the corners, bastions etc. Their courtyard was much larger, in order to accommodate animals, and the domed chamber was often missing. The outer walls were usually bare and blind, though there are some cases of architectural decoration (pilasters, blind arches) being used.[25]

The mausoleum was either a square domed chamber or a tomb tower which could be round, square or polygonal. Such towers were topped by a round or conical cupola. Over the chamber was an inner dome, and there was often a *mihrab* inside. The tomb was placed on the floor of the chamber or in a crypt below. At a later stage an ornamental portal or *iwan* was added to the original structure. According to Grabar,[26] the mausoleums were among the first buildings to acquire monumental gates.

The minarets were of various shapes and heights, ranging from the circular and conical Transoxanian types to the star-shaped towers of Ghazni or the three-storey gigantic minaret of Jam. In the West, in Samarra and Fustat, spiral minarets were no doubt built on Sasanian models going back to the Babylonian *ziggurat*. They were either free-standing or connected with the mosque. In Seljuk times, two minarets were used to flank the entrance gate. In some places in Iran, Anatolia and Egypt, the function of the minaret was fulfilled by a small baldachined platform on the roof of the mosque.

Building in brick was an old tradition in the East, whereas stone buildings belong rather to Anatolian, in particular Armenian, traditions. Stone-built Seljuk mosques may have been built by Armenian master builders.[27]

Various types of vault were used for roofing. *Iwans* had been roofed by barrel vaults since Parthian times, and in the early mosques the same system had been used to cover the bays behind the court arcades. Square or rectangular premises in the corners of the court posed certain problems, and new types of vaulting had to be devised, most of them structural variations of the barrel-vault principle.

Another ancient type of roofing which passed into Islamic architecture was the dome or cupola. The single dome was a direct development of the Sasanian dome. Some time in the twelfth century the double dome appeared, but it became widely used in the Timurid period only.

The squinch, which was also known from Parthian and Sasanian times now became used in an astonishing variety of shapes and forms. In principle, it was an arch built across each corner of the square, thus providing a zone of transition and reducing the square to an octagon. If necessary, small arches could be further built to bridge its corners, thus producing a sixteen-sided figure which nearly approximated the ring of the dome. In the earliest examples of this type of construction, the squinch was rather crude and compressed, and the arch created a small trumpet-shaped hollow in each corner of the angle, which had to be filled or masked. Various ingenious ways were devised to do this.

The *mukarnas*, or stalactite vault, may have had a structural function in the early period, but later became a purely decorative device. It consisted of clusters and tiers of cells that softened and enriched the broad expanses and simple contours of buildings. It became used almost universally, although, in Pope's words, it was difficult to describe or record, and its planning was a baffling task. Briefly, it was formed by 'rows of superimposed out-curving panels, generally miniature quarter-domes, the apexes apparently leaning on empty space, the point of each support being the dividing line of the row above'.[28]

Architectural decoration in carved stone goes back to Achaemenid times, but it was more often designed to fill the surface of the wall than to become part of its fabric. Brick decoration, on the other hand, was more likely to achieve the result that the decorated surfaces became parts of architectural volumes (walls, towers, arches) of brick constructions. Variations in brickwork could emphasise

12. Khiva (view from the Kunya Ark)

13. Kalta Minar, Khiva

14. Tash Hauli Palace, Khiva

15. Mausoleum of Sultan Tekesh, Kunya Urgench

16. Mausoleum Gur Emir, Samarkand (front view)

17. Mausoleum Gur Emir, Samarkand

18. Mausoleum Gur Emir, Samarkand (general view)

19. ABOVE. Madrasa Tilla Kari, Samarkand (restored)

20. BELOW. Mosque Bibi Khanum, Samarkand (under restoration)

architectural lines and distinguish surfaces which were to be decorated. Decorative designs could be obtained by the way in which bricks were laid. According to Grabar,[29] brick decoration spread from Central Asia to Iran and Anatolia.

Stucco was used to fill gaps between bricks, and stucco panels were eventually used as parts of brick ornaments. Stucco was known in pre-Islamic times (for example in the palaces of Ctesiphon, Varaksha etc.), and early Iranian motifs were used on Umayyad palaces.[30]

Pre-Islamic motifs can also be discerned on the decorative slabs from the early eleventh century palace of Termez, on some of the ninth to tenth century panels from Afrasiyab (Samarkand) and in the eleventh century mausoleum Nasr ben Ali in Uzkend, as well as on the mosques of Samarra, Nayin and No Gumbad.

The technique of terracotta – ceramic fragments formed to fit certain areas or to form patterns – was also known in Central Asia in Parthian times. Its motifs were no doubt inspired by stucco patterns. According to Grabar, it reappeared in Uzkend and Bost.[31] It further developed into mosaic faience, which became widely used from the fourteenth century onwards, when 'stucco and brick began to lose their effectiveness'.[32]

It was manufactured in the town of Kashan, in Iran, with the use of cobalt, sulphur, arsenic and metallic oxides. Originally, small glazed bricks were used to form inscriptions or inscriptional friezes. The earliest of these is believed to be in Damghan (eleventh century). This technique was suitable for Kufic inscriptions and geometrical patterns, but for inscriptions in Naskhi or Thulth, and for vegetal ornamental patterns, a different technique was required. It was found in larger ceramic tiles, or panels, with under-glaze painted or carved decoration. Whole surfaces could then be filled with ornamental designs. The first large surface decorated in mosaic faience dates from the mid-thirteenth century and is on the Sircali Madrasa in Konya.

Up to the Mongol invasion, architectural decoration was strictly monochrome, with few exceptions just mentioned. In the fourteenth and fifteenth centuries the use of colour became virtually universal, with an ever increasing range. The first colours were turquoise, royal blue and white. The peak was reached in the Timurid period in Samarkand, Herat and Balkh, after which a decadence set in, the quality deteriorated and the range of colours shrank again.

The two main parts of religious buildings to be decorated in this way were the *mihrab* and the entrance gate. Bands of decoration, ornamental or inscriptional, were used on minarets from earlier times (Jam, Kalan-Bukhara, Vabkent, Dawlatabad, Ghazni etc).

The ornamental motifs were classified by Grabar[33] in five categories. Human and animal features were rare. Some stucco figures exist in museums only; there seemed to be a limited range of figural wall-paintings, and many more appeared in manuscripts, thus responding both to the Iranian and Indian traditions. At a later stage, some highly stylised bird and animal shapes appeared, probably under Chinese influence, on some buildings in Samarkand and elsewhere. Architectural elements, columns, pilasters, blind arches, cornices, capitals and bases were more frequent. The *mukarnas*, mentioned above, would fall into this category. Geometrical ornaments consisted first of simple forms and patterns, usually combinations of squares, triangles and circles. More sophisticated ornaments in the form of knots (*girikh*) appeared later. Calligraphy, first Kufic and later Naskhi and Thulth, was frequently used and was generally of a very high standard. Indian influences can be found in some decorative elements in inscriptions, for example on the tomb of Mahmud of Ghazna, and later on the tombs of the Sultans Masud and Ibrahim. Floral and vegetal ornament on its own was rare before the Mongol period. Vegetal motifs were mainly used as a background to inscriptions, and only at a later stage they formed independent panels and patterns. Finally, some abstract designs may be discerned, in particular in the form of medallions, sometimes incorporating pre-Islamic symbols and signs. Three-dimensional abstract designs composed of bevelled curved lines were first used in the ninth century in Iraq to carve in stones, stucco and wood. Later they were also used in Iran and Central Asia.[34] There was, no doubt, a close connection between ornamental motifs used in architecture, in carpets, in book illumination and in various other crafts, such as pottery, metalware etc., although it is not easy to determine their mutual influence. It seems that in certain periods architectural decoration was inspired by motifs used in carpets or pottery, whereas in others the inspiration went in the opposite direction.

Very few wall-paintings have survived, but in those from Lashkar-i Bazar Schlumberger finds a strong influence of Buddhist art.[35]

Wood carving was, no doubt, extensively used, but only a few specimens survived, among them the famous 'Somnath door' at Agra, and some of the columns in the Djuma mosque in Khiva.

Although all artistic activity on the territory of Afghanistan was interrupted by the Mongol invasion, the Seljuk (Ghaznavid, Ghorid) architectural tradition lived on in India under the rule of the sultans of Ghor. A series of remarkable buildings were erected in Delhi, in particular, which provide an interesting blend of Iranian Muslim and local Hinduistic features.

TIMURID AND LATE ISLAMIC

In the first half century or so after the Mongol invasion, hardly any new buildings were erected. In two generations of inactivity, specialised skills and crafts tend to disappear or to deteriorate. It was therefore natural that when some activity was resumed towards the end of the thirteenth century, the leading craftsmen should come from Shiraz and other cities in Southern Iran, a part of the country which escaped destruction and where at least some building, however limited, had continued. In Transoxania the gap was longer, and in Afghanistan longer still. In Transoxania there were a few edifices from the middle of the fourteenth century, but in the last quarter of the century building activity was already in full swing under Timur's personal patronage. In Afghanistan, with the exception of the reconstruction in the early fourteenth century of the Great Mosque in Herat, virtually no monumental building was carried out until the reign of Shah Rukh at the beginning of the fifteenth century. (It seems that the Eastern Islamic outpost in the sultanate of Delhi, where some remarkable monuments were constructed in the fourteenth and fifteenth centuries, had little to contribute to the artistic revival of Afghanistan). Local craftsmen had therefore to bridge a gap of nearly two centuries, and it is safe to assume that most of Shah Rukh's architects and craftsmen came either from Iran or from his father's Samarkand. Many of them would again be from Shiraz, given the fact that Timur occupied that city in 1393 and deported all its artists and craftsmen to Samarkand. The ideas and the models came with these architects, masons and decorative artists. Thus the architecture of fourteenth-century Iran, which was itself a continuation of a pre-Mongol Seljuk architecture, became an inspiration for the construction of Timur's Samarkand which, in turn, served as a model for Shah Rukh's Herat.

Architectural forms remained more or less the same as in the pre-Mongol period. The double dome now became frequently used. The two domes usually had different profiles. As a rule, the outer one was raised much higher than the inner one, to enhance the outside effect of the building. To increase this effect still further, the outer dome was given a bulbous shape and was raised on a high drum. The drum, which in earlier times was hardly more than a zone of transition between the base and the dome, now helped to enlarge the interior covered by the dome. The drum as such was well known in Buddhist architecture, where it was used to raise the cupola of the *stupa*, but in Islamic architecture it acquired real significance only in the Timurid period.

An isolated innovation was the triple dome used in the mausoleum of Gawhar Shad in Herat, but the added inner dome was purely decorative, with no structural function.

The *iwan* now acquired the function of a monumental entrance hall. Two *iwans* were usually built back-to-back, one facing into the courtyard, the other turned outwards. A splendid decorated facade, with the *iwan* in the middle, was part of the general emphasis on the outer appearance and visual impression, which went hand-in-hand with the colossal dimensions of the buildings.

Generally speaking, this trend towards the colossal and the conspicuous became the characteristic features of the Timurid period, often to the detriment of the quality of construction or the attention to detail – although some scholars find the combination of architectural masses, decorative designs and colour-schemes to be in perfect balance.[36]

This may be true of some of the smaller and more intimate buildings in Samarkand (Ishrat Khana or Shah-i Zinda), but it could hardly apply to such rambling structures as the Bibi Khanum mosque, and even less to the much cruder buildings and their decoration in Herat or in Balkh.

This tendency towards the colossal continued for some time under the Uzbek khans in Transoxania, where a notable addition to the previous style was the exceedingly high *pishtak* wall (the front wall of the *iwan*). Buildings of this kind were contemporary with the Safavid monuments in Isfahan, but on the whole lagged behind them both in their design and in their decoration.

In urban design, the Timurid and post-Timurid era contributed the notion of the monumental square, an open space surrounded by large, impressive buildings and conveying a sense of proportion and harmony, as well as greatness. The Registan in Samarkand, the somewhat later Labi-Hauz complex in Bukhara and the Maydan-i Shah in Isfahan (laid out in 1598) were expressions of the same idea.

The Timurid gardens were based on the Iranian principle of the *chahar bagh* (four gardens), that is symmetrically laid out squares divided by water channels, with straight rows of trees and shrubs lined with flower beds. They can still be seen in the Babur Gardens in Kabul and in their later imitations in Srinagar, Lahore and elsewhere in India.

Finally, a special bazaar building made its appearance in this period. Its standard plan was the so-called *chahar-su* (four rivers) – sometimes rendered as *chahar-suq* (four markets) – consisting of two passageways intersecting each other at right angles, covered by a dome at the crossing. Small apertures in the vaulted roof let in sufficient light, yet kept out the intense heat in summer and retained warmth in winter. Buildings of this kind seem to have had a long tradition in the area.

In contrast to architecture, the decoration, and in particular the ornament, changed considerably.

The main new factor was the introduction of glazed tiles and the ever increasing range of colours. The basic three colours, turquoise, royal blue, and white, were followed by black, red and yellow, as well as other shades of green and blue. The larger ornaments were again executed in small bricks which were not glazed (the so-called *banai*-technique). More sophisticated ornaments were composed of mosaic panels made of a number of small particles of various sizes and shapes. The monochrome carved, or incised, terracotta of the previous period was now glazed and polychrome. As for the motifs, *banai*-technique was mainly used for geometrical ornaments and large Kufic inscriptions. Complicated *girikhs* based on intertwined patterns of pentagons, hexagons or octagons appeared on flat and spherical surfaces. Floral motifs were widely used, in particular on arches, vaults and spandrels. Chinese motifs, stylised dragons, clouds and mountains, sometimes appeared among purely vegetal ornaments. In calligraphy, the highly decorative Thulth style was added to the Kufic and Naskhi, but in general the inscriptions of this period are inferior to the elegance and variety of the monochrome bands of the previous age.

Painted decoration seems to have been fairly rare. Few specimens have been preserved, some in Samarkand and Shahrisabz, in the Masjid-i Shah in Mashad and in the Zarnigar Khana of Gazurgah in Herat, all dating from the second half of the fifteenth and the first half of the sixteenth century. The motifs were mainly floral, in medallion and band form, with some affinity to carpet design and miniature painting.

The trend seems to have been reversed as regards the origin of the motifs. Whereas in the previous period architectural ornaments were often imitated in other crafts, pottery, textiles etc., it now seems as though architecture preferred to use motifs already developed elsewhere, especially in carpet-knotting and book decoration.

The totally flat decoration inspired by book illustration dominated the field. To quote Melikian-Chirvani,[37] the decoration became 'totally independent from architecture itself... in accordance with the general tendency of the Timurid century where art of the book prevailed over all other arts'. It was the surface alone that mattered, and it had to be a flat surface. Consequently, all architectural decoration disappeared, except some examples of corner colonettes with capitals, which can be seen on the Timurid mausoleums in Samarkand and in a much cruder form on the Green Mosque in Balkh.

Under Shah Rukh and Husayn Baykara, the art of the miniature and book illumination reached its peak. In Herat, a distinct Timurid style developed, with the famous Bihzad as its supreme master. After Herat fell to the Uzbeks in 1507, Bihzad moved to Tabriz, to the court of Shah Tahmasp who, as a boy, had spent several years in Herat. Tabriz had been, for some time, the home of a rival miniaturist school, that of the Turkmen, which was considerably influenced by Chinese and Indian art. Under the shah, who became acquainted with its artists

and himself became a keen painter during his stay in Herat, the refined classical
Timurid style coexisted in Tabriz with the much wilder and rougher Turkmen
idiom. Eventually, a synthesis of the two styles emerged in the person of Sultan
Muhammad, a Tabriz painter whose pictures, in their refinement and psycho-
logical characterisation might even surpass Bihzad's.[38]

Little is known about carpet-knotting and design in the Herat period.
However, the change brought about in the traditional carpet patterns in Tabriz
by the arrival of Shah Tahmasp was in many ways similar to the change in the
art of the miniature. The early carpets which were introduced to Western Asia by
the Turkish tribes had a geometrical, primitively abstract decoration which, by
repeating the same motif, tried to break out of the limited space available. The
Turkish abstract patterns that dominated all rug design up to the end of the
fifteenth century were enlivened by floral ornaments, while in Iran they were
replaced by figurative and floral motifs, often set within a pattern of arabesques
surrounding a central medallion. The medallion style was created not by the
weavers but rather by the painters and illuminators of the court school. The large
characteristic central medallions served to give the rugs a monumental character.
Some of them were of supreme simplicity and austerity, others were more
elaborate, with a great variety of decorative motifs. The carpet design was often
taken from drawings by well known painters. Persian workshops were producing
carpets with magnificent compositions, sumptuous decor and dazzling colours,
in which the subject became more and more important. Hunting carpets and
animal carpets developed at that time, showing scenes of animals fighting among
trees and plants, or being chased by hunters.

When Babur became the first Moghul emperor of India, Kabul and eastern
Afghanistan were open to an ever increasing Indian influence. This lasted until
the invasion of the Persian Nadir Shah in the eighteenth century, after which the
local Turco-Iranian traditions again prevailed.

Little of historical interest remains of that period except the Babur Gardens in
Kabul, already mentioned. In architecture, the most remarkable building showing
strong Indian influence is the mausoleum of Hazret Ali in Mazar-i Sharif. It
was originally built in the Timurid style, but acquired an increasingly Indian
appearance as a result of subsequent additions, restorations and rebuilding,
which has gone on until recently.

In the seventeenth and eighteenth centuries wall-paintings with subjects
such as landscapes and buildings appeared alongside purely ornamental motifs.
The holy places of Islam seem to have been the favourite subject. Golombek[39]
distinguished between two different styles, one from the mid-seventeenth century,
the other from the eighteenth or even early nineteenth century, the main
difference being the emphasis on line in the first, on area colour in the second.

Paintings of both styles have been preserved in the shrine of Gazurgah in Herat.

Although in the nineteenth century Khiva wood carving on doors and wooden support columns of the traditional *ayvan* (*iwan*) was of a very high quality, few comparable specimens can be found in contemporary Afghanistan.

In Afghanistan, the period from the middle of the eighteenth century onwards may be regarded as a period of national independence, but culturally it was an era of decadence. The tribal oligarchy which ruled the country had neither the financial means nor the cultural background to foster artistic activity of any significance.

Although not in any way outstanding, the mosque of Takht-i Pol near Balkh, with its Indianised architecture and interior decoration, is the most interesting building from that period.

And yet, while all artistic activity seemed to be at a standstill in Afghanistan from the early sixteenth century onwards, this was not the case in the neigh-bouring territories of Turkestan and northern India. The Uzbek khans, when forced to retreat beyond the Amu Darya, established their residence in Bukhara, and it was in this city as well as in post-Timurid Samarkand that the first two centuries of Uzbek rule brought about a number of interesting contributions to the local brand of Islamic architecture and ornament. There was little innovation in the art of building itself, as all monumental structures of that period continued to be built by traditional methods and in the traditional idiom, but the range of ornamental motifs and the techniques of decoration changed and expanded considerably until, in the eighteenth century, decadence set in and the general atmosphere began to resemble that of Afghanistan. After that, with the exception of some isolated specimens, like the khan's palace in Kokand (1876), it was the curious, unexpected and short-lived flowering of nineteenth-century Khiva, an isolated oasis near the Aral Sea, that kept the Persian creative genius alive in all that enormous area east of Iran itself.

An entirely different picture emerged in northern India, where Moghul archi-tecture appeared as an entirely new style. It blended Islamic traditions ranging from the Ghaznavid and Ghorid to the late Timurid with the indigenous Indian, or Hinduistic, ones. The traditional Iranian models were either abandoned or changed beyond recognition. The four-*iwan* mosque gave way to the three-hall mosque (itself perhaps a late reappearance of the ancient triple-*iwan*), the bulbous cupola became onion-shaped, the broken arch gave way to the horse-shoe arch. The Iranian sobriety, linearity and flatness were supplanted by the Indian profusion or ornamentalism, naturalism and a much less thorough attention to architectural and technical detail. The Iranian technique of mosaic faience was replaced by inlaid stone, first sandstone inlaid with marble, and later marble inlaid with semi-precious stones. The glazed tiles persisted for some time, mainly as painted medallion panels, but in a much cruder and less refined form. Red sandstone inlaid with white marble became a typical, and effective, element of flat wall decoration. Ornamental panels composed of simple geometrical patterns of clearly Islamic origin were still to be found. Next to them, however, other panels of the same material carried symbolic images and motifs of a pre-dominantly indigenous Hinduistic character.

NOTES ON CHAPTER IV
Full details of abbreviations and publications are in the Bibliography

1 Ghirshman, *Iran*, p. 135.
2 Ghirshman, *Iran*, p. 165.
3 Ghirshman, *Iran*, p. 166.
4 Ghirshman, *Iran*, p. 167.
5 Ghirshman, *Iran*, p. 232.
6 Franz, G.H., 'Der Buddhistische Stupa in Afghanistan', *AFJ* 4/4/1977 and *AFJ* 5/1/1978.
7 Fischer, K., *Schöpfungen der indischen Kunst.*
8 Barthoux, J.J., 'Les Fouilles de Hadda', *Mem. DAFA* IV, 1933.
9 K. Fischer sees in the lantern ceiling an element of Central Asian wooden architecture: *Schöpfungen der indischen Kunst.*
10 Dupree, L., *Afghanistan*, p. 296.
11 Frumkin, G., 'Archaeology', *CAR* XIII, p. 253.
12 Marshall, J., *Taxila* I, p. 75; II., p. 520.
13 Ghirshman, *Iran*, p. 273.
14 Ghirshman, *Iran*, p. 276.
15 Frumkin, *CAR* XIV, p. 77.
16 For a detailed description of the squinch, see Pope, *Persian Architecture*, p. 256.
17 Ghirshman, *Iran*, p. 322.
18 Ghirshman, *Iran*, p. 322.
19 Frumkin, *CAR* XIII, p. 252.
20 Bosworth, C.E., *The Development of Persian Culture*, p. 34.
21 Bosworth, *Culture*, p. 34.
22 Creswell, K.A.C., *Early Muslim Architecture.*
23 Ettinghausen, R., 'The Man-made Setting', in *The World of Islam*, p. 72.
24 Vogt-Göknil, U., *Les grands courants de l'architecture islamique*, p. 72.
25 See Rabat-i Malik, nr. Bukhara, described by Pope in *Architecture*, p. 129.
26 Grabar, O., *Islamic Architecture*, p. 76.
27 Vogt-Göknil, *Les grands courants*, p. 121.

28 Pope, *Architecture*, p. 259.
29 Grabar, *Architecture*, p. 74.
30 Grabar, *Architecture*, p. 75.
31 Grabar, *Architecture*, p. 75.
32 Grabar, *Architecture*, p. 75.
33 Grabar, *Architecture*, p. 77ff.
34 Ettinghausen, *Man-made Setting*, p. 58.
35 Schlumberger, D., 'Le palais ghaznévide de Lashkar-i Bazar', *Syria*, XXIX, 1952.
36 Grabar, *Architecture*, p. 75.
37 Melikian-Chirvani, 'Eastern Iranian Architecture', *BSOAS* XXXIII, 1970.
38 Welch, S.C., *King's Book of Kings*, p. 54.
39 Golombek, L., *The Timurid Shrine at Gazur Gah*, p. 67ff.

V

THE SOURCES

THE SOURCES PROVIDING INFORMATION about the country's past can be classified into four different categories: the accounts of travellers; geographers; historians; and authentic local documents.

Important deposits of ancient documents were found in various places in Xinjiang, mostly in cave-temples, at Mount Mug near Pendzhikent, and also, to some extent, at Toprak-Kala in Khorezm. They relate on the whole to the Kushan and Soghdian periods and deal mostly with religious and commercial matters. They are written in various languages and scripts, and many of those discovered have not yet been deciphered; others, although deciphered and translated, still await publication. More about these may be found on pp. 76 and 179, but the formidable philological problems that they pose are beyond the scope of this book.

For the ancient period we have isolated remarks on the Scythians in Herodotus, Ptolemy, and Strabo. Ammianus Marcellinus and Sidonius Apollinaris wrote about the history of the Hunnic invasion of Europe. The invasion of China by another tribe of Huns was the subject of a work by the Chinese historian Sseu-ma Tsien and all three have left an extremely valuable description of these fifth-century nomads.

There is no evidence of any historical treatises in Central Asia in the pre-Arab period. If al-Biruni (eleventh century) is to be believed, the Arabs systematically exterminated all priests – that is literate and learned people – in Persia, Soghd, and Khorezm and their books perished with them. All we have, therefore, are accounts of pilgrims, like Fa-Sien, a Buddhist monk, who with some of his fellow-students set out across the Gobi desert in A.D. 399, reached India, and returned to China by sea ten years later. Other Chinese Buddhists, Song Yun in 518–21, and Suen-Tsang (Hsuen-tsang) in 629–30, travelled to India and back by the land-route. There are also the reports of Byzantine envoys, Zemarchos,

Eutychios, Valentinos, Herodian, and Paul of Cilicia, who were all sent, one after the other, by the emperor to the khan of the Turks, in the second half of the sixth century. Theophylactes Simocatta summarised Byzantine-Turkish relations in his historical work. Other sixth-century historians, Procopios of Cesarea and Menandros Protector, give some information about the Hephthalites. There is also the Armenian chronicle of Sebeos. The Chinese chronicles *Suei chou* and *T'ang chou* contribute their side of the picture.

With the arrival of the Arabs there begins a steady flow of historical and geographical literature, written both in Arabic and in Persian, and admirably summarised by Barthold.[1] Unfortunately, most of it is obscured by frequent rewriting and compilations. So, for example, the work of the fourteenth-century compiler Abu'l Fida is based almost completely on a previous compilation from the early thirteenth century by Ibn al-Athir, who in his turn used texts of yet earlier compilations, especially that of Tabari (late ninth and early tenth centuries). Another compilation is that of Ibn Khalikan (thirteenth century), which has been translated into English under the title *Biographical Dictionary*. A list of Arabic historians can be found in Masudi's tenth-century encyclopaedia, *The Golden Meadows*, and in the vast bibliography of the same century called *The Fihrist*. The Arab conquest is the subject of a ninth-century historian, Baladhuri. Other ninth-century histories are those of Yakubi and Abu Hanifa. Ibn Khurdadbih, also writing in the ninth century, may be described as the earliest Arab geographer.

In the tenth century, the Samanids patronised writers, scholars, and especially Persian poets. Tha'alibi, who died about 1037, produced an anthology of the poets of Khorassan and Transoxania. He described Bukhara as 'the home of glory, the Ka'aba of sovereignty, the place of assembly of all eminent people of the age'. He quotes in his autobiography his contemporary, the famous Avicenna (Ibn Sina), who described the library of the Samanids:

> I entered a house with many chambers; in each chamber were coffers of books piled up one upon another. In one chamber were Arabic books and books of poetry, in another books on law, and so on, in each chamber books on one of the sciences. I read a list of books of ancient authors and asked for those I needed. I saw books whose very names are unknown to many people. I have never seen such a collection of books either before or since. I read these books, profited by them, and learned the relative importance of each man in his own science.[2]

Geographical literature was more highly developed than historical literature in the Samanid kingdom. Balkhi, Istakhri, and Ibn Haukal produced a detailed description of Transoxania based on first-hand accounts. Makdisi, one of the greatest geographers of all time, also visited the country and 'his information on the climate, products, trade, currencies, weights and measures, manners, taxes and contributions of each country belongs to the most important data for the history of Eastern Culture'.[3]

The earliest monographic description of Bukhara comes from the pen of Narshakhi (died 959). Some sixty years later Idrisi produced a history of Samarkand.

At the Court of the Ghaznavid sultans lived the great Khorezmian scholar al-Biruni (died about 1048), whom Barthold does no hesitate to call 'perhaps the greatest Muslim scholar'. His special studies were in mathematics and astronomy, but he also wrote historical works. His *History of Khorezm* has not come down to us, but there is some valuable information about Khorezm in Biruni's chronological work, published in English in 1879 under the title *The Chronology of Ancient Nations*. His contemporary was the Persian historian Gardizi whose work includes a chapter on the Turks, one on India, the history of the Caliphs, and that of Khorassan down to the year 1041. A candid picture of court life under the Ghaznavids is presented by the memoirs of Bayhaki (died 1077), which also include a fairly detailed account of external relations. The author was himself for some time in charge of the sultan's office of diplomatic documents.

So far as is known, there were no compositions written in the eleventh century that can properly be called historical, but some idea of the organisation of the state and general conditions of life at this time is given in *The Book on the Administration of the State* (Siyasat-namah) by the famous *wazir* Nizam al-Mulk (died 1092). It deals with the duties of various officials and gives advice on all branches of administration. It is incontestably the chief source for the study of the political structure of the Eastern Muslim states.[4]

The second half of the twelfth and the beginning of the thirteenth centuries belong on the whole to the darkest pages of Central Asian history. The testimony of sources is contradictory in the extreme and the establishment of chronology presents great difficulties. Yet the events of this period were of marked importance: the decline of the Seljuks, the invasion of the Kara-Khitai, the rise of the Khorezmshahs, and the union under their rule of the whole Eastern Muslim world; the formation of the empire of the Khorezmshahs, to all appearances powerful, but whose internal weakness was speedily revealed at the first serious confrontation with an external foe.[5] The history of the Khorezmshahs occupies a considerable part of the work of Juvayni, who wrote in the thirteenth century (died 1283). For the earlier history of Khorezm great importance is attached to the enormous work (eight volumes) of al-Khorezmi (died 1172). This is in a way the only historical information we have of this period although it is supplemented to a limited extent by the accounts of travellers. After the tenth century, Arabic geographical literature was chiefly of a compilatory character. Among the few travellers was a native of Spain, al-Gharnati, who visited the Eastern countries and went as far north as the Volga and Kama Rivers.

An exception here is the work of Yakut (died 1229), author of a well-known geographical dictionary. He collected abundant material, mainly in the libraries of Merv and in his work he enumerates almost all the towns and the more important villages in the Muslim lands. He himself visited Khorezmia but not Transoxania. Yakut also compiled a 'dictionary of learned men' containing extracts of many treatises which have been lost.

Juvayni has also a short historical passage on the Kara-Khitai, but this is neither very clear nor accurate. A far better source for this subject is the work of Ibn al-Athir, mentioned above. On the other hand, Juvayni's work deserves full credit for its part devoted to the Mongols down to the reign of Hulagu and the conquest of Baghdad. His superiority over other writers on this subject lies in the fact that he lived at a time when the Mongol Empire was still united. He also visited Turkestan, Mongolia, and Uighuria. He endeavoured to relate the history of the empire as a whole and used for this purpose some oral Mongol narratives, and possibly also some written ones. Other Muslim writers who dealt with the Mongol invasion were Ibn al-Athir, Juzjani, and Nassavi, who wrote a biography of Jalal ad-Din. Their works are far less reliable than Juvayni's, mainly because they lack first-hand knowledge of the facts in all other parts of the empire but their own.

Among the Chinese travellers of the Mongol period there is the report of Meng Hung, who was sent in 1221, as an envoy by the Sung government, to conclude an alliance with the Mongols against the Jurchat. More interesting, however, is the diary of the Taoist hermit Ch'ang Ch'un, written by his disciple Li Che-chang in 1229 and called *The Travels of an Alchemist*. Ch'ang-Ch'un was invited to the Court of Chingiz-Khan and followed him as far as Afghanistan. Like the Muslims, the Chinese portray the cruel devastations of the Mongols in vivid colours; but where the Muslims, with a few exceptions, fail because of religious fanaticism to observe the features by which the nomads were favourably distinguished from the settled population, Chinese were often attracted by the simplicity of nomadic manners and, like Meng Hung, praised the unspoiled customs of antiquity that prevailed among them.

A valuable source of information on Mongol habits and traditions, in addition to the history of Chingiz-Khan's campaigns, is the so-called *Secret History of the Mongols*, written in Uighur in 1240 and preserved in Chinese translation and transcript. The events are unfortunately not recorded by years and the chronology is very vague and confused. There are also many mythical elements in this history which make the whole work look more like a heroic epic. An official history of the Mongols was written in China early in the fourteenth century and after the fall of the Yuan dynasty the history of the Mongols was compiled under the title *Yuan-shi.*

The chief source of Mongol history in Persia is Rashid ad-Din (late thirteenth-early fourteenth centuries), who was *wazir* to the Mongol khan in Persia and was entrusted by him to write a history of the Mongol Empire and, further, a history of all nations who had come into contact with the Mongols. The work took the form of a vast historical encyclopaedia, such as no single people possessed in the Middle Ages either in Asia or in Europe. The very possibility of the creation of such a work with the assistance of learned men of all nations show what might have been the results, under more favourable conditions, of the Mongol invasion, which had connected the most distant civilised peoples with one another.[6] Rashid ad-Din himself translated all his Persian works into Arabic and all Arabic into Persian, and arranged for copies of them to be made annually, but he was executed in 1318 and a part of his work was lost.

Among the European reports on the Mongol invasion, we have already mentioned John de Plano Carpini and William of Rubruck (above). Carpini, who was sixty-five at the time of his journey was obviously an experienced diplomat with a thorough knowledge of military affairs. The bulk of his report is in fact an attempt to produce a critical – we may even say scientific – assessment of the Mongols, their government and organisation, religion and laws, strategy and arms, and, of course, the history of their campaigns and the means of possible defence against them. Rubruck's report is a personal account of his journey, full of interesting observations on languages, religious rites, trade etc. He was obviously well versed in geography, and as far as history is concerned, he is more critical and reliable than Carpini.

There were other contacts as well: the two Franciscans Lawrence of Portugal and Anselm (Ascelin), who were dispatched by Pope Innocent IV to the Mongol commanders in the Caucasus; André de Longjumeau, who was sent by St Louis in 1249 to the Mongols, but only got as far as the Talas. The Russians and the Armenians had frequent contacts with them and the most valuable source here is the chronicle of the Armenian king Hethum (Haythum). A few decades later came the famous journeys of the Venetian merchants, the Polos - first that of Niccolo and Matteo to Karakorum and, after that, Marco Polo's epic journey to China.

Among the fourteenth-century sources, the work of Kazvini, written in the 1330s, consists both of geographical and historical treatises. It is an important source of information for the administrative and fiscal division of Persia and, for the linguists, it offers some very rare information on the Mongol language; in the cosmographical section the names of various animals are given in Persian, Turkish, and Mongol.

The history of Transoxania was unfortunately recorded even less than that of Persia. Political disturbances among the Chagatayids did not favour the development of science and literature. Besides, Persian culture did not even attain complete supremacy there. The Uighur alphabet was widely used as well as the Arabic. There were Uighur scribes even at the Court of the Timurids down to the last representative of that dynasty. There were definitely some Uighur writings, but there is no evidence of a single literary composition in either Arabic or Persian written at the behest of any Chagatay khan.[7] So we have for the first half of the century only a traveller's report, the narrative of Ibn Battuta, the famous sheikh of Tangier, who crossed Central Asia on his way from the Volga to India. We find in Juvayni an angry comment on the preponderance of Uighur writing over Persian in Khorassan: 'All educated people perished, were exterminated, and those nobodies who replace them know nothing but to speak and write in Uighur'.[8]

In 1425 a history of Timur's campaign was written in Persia by Sharaf ad-Din Ali Yazdi, called *The Book of Victory* (Zafar-namah). The same title, devised by Timur himself, had already been used by Nizam ad-Din Shami for his own book written in Timur's lifetime (1403-4), but Sharaf ad-Din also made use of the Uighur verse-chronicle of Timur's campaigns, which Nizam ad-Din did not. This chronicle did not survive in its original form. Nizam was a scholar from Tabriz who was in Baghdad in 1393 when the city surrendered to Timur. He was among the first to pay homage to the conqueror. He was in Aleppo during the Syrian campaign, and the following year was summoned to Timur and asked to write a history of his reign. He completed his work and presented it to Timur in the spring of 1404, before the Court returned to Samarkand.[9] Sharaf was one of the scholars who received patronage at the Court of Shah Rukh. His work, based on a collection of records and eyewitness accounts, was regarded as a model of literacy and historical composition, and is one of the most useful and comprehensive court histories.

A world history called *The Cream of Chronicles* was composed in 1423-24 by Hafiz-i Abru, a scholar at Timur's Court and later Shah Rukh's court historian in Herat. Further works originated in Herat include *The History of Mawarannahr and Persia* by Abdar-Razzak Samarkandi and, somewhat later, a world history called *The Garden of Purity* by Mirkhond. All these works were of an official or semi-official character and all include, to a greater or lesser degree, flattery of patrons. Similarly tendentious are the histories of hostile scholars, especially from the countries overrun in the Syrian and Turkish campaigns of Timur. The most important hostile source is that of Ibn Arabshah, who was taken captive as a boy in Damascus and carried off to Samarkand. He later studied and travelled widely, and died in Cairo in 1450. His history is rich in evidence, especially relating to the later part of Timur's life and events following his death. Despite its bitterness, Arabshah's work contains much sober commentary.[10]

Among the travellers of this era we have already mentioned Ruy Gonzalez de Clavijo, whose report is by far the most important and impartial. A completely different matter is the story of Schiltberger of Bavaria. He started out as a squire on a crusade, was captured at Nicopolis, and became slave to the Ottoman sultan Bayezid. After the defeat at Angora, he became captive to Timur, survived him and lived to serve his son and grandsons. Finally he escaped and made his return to Bavaria. His story is subjective but important, written from an entirely different viewpoint to that of the court historian.[11] The next traveller of importance comes only 150 years later. He is Anthony Jenkinson, an Elizabethan merchant and sailor who was probably the first Englishman to enter Bukhara (1558), after a journey from London to the White Sea, to Moscow, and down the Volga into the Caspian. We may conclude this survey by mentioning another Englishman, Alexander Burnes, who almost three centuries later arrived in Bukhara from the opposite direction, from India and Afghanistan, in 1832.

NOTES ON CHAPTER V
Full details of abbreviations and publications are in the Bibliography

1   Barthold, *Turkestan*, p. 1–58.
2   Quoted by Barthold in *Turkestan*, p. 9–10.
3   Quoted by Barthold in *Turkestan*, p. 11.
4   Barthold, *Turkestan*, p. 25.
5   Barthold, *Turkestan*, p. 31.
6   Barthold, *Turkestan*, p. 46.
7   Barthold, *Turkestan*, p. 51.
8   Grousset, *L'Empire*, p. 425.
9   Hookham, *Tamburlaine*, p. 319.
10   Hookham, *Tamburlaine*, p. 320.
11   Hookham, *Tamburlaine*, p. 321.

21. Mausoleum of Pahlavan Mahmud, Khiva

22. Mosque Hazret-i Hizr, Samarkand

23. Mosque Bibi Khanum, Samarkand. Main iwan

24. Madrasa Ulug Beg, Samarkand (detail)

25. Shah-i Zinda, Samarkand (general view)

26. Mausoleum No. 9, Shah-i Zinda, Samarkand

27. Ak Saray Palace, Shahrisabz (detail)

28. ABOVE. Mausoleum Chashma Ayub, Bukhara

29. BELOW. Tash Hauli Palace, Khiva

PART II
CENTRAL ASIA

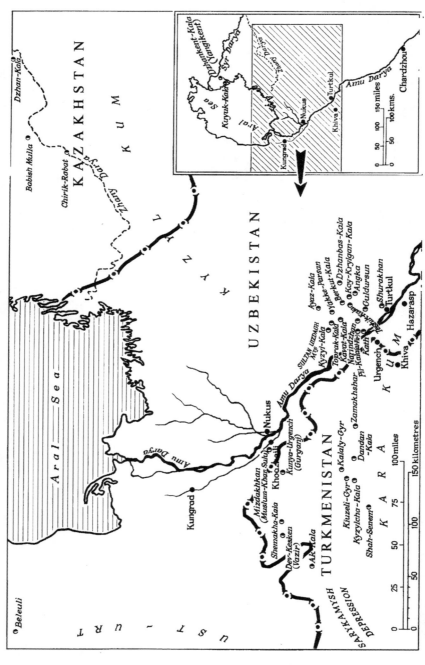

MAP 4 Khorezm

VI

KHOREZM

GEOGRAPHICALLY, THE OASIS OF KHOREZM lies east and south of the Aral Sea, on both sides of the lower reaches of the Oxus (Amu Darya), and round its delta estuary. It also comprises the formerly inhabited areas between the Amu and the Syr Darya as well as the southern part of the arid plateau Ust-Urt, south-west of the Aral Sea.

Politically, it is now divided between Uzbekistan and its Karakalpak Region and Turkmenistan's Region of Tashauz. Tashauz has an air connection to Ashkhabad.

The western, Karakalpak, part is centred around the capital, Nukus, which has a scheduled air service to Tashkent. The same applies to Urgench, in the eastern part. A railway line runs along the Amu Darya, from Chardzhou to Khodzheili in the delta, and provides a direct link with Bukhara, Samarkand and Tashkent. In Chardzhou, where the line crosses the river, it meets the Transcaspian line to Ashkhabad and Krasnovodsk on the eastern coast of the Caspian. Recent rail-links connect Khodzheili with the Volga region of Russia and Chardzhou via Mary with Mashad in Iran.

Throughout its long history Khorezm was an isolated oasis accessible only by long and hazardous caravan-routes across the formidable deserts Kara Kum and Kyzyl Kum (Black and Red Sands), or across the equally dangerous, lifeless plateau Ust-Urt. This was why the course of events here frequently ran separately from the mainstream of history, and it will therefore be necessary to give it a little more attention in this chapter.

It should be emphasised here that owing to a division of labour among Soviet archaeologists, each region was the exclusive domain of one person or one school. No foreign expeditions were permitted. It is extremely difficult to check the views and interpretations of the work carried out in a particular area. For Khorezm, Professor S.P. Tolstov and his school have thus had a virtual monopoly of access to, and of publication on everything that concerns history, ethnography, archaeology etc. of this vast and complex sector of Central Asia.

According to Tolstov, in the fourth and third millennium B.C. the country just east of the Aral Sea was quite different from what it is now. The climate was probably much drier, the Amu and Syr Darya had less water and could not force their way through the hilly region of Sultan Uizdagh to reach the sea. Instead, the whole area between the lower reaches of these two rivers and the hills was probably a vast marshland, interwoven with channels and lakes and covered with reed and jungle forest. Here, on the sandy islets in the marshes and on the dry foothills of the Sultan Uizdagh were the homes of the Neolithic hunters and fishermen whose culture, probably the earliest in the area, Tolstov calls Kelteminar. These hunters and fishermen lived in large houses, some 70 by 50 feet, oval-shaped and built on a skeleton of wooden poles, with walls and roofs of reed. A whole tribal family, between 100 and 200 people, lived in such houses. Similar houses were found in Neolithic layers in southern Xinjiang and, more recently, in western Kazakhstan and in the lower Volga region.

Later, the drain to the Aral basin was established and the marshes and lakes dried up. Ever since then the agricultural communities that subsequently settled in this area became dependent on artificial irrigation. The network of canals using the water of the Amu Darya shrank and expanded in a way curiously connected with historical events, with the wealth of the country, the growth and decline of the population, the flow of world trade, internal and external security, and other phenomena.

In the time of the Achaemenids, Khorezm was in the hands of the Massagetae, a nomad tribe of Scythian origin, against whom Cyrus sent a military expedition around 530 B.C., subdued them, and made Khorezm the sixteenth *satrapy* of the Persian Empire. It is very likely that after the fall of the Achaemenids, the local ruler or rulers gained some independence, and we know that Alexander, when he arrived at Marakanda (Samarkand), after his victory over the Soghdians, was visited there by a 'a king of Khorezmians' named Farsman who, according to Ammianus, offered him his help against 'peoples living at the Black Sea'. This information is, of course, very vague, but at least it shows that Alexander's power never reached as far as Khorezm. After that, for several centuries, we have no direct information at all.

However, there are legends. In one legend, al-Biruni, the famous medieval historian (972–1048) from Khorezm, tells the story of a mythical hero, Siyavush, founder of a Khorezmian dynasty that ruled the country up to the tenth century A.D. This Siyavush also appears in the *Avesta*, a Zoroastrian religious text, where his name is Siyvarshana. He went from Iran to Turan and there married a local princess, acquired some land, and built a fortified town, Kang-i Siyavaksh; finally, he was treacherously murdered. The figure of Siyavush on horseback can be seen on Khorezmian coins from the first century B.C. to the eighth century A.D. From this and other myths ethnographers conclude that in Khorezm three kinds of population were mingled: Indo-Iranian tribes who occupied the area between the Iranian plateau and the upper Amu Darya; some tribes from the Thracian-Kimmerian family whose territory was west of the Aral Sea and north of the Caspian as far west as the Danube; and finally the Saka or Scythians, who originally lived in the steppes north and north-east of the Syr Darya and gradually penetrated into the territory of the Thracians and Kimmerians. Al-Biruni puts the arrival of Siyavush at Khorezm in the year 1200 B.C., but the first semi-historical name of this dynasty, Afrigh, appears only around A.D. 305. From then on, al-Biruni gives twenty-two names covering the period between A.D. 305 and 995.

Archaeological sites dated around 500 B.C. show fortified settlements of rectangular shape with a huge inner yard that apparently was completely empty and served most probably as a corral for cattle. The walls were very thick and within them were two or three parallel gang-ways used for habitation. There is a text in the *Avesta* which confirms this. The inhabited gangways or corridors were in fact an enormous long house where several thousand people lived. Apart from the *Avesta*, we find some information about Khorezm and its inhabitants in Herodotus, Strabo and Ctesias of Cnidos. It seems that both Herodotus and Strabo based their narrative on Hekataios of Miletus (around 500 B.C.).

Next to the sites of the 'settlements with inhabited walls' period are numerous sites of the so-called Kangha, or Kang-yue, period. Kang-yue, according to Chinese sources, was a vast empire, but no such name is found in other records. Some scholars are inclined to believe that it means Khorezm between the Achaemenid and Kushan periods. The expansion of towns and also of agriculture and irrigation was remarkable. As can be seen, for example on the site of Dzhanbas-Kala, the type of settlement changed considerably. Instead of inhabited walls we now find several long collective houses, each with 150 to 200 rooms. These houses themselves are not fortified, but the whole settlement is surrounded by walls. At Dzhanbas-Kala, there are only two such houses with a street between them, while at Toprak-Kala, at the height of the period, there were no less than ten or twelve, grouped on both sides of a main street and separated by narrow lanes. The street ran from the city gate to the temple of fire-worshippers on the opposite side, next to which was a marketplace and a royal castle.

Toprak-Kala, situated twenty miles north of the Amu Darya opposite Urgench, is perhaps the most significant archaeological site in this area, or at least the best explored. It lies in a lifeless desert and can be approached only by air in small air-craft, which can land on the hard surface of a *takyr* (dry salt-lake). Dating from the third or fourth centuries A.D., Toprak-Kala belongs to the Kushan period and seems to have been relatively short-lived.[1] The city walls, built of clay, form a rectangle 1650 by 990 feet. Towers and vaulted corridors were built of sun-baked bricks of trapezoidal shape. The three-towered castle, occupying about 2.7 acres and originally on three floors, contained a range of palatial halls, among which the so-called Hall of Kings (about 3000 square feet) had walls covered with paintings and many big statues of unburnt clay representing the Khorezmian rulers, their wives and guardian deities.[2] Statues of kings and of dark-skinned, armour-plated warriors of an exotic, possibly southern Indian type were a distinctive feature of the so-called Hall of the Black Guards. This suggests that there were Indians among the Khorezmian troops at that time. The con-currence of exquisite friezes of deer and griffins, which decorated another hall, was typical of the more ancient Scythian art.[3] Among the numerous documents written mostly on leather and wood in ancient Khorezmian script, which is related to Aramaic, some were apparently dated according to an Indian calendar.[4] There was also a great quantity of coins, from the Kushan and other periods, dating from the third to the fifth centuries A.D., with portraits of ancient Khorezmian rulers. Another feature of interest was the 'armoury' – a workshop for the manufacture of bows. (See Plates 4 and 5.)

Somewhat older, but of a different design, was **Koy-Krylgan-Kala**, a few miles to the south-east of Toprak-Kala. It forms two almost perfect concentric circles, of which the inner one is much better preserved than the outer. The outer circle, with a diameter of 276 feet, appears to have consisted of dwellings. The inner circle, 138 feet deep, was probably a burial-ground for the rulers and a temple of a dynastic cult. The site was inhabited from the fourth century B.C., but came to a sudden end in the first century A.D., when Khorezm was incorporated into the Kushan Empire.[5] Here, too, some small but colourful wall-paintings were found, as well as terracotta statuettes and fine ornamental pottery. The archaeological evidence from Toprak-Kala and other Khorezm towns points to a knowledge of metalwork, of specialised handicrafts, and to a high standard of artistic production.

The dense population provided sufficient labour for the installation and maintenance of irrigation systems necessary for prosperous agriculture. The maintenance and extension of the complex irrigation network required an enor-mous amount of manpower and money. Only populous and rich communities could afford it. Prosperity and irrigation were inseparable, and whenever wars, nomad invasions, or natural catastrophes decimated the population the canals were immediately shortened and the more distant settlements were abandoned,

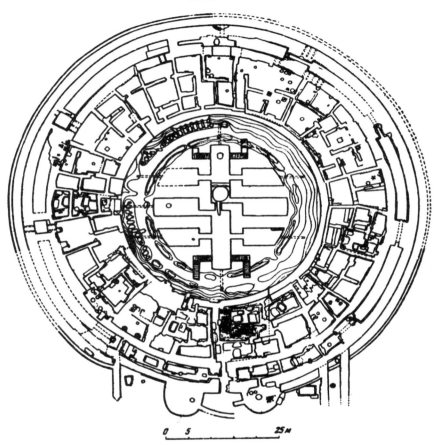

PLAN 1 Koy-Krylgan-Kala

left to be swallowed by the deserts. As one flies over the right bank of the river, the pattern of the ancient canals can clearly be seen. Every now and then there is a sandy hillock reminiscent of the *tells* in Syria and Iraq, which in Central Asia are called *tepe* or *kala* (castle), and within which is a dead village or town. This once fertile and populous country stretches in a vast semicircle some 600 miles to the north-west, as far as the lower Syr Darya. On the left bank of the Amu Darya the situation is a little better. Some of the huge ancient canals still exist and are still in use. They are much shorter now than a thousand years ago and whole stretches of abandoned settlements and sand-covered fields can be found on and beyond the fringes of cultivated areas. The water of the Amu Darya is thick with sand, and continuous dredging has added considerably to the dykes, so that now the canals lie several feet above ground level.

After the fall of the Kushan Empire, which collapsed under the pressure of the Hephthalites, Khorezm was on the periphery of the protracted struggle between the Hephthalites and the Sasanians. For centuries there was neither peace nor prosperity. Trade-routes were cut and the oasis once again almost disappeared. Most cities were abandoned and the remaining people lived in heavily fortified farmhouses on a much reduced irrigation system, their protection being provided by the scattered castles that belonged to the feudal lords who were emerging at this time.

> This happened under King Afrigh, who was one of that dynasty. And he deserved his bad reputation, as Yezdegerd had deserved it among the Persians... And Afrigh built his castle inside al-Fir 660 years after Alexander. Al-Fir was a fortress near the town of Khorezm, with three walls of clay and unbaked bricks, one inside the other and one higher than the other, and the King's Castle was higher than all three. And al-Fir could be seen from a distance of ten miles and more.

This is how al-Biruni describes the capital of Khorezm at the beginning of the last pre-Muslim period of its history.

In the dead oasis Berkut-Kala (seventh to eighth centuries A.D.) there are, in a belt fourteen miles long and one to two miles wide, almost a hundred strongly fortified castles of various sizes. They were all built on the same principle: high walls of clay (sun-baked bricks became rare and are also smaller in size), and a *donjon* (turret), with living quarters. Everybody seemed to live in a fortress. Open villages disappeared, clear evidence of a general decline in security. Water was scarce, and therefore those who controlled its supply became the rulers. This is why we invariably find the big castles of the lords situated where smaller canals branch off the main one. Excavations show that at the same time crafts-manship was also deteriorating. In the fifth century, crude, home-made pottery replaced the elegant forms of the preceding period. Even the potter's wheel seemed to be forgotten; the firing was poor, the range of forms greatly reduced, the decoration became poorer and cruder, and glazing, polishing, and varnishing disappeared altogether. Decline in trade was reflected in the non-existence of imported goods. A little later, at the beginning of the eighth century, the Arab historian Tabari records only three towns in the whole of Khorezm. And Makdisi, writing in the tenth century, mentions 12,000 castles and forts in the vicinity of one single town. There was no unifying force, either political or cultural. The particularism of areas and regions was reflected in the crafts, in a diversity of motifs and shapes that did not exist before. Such a situation naturally invited foreign intervention, which came to Khorezm in 712 in the form of the Arab invasion.

There were two Arab expeditions against Khorezm at the end of the seventh century, but only a systematic conquest, undertaken by the Governor of Khorassan, Kutayba ben Muslim, marked the end of the independent rule of the kings, or Khorezmshahs. According to Tabari, shortly before the invasion there was a revolt in Khorezm against the legitimate Khorezmshah. The shah, hard pressed by the rebels, appealed to Kutayba for help. This was readily given, the rebels were defeated, and the shah reinstated with an obligation to pay tribute to his rescuers. As soon as the Arabs had left, another revolt flared up, in which the shah was killed. The Arabs returned and this time they stayed. Kutayba even went so far in his persecution of the rebels as to order all Khorezmian literature to be destroyed and all educated men banished from the country. Al-Biruni writes:

> And by all means Kutayba dispersed and destroyed all who knew the writings of Khorezm, who preserved the traditions of the country, all learned men who were among them, so that everything became covered in darkness and now we do not know for certain anymore, what of their history was known in times when Islam came to them.

Throughout the eighth century, Arab sources are silent about Khorezm. But from other sources we know for instance that in 751, when the Arabs were engaged in a decisive struggle with the Chinese army, the Khorezmshah Shavushafar sent his envoys to China.

The scholars and intellectuals, chased by the Arabs from Khorezm, mostly turned west – to southern Russia, which by then was the territory of the Khazars. There were many Jews among this intellectual elite, and they quickly made their impact on the primitive Khazar society. Jews occupied leading positions in the army and in the council of the khan, who was gradually reduced to a mere puppet king. Judaism, as far as we know, became the official religion.[6] Even after a domestic rebellion in Khazaria forced the Jews to emigrate further west in the second half of the eighth century, the flow of refugees from Khorezm continued. The Arabs gradually established their rule over the country, and in the last decade of that century Khorezmian coins already bore the names of the Arab governors of Khorassan in Kufic characters. Economic depression is shown both by a considerable deterioration in the weight of these coins (reduced to almost one-third of their former weight) and by further shrinking of the irrigation network.

The continuously cultivated land began with a narrow strip just below Chardzhou (then Amul). It was here that the first of the major left-bank canals originated. It supplied with water the town of Hazarasp, situated, according to contemporary sources, nine days' journey downstream (north-west). The town and the canal still exist. Lower down was the *aryk* (canal) of Khiva, which, according to Makdisi, was the largest and could be used by boats as far as the town. Below the heads of these canals the river passed through a mountainous gorge where it narrowed to one-third of its original width.[7] The right-bank irrigation began only below this gorge, with the large Gawkhore or Cow-fodder canal, but continuous cultivation began still lower down. Between this canal and the main river-bed was the capital city of Khorezm, Kath or al-Fir. Kath was situated on the right bank of the river and, at the time of the Arab invasion, consisted of three parts, of which the most strongly fortified was the citadel, called al-Fir. This citadel was gradually undermined by the waters of the Amu Darya. At the beginning of the tenth century, the citadel and the whole of the old town had already been abandoned, the gates had been carried away by the water, and the citadel was threatened with complete destruction.

The inhabitants built themselves new quarters further east, and the last traces of Fir had disappeared by the end of the century. According to Makdisi, the palace of the emir was in the centre of the town. By then the citadel had already been destroyed by the river. There were *aryks* flowing through the very centre of the town.

> The town is magnificent. It contains many learned men and men of letters, many wealthy persons and many fine commodities and merchandise. The architects are distinguished for their skill. On the other hand the town is constantly flooded by the river, and the inhabitants are moving away from the bank. The town is dirtier than Ardabil and contains many refuse drains which everywhere overflow the high road. The inhabitants use the streets as latrines and collect the filth in pits, whence it is subsequently carried out to the fields in sacks. Because of this enormous quantity of filth strangers can walk about the town only by daylight. The inhabitants kick the filth in heaps with their feet.[8]

We know from al-Biruni's eyewitness account that in 995 the last Khorezmshah of the Afrighid dynasty was captured and killed by the Emir of Gurganj, or Urgench (not to be confused with the modern Yanghi-Urgench). The country had obviously been split for some time between the two rival states – the Afrighid in the east, with Kath as capital, and that of the usurpers of Gurganj nearer to the delta and south of the Aral Sea. Now, after the assassination, the country was reunited again in the hands of the emir, who resumed the traditional title of Khorezmshah. The importance of Kath declined and the place is last mentioned by Ibn Battuta in the early fourteenth century.

> We entered the desert which is between Khorezm and Bukhara, an eighteen days' journey through sands, with no settlements on the way except the small town of Kath which we reached after four days.[9]

On the other hand, Gurganj became a thriving capital and remained for four centuries to come one of the most important cities not only in Central Asia but also in the whole world of Islam. Gurganj, called by the Arabs Jurjaniya, and by the Mongols and Turks Urgench, was situated about a mile from the river, at some distance from a wooden dam, which was built in the river to deflect its course to the east; the water had formerly come up to the town itself. This was obviously a device to spare Gurganj the fate of Kath. Also, all *aryks* came only to the city gates, but no water flowed through the city. The first period of splendour for Gurganj was during the reign of Ma'mun II, in the early eleventh century, when scholars like al-Biruni, Avicenna (Ibn Sina) and many others formed the 'Court Academy' of the shah and added to the renown of the city, which was 'second to none in the world of Islam'. Baghdad was already past its zenith and Cairo and Cordoba had not yet reached theirs. For a short time, therefore, Gurganj was the undisputed centre of Islamic wisdom and civilisation.

The works of al-Biruni show the astonishing knowledge of their author. Al-Biruni was poet, historian, geographer, astronomer, mineralogist, and ethnographer. He was also a courageous and independent thinker, and his theories, for example on the historical and geological origins of the North Indian plain, or on the changes of the river-bed of the Amu Darya, come very close to modern opinions. Some of his papers still exist only in manuscript, and his most important work, *The History of Khorezm*, was lost. However, al-Biruni was not destined to live long in his own country. In 1017 Ma'mun II was faced with an ultimatum from the powerful Ghaznavid ruler Mahmud to send his brilliant scholars to Ghazna. The shah was unable to resist, but the scholars showed little enthusiasm for the new despot. Some, like Avicenna, left Khorezm and escaped to Persia. What Biruni did is not quite clear. At any rate, when Shah Ma'mun died in the same year and Khorezm was subsequently subdued by Mahmud, Biruni came to Ghazna as a captive to spend the remaining thirty years of his life at his court.

The rule of the Ghaznavids over Khorezm was short-lived. It was still in Biruni's lifetime that the Turkish Seljuks infiltrated into Khorassan from the steppes and in a decisive battle in 1040 defeated the Ghaznavids. Thereafter, Khorezm became once again a faraway province of a vast and loosely-knit empire. From the eleventh and twelfth centuries there is no detailed information on either Kath or Gurganj. In the thirteenth century Gurganj acquired fresh importance as the capital of the powerful dynasty of the Khorezmshahs. When this dynasty became the most powerful in the Muslim world, its capital city must have been enriched by the treasures of the conquered lands. Yakut, who lived there between 1219 and 1220, considers it perhaps the most extensive and richest of all the towns he had seen.

Meanwhile, the economic situation seemed to have greatly improved. Many abandoned settlements were revived, and quite a few can be found on re-irrigated ground reclaimed from the desert. Crafts, especially pottery, had also recovered.

New forms of richly decorated jars are typical of this period and, apart from unglazed pottery, we find ample evidence of glazed ceramics with decoration painted under the glaze in cinnamon, red, ochre or yellow on a white or yellowish background. Trade had revived on all main caravan-routes and for Khorezm the western routes were now of particular importance. The amount of trade in this direction was growing steadily, first with Khazaria and later with the emerging Kievan Russia, as well as with the so-called Great Bulgaria on the Volga. Slaves and furs are named by Arab and Persian historians as the main goods, but amber, nuts, timber and cattle are also mentioned. Makdisi even mentions boats, cheese, fish, and 'extremely strong bows' among items exported from Khorezm into the lands of the caliphate. Khorezm evidently acted as a transit place for goods coming in from the north and west to be shipped to the south. This trade, traversing the Ust-Urt, naturally favoured the western outposts of the country, and Gurganj was most conveniently situated to benefit from this. To protect this route against the raids of the nomad Turks, the Oghuz or Ghuzz, the Khorezmians built a belt of fortifications, signal towers and small forts, along the whole border of the high plateau that protected all descents into the delta and the Khorezmian plain. Stone-built caravanserais and wells were spread all along the route from Gurganj to the lower Volga. The best preserved is known as Beleuli, west from the Aral Sea, with four wells. Each well was surrounded by a walled yard and had a large watering trough, hewn from a stone block. The serai itself is of the tenth or eleventh centuries. It is a square building of hewn stone with round turrets in the corners and with a high stone portal decorated with flat reliefs of lions.

At the beginning of the twelfth century the Seljuk governors of Khorezm had acquired more and more independence from the sultans. It was increasingly difficult to rule the distant province; therefore more power was delegated to the governors who, after a time, revived the traditional title of Khorezmshah and reduced their dependence on the sultan to a nominal tribute. Under the Seljuk dynasty Khorezm defended itself successfully against the nomad incursions, and expanded again into its former territories, both east and west of the Aral Sea, which had been lost in times of decadence. Atsyz (1127–56) succeeded in making the country independent. His grandson Tekesh (1172–1200) transformed it into a great power, conquering Khorassan and Iraq and defeating the caliph. Tekesh's son Muhammad II (1200–20) completed the conquest of Transoxania and extended his power as far as Ghazna, western Iraq, and Azerbaidzhan. Proud of his genius, Muhammad looked upon himself as a second Alexander. His most ambitious project was to deprive the Abbasid caliph of his remaining power. He was preparing a major campaign against Baghdad when news reached him that the Mongol armies were appearing on the eastern flank of his empire.

We find a detailed description of thirteenth century Khorezm in Yakut, who writes:

> I don't think that anywhere in the world can be found larger countries than those of Khorezm and more populous in spite of the inhabitants being subject to a laborious life and a modest standard. Most settlements in Khorezm are towns with markets of foods and with shops. You seldom find a village without a marketplace. And all this while there is general security and undisturbed peace... There is hardly a town in the world comparable to the capital of Khorezm for its riches and metropolitan grandeur, its number of inhabitants, and its proximity to wealth and fulfilment of religious aspirations and regulations.

The irrigated areas expanded once again and the main left-bank canal was even extended some fifty miles into the desert. On the right bank whole new oases grew on reclaimed grounds. Villages were close to each other and Tolstov estimates that the density of population had quadrupled since Afrighid times, 250 years before. **Kavat-Kala** on the right bank is perhaps the best example of a settlement of that time. It lies only a couple of miles east from Toprak-Kala and was probably situated on the *aryk* which a thousand years earlier had watered the fields around Toprak-Kala. The centre of the Kavat-Kala area is a fortified town of modest size. Inside is a ruined palace with engraved stucco ornaments. Nearby, at the canal, are four square castles with pointed arches and decorative turrets in the corners. There are no habitable towers here, and the houses flanking the walls form a square with a large open space in the middle. The walls are thin and could hardly have served any defensive purpose. All around were innumerable little farmhouses fenced with low clay walls. Feudal society is shown here in miniature. The prince who governed the area lived in the town. Local lords had their castles walled purely for prestige. The farmer-serfs lived in their own little houses. However, the fortifications of the important government strongholds were far from decorative and, in fact, showed a considerable improvement in fortification techniques compared with previous periods. Protective outposts, a double row of bastions covering the flank approaches to the walls, and powerful semicircular battlements sheltering the gates, show an inventive spirit just as their huge dimensions give convincing evidence of the power and wealth of the rulers. 'It was a short period of prosperity, of a refined civilisation flourishing in cities and unfortified mansions protected by a system of strongholds built by the ruler who concentrated all means of defence in his own hands.'[10]

Chingiz-Khan dispatched only a detachment of his main army to Khorezm after the fall of Bukhara. Commanded by his two sons Jochi and Chagatay, the army besieged Gurganj for several months. The inhabitants put up a bitter resistance. Quarter by quarter, house by house, the Mongols took the town, destroying the buildings and slaughtering the inhabitants. Then they drove the survivors out into the open. Artisans and craftsmen, of whom there were more than 100,000, were separated from the rest. The children and young women were taken into captivity as slaves. The men who remained were divided among the soldiers, and each fighting man was to execute twenty-four. After the massacre the Mongols destroyed the dam and water flooded the town. 'Khorezm (Gurganj) became the abode of the jackal and the haunt of the owl and the kite,' writes Juvayni.[11]

The destruction of Gurganj seems to have been complete. The lands of Khorezm again became distant provinces of a vast empire which, for their lack of pastures, had no interest for the new rulers. Yet another period of decay and oblivion followed, and when Ibn Battuta travelled to Khorezm more than a hundred years later on his journey to Bukhara, he did not see a single inhabited place east of Kath.

Until this day the desert on the right bank can be found strewn with remnants of the Mongol destruction. Kavat-Kala, Guldursun, and many others were pre-Mongol fortresses that ceased to exist after the invasion. After Toprak-Kala, Berkut-Kala etc., they represent to the archaeologist yet another layer of cultural ground – but the last in this region, for in the whole area there was hardly any post-Mongol settlement at all.

The picture is somewhat different in the north-western part. The Volga region became an important centre for trade with the Golden Horde, and caravan-routes that linked it with Khorassan and Transoxania had to pass through western Khorezm. That is why Gurganj, despite previous total destruction, was again before long a bustling, thriving city. Ibn Battuta recalls it as 'the largest, greatest, most beautiful and most important city of the Turks, shaking under the weight of its populations, with bazaars so crowded that it was difficult to pass'. Knowing that Ibn Battuta had just come from Itil, capital of the Golden Horde, this description is really worth noting.

Very few buildings survived relatively undamaged from the pre-Mongol or immediately post-Mongol periods. For example, it is known that a palace was built in Gurganj at the same time as the palaces of Termez and Samarkand – Afrasiyab. However, nothing has yet been found of the Gurganj palace. Two mausoleums survived at **Kunya-Urgench**, which is the site of Gurganj.

The mausoleum of **Sultan Tekesh** is a cubic structure with a sixteen-sided drum surmounted by a high conical cupola decorated with turquoise tiles. The entrance *iwan* is decorated with a *mukarnas* wedge-shaped vault. Inside, the spherical inner dome rests on a richly decorated drum. (See Plates 11 and 15.)

The mausoleum of **Fakhr ad-Din Razi** is also cube-shaped, with a twelve-sided drum and a conical cupola with tiled ornamental decoration. The entrance is on the eastern side and the eastern facade is beautifully decorated with monochrome ornaments arranged in three rectangular sections with a frieze of Kufic script around them. Both were built either at the end of the twelfth or at the beginning of the thirteenth century. (See Plate 10.)

Other monuments preserved on the Kunya-Urgench site are a high minaret (almost 200 feet) and two mausoleums. The **minaret** is high and slender with its top section damaged. It is believed to have been built around 1320–30. (See Plate 9.) Its decoration consists of monochrome horizontal bands of baked bricks alternating with inscription bands of stylised Kufic. Some bands, probably of coloured tiles, are now missing.

The fourteenth-century mausoleum of **Najmaddin Kubr** (1320–30) has an undecorated spherical dome of baked bricks and an entrance *iwan* with segments of blue-and-white tile ornaments and inscriptions. Inside is a cenotaph with specimens of early Khorezmian majolica.

The mausoleum of **Turabeg Khanum** (second half of the fourteenth century, now in restoration) consists of a high entrance *iwan* with some tiled *mukarnas* decoration, a twelve-sided building with a round dome on a low drum and a small six-sided annex in the rear. There are some of the first, and surprisingly mature, specimens of ornaments in tiled mosaic, executed mainly in blue, turquoise, white and brown with black, green, red and some other colours. This mausoleum was the burial-site of the Sufi dynasty which ruled Khorezm between the disintegration of the Mongol Empire and the conquest of Timur.

On the site of the former citadel a trench through a mass grave can be seen, probably dating from Timur's destruction of Gurganj.

The site of **Tash-Kala**, where most of the excavations were carried out, was one of the districts of Gurganj, which was resettled and lived in until the seventeenth century. Among the finds were foundations of an eleventh-century minaret, a gate of a caravanserai, and numerous houses of craftsmen and merchants dating from the fifteenth to the seventeenth centuries. Chinese porcelain and *celadon*-ware of the sixteenth and seventeenth centuries prove that trade relations with China existed at that time. Ak-Kala is a fortress of the same period.

Nearby, on the site of **Mizdakhkan**, about one mile from Khodzheili, is another interesting mausoleum. Mizdakhkan was an important medieval town, almost equal in size to Gurganj. The mausoleum, built in 1320–30, is called **Muzlum-Khan Sulu** and contains some floral ornaments executed in incised terracotta, subsequently glazed with a pale-blue glaze. The cenotaph inside, like the cenotaph of the mausoleum of Khoja Alauddin in Khiva (first half of the fourteenth century), has excellent ornaments in majolica, similar to those of Najmaddin Kubr. Their basic colour is blue, while the floral design and the inscriptions are executed in white and some of the motifs (rosettes) add black, red and golden tones to the scale. In one case white letters have brown borders, in another green and yellow. Rempel[12] considers Khorezmian majolica of the years 1320–60 to be the best specimens of decorative tiles in the whole history of Central Asian ornament. On monuments like the Khoja Alauddin in Khiva, local potters, designers and calligraphers were not originators, but proved themselves accomplished masters of their craft. No wonder, therefore, that in the artistic revival of Khiva in the nineteenth century artists frequently looked back to this period for inspiration.

The Sufi dynasty came to power in Gurganj in the second half of the fourteenth century, when the Golden Horde was weakened by internal dissent. It soon extended its domination to the southern parts of the oasis, occupying Kath and Khiva, but in 1372 clashed for the first time with the rising power of Timur. According to Hookham[13] the Sufi possessions endangered Timur's interests in the caravan trade between Transoxania and the West; they also represented a dangerous political challenge.

The campaign of 1372 resulted in the sacking of Kath and the defeat of the khan, Husayn Sufi. Peace terms agreed with the khan's brother were not kept, and next year Timur launched a second campaign. This time the Sufi khan was brought to heel and the southern part of the oasis was annexed to Transoxania – or, according to contemporary opinion, reunited with the former Chagatay *ulus*. But in 1379 the Sufis rose again. Timur besieged Gurganj, and an anecdote about this is told by Hookham:[14]

> ... the khan, Yusuf Sufi, boasted that he was prepared to meet Timur in personal combat. Why should the world face ruin and destruction because of two men? Better that the two of them should find themselves face to face in an open field to prove their valour. The challenge was accepted and Timur, in his light duelling armour, galloped towards the moat surrounding the walls. But Yusuf Sufi did not appear. Timur called out for him again and again, saying that death was preferable to a breach of faith. But Yusuf preferred life to honour. Soon after, Timur received the first melons of the season from Termez. Thinking it an incivility not to share the fruit with his neighbour who was deprived of such a pleasure, Timur put some in a golden dish and ordered them to be taken across the moat and handed to the guards for Yusuf. Khan Yusuf did not appreciate the gift. The dish was given to the gate-keeper and the melons flung into the moat.

The siege lasted over three months, but finally the city was captured and pillaged. Another revolt followed nine years later, and in 1388 Timur mounted his final campaign to crush these indomitable foes. This time Gurganj was razed to the ground and the entire Sufi family was put to death. After a systematic destruction of the city, Timur ordered barley to be sown on the site.

Anthony Jenkinson stayed twice in Gurganj in 1558–59. At that time the place was a mere caravan-halt, where duties were levied for men, horses, and camels.

30. Madrasa Shir Dor, Samarkand

31. Mausoleum Numbers 2 and 3, Shah-i Zinda, Samarkand

32. Shah-i Zinda, Samarkand (general view, inside)

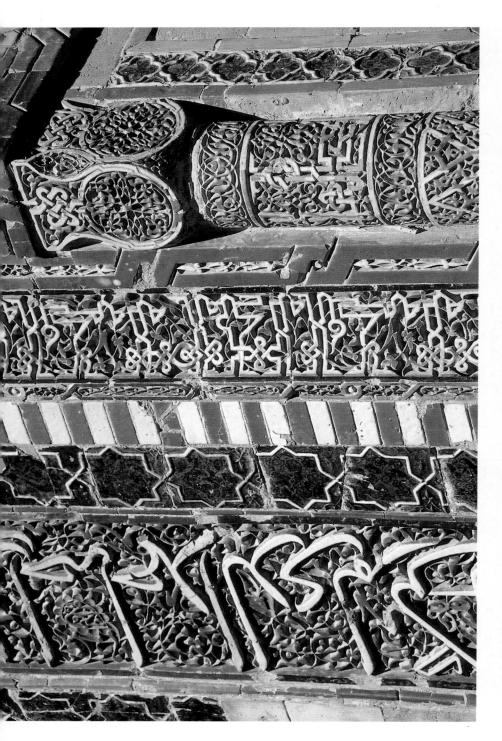

33. Mausoleum Number 14, Shah-i Zinda, Samarkand

34. Mausoleum Gumbaz-i Zaidin, Shahrisabz

35. Ak Saray Palace, Shahrisabz

36. Ak Saray Palace, Shahrisabz

37. Mosque Kok Gumbaz, Shahrisabz

This Citie or towne of Vrgence standeth in a plaine ground, with walles of earth, by estimation 4. miles about it. The buildings within it are also of earth, but ruined and out of good order: it hath one long street that is couered above, which is the place of their market.[15]

Ibn Arabshah says:

There used to advance convoys of travellers from Khorezm, making the journey in waggons as far as the Crimea, securely and without fear, a journey of about three months... But now through these places from Khorezm to the Crimea nothing moves or rests and nothing ranges there, but the antelopes and the camels...[16]

About thirty miles west from Kunya-Urgench, near the border of the Ust-Urt plateau, are the ruins of another dead city. This, however, seems to have been abandoned rather than destroyed. It is called **Shemakha-Kala** and in the Middle Ages its name was probably Tersek. It is a strongly fortified, early medieval town, which was probably sacked by the Mongols, but continued to exist until the sixteenth or seventeenth centuries. The fortifications were destroyed and only a few lonely towers, some square and some round, still exist. The whole pattern of streets, lanes and avenues of the rectangular, post-Mongol plan is clearly visible. Some stone-walled houses still stand; there is a ruined mosque in the centre with its yard and several rows of columns; and we can even discern the quarters of various crafts – the potters' district with kilns and heaps of slag, the district where iron-founders, blacksmiths and others lived and worked. Glazed pottery, china and other domestic hardware were found in profusion, but a systematic archaeological survey has not yet been carried out. Shemakha, of course, is not the only city dating from that period. There are so many ruins all around that it will take considerable time to identify them from literary references alone. Excavations, even if concentrated on essential sites only, may last for generations.

Close to Shemakha, for example, there was another town, **Vazir**, which was also visited by Anthony Jenkinson in 1558.

This Castle of Sellizure [Shahr-i Vazir] is situated upon a high hill where the king called the Can lyeth, whose palace is built of earth very basely, and not strong: the people are but poore, and little trade of marchandise among them. The South part of this Castle is lowe lande, but very fruitfull, where growe many good fruites among which there is one called a Dynie of a great bignesse and full of moysture, which the people doe eate after meate in steade of drinke... The water that serueth all that Countrey is drawen by diches out of the riuer Oxus, vnto the great destruction of the said riuer, for which cause it falleth not into the Caspian sea as it hath done in times past, and in short time all that lande is like to be destroyed, and to become a wilderness for want of water, when the riuer of Oxus shall faile.[17]

Tolstov identifies Vazir with the ruins called **Dev-Kesken-Kala** on the southern tip of the Ust-Urt. He describes it as a mighty rectangle of walls built of unhewn stone, with many towers and bastions, and a deep moat cut into the rock. Inside the walls can be found many remnants of stone buildings, dating from the late Middle Ages. The foundations of the walls and the citadel may be ancient, but the last period of the city's life was during the sixteenth and seventeenth centuries. Below the upper town and close to the rock is a second rectangle, the lower town, with mediaeval walls of unbaked bricks and surrounded by the dry river-bed of what once was a branch of the Amu Darya.

Water, as well as trade, played a decisive role in the final destiny of western Khorezm. After an invasion, which resulted in large-scale slaughter of the inhabitants, the reduced population was unable to maintain the canals, which quickly fell into disuse. On the one hand, the irrigated area shrank and caused a further departure of the people. On the other hand, excess water, not used for irrigation, caused floods and even changes of the whole geography of the country. So after the Hunnic raid in the fourth century, the Mongol invasion in the thirteenth, and Timur's devastation in the fourteenth, the Amu Darya burst its banks and, rushing through old dried river-beds, flooded the large Sarykamysh depression south-west of the delta.[18] This has been the source of legends that have spread far and wide about the river once emptying into the Caspian; but it has also been the reason why, on the southern fringes of the Ust-Urt west and south-west of the river delta, in certain periods of history short-lived settlements or even big cities appeared, built on an irrigation network that dried up as soon as the dams on the river were repaired, and the irrigation area of the main oasis again expanded.

After the devastations effected by Timur, and the changes in the water system, the population shifted eastwards, upstream, where **Khiva** became the new capital of what emerged, in the late fifteenth century, as an independent principality of the Uzbeks. Some time in the seventeenth century one of the Uzbek khans, Abulghazi, finally transferred the remaining population from the Gurganj area to the neighbourhood of Khiva, where the present Urgench – New Urgench – was founded.

The Uzbek khanate of Khiva was, up to the late eighteenth century, hardly more than a nest of caravan-robbers, safely hidden behind the formidable barriers of the desert. At that time, however, and perhaps in connection with the raid of the Persian conqueror Nadir Shah on Central Asia, there was a sudden revival of artistic and cultural activity in Khiva.

It almost seems as if the creative genius of Persia, unable to express itself at home, sought and found refuge in that isolated little world behind the Kara Kum sands. For Khiva, having surprisingly survived undamaged so far, is a genuine oasis of art, a relic of the past in a different world and a unique gem of city architecture.

The Russians were interested in Khorezm as early as 1715, when Peter the Great dispatched Aleksander Bekovich to find the old river-bed of the Amu Darya leading to the Caspian. The purpose was to establish an easier route to India by cutting off the existing opening to the Aral Sea and bringing the river back to the Caspian, where a port and a fortress were to be built. Bekovich's mission failed and almost all his people perished. Several punitive expeditions against the Khiva brigands also failed, and it was not until 1873 that the Khan of Khiva accepted the suzerainty of the tsar.

Ichan-Kala (the Inner City or Fortress of Khiva) has a completely preserved belt of walls with ramparts, bastions and gates, built partly of clay and partly of sun-baked bricks. (See Plate 12.) Only the gateways and the flanking towers are of burnt bricks. Outside the walls, the suburbs and gardens form a green ring with mulberry trees, orchards and small vineyards; further out lie the fields irrigated by a cobweb of tiny *aryks* and then, quite abruptly, come the sand-dunes of the Kara Kum dotted with tufts of long dry grass or some thorny bushes, an endless grazing ground for the herds of Khivan sheep.

In Ichan-Kala there are two palaces, the older, eighteenth century, **Kunya-Ark** (Old Castle) and the newer **Tash-Hauli** (Stone House) built c.1830. The mosque inside the Kunya-Ark dates from 1838 and has a very fine *iwan* with majolica tiles. (See Plates 14 and 29.) The Tash-Hauli has three courtyards (a harem, a banqueting hall and a court of justice) and six *iwans*, all richly decorated with glazed tiles and typical Khorezmian ornamental motifs, stylised cloves of garlic, for example, in navy blue and white, with a touch of pale blue and brown. The majolica is of indifferent quality, the patterns lack definition, the colours are muted, and there are inaccuracies in design, but the architecture of the ensemble as a whole is distinguished by its purity. The yards are surrounded by two-storey buildings. The rooms on the upper floor form a gallery that opens into the yard and is supported by carved wooden columns. The *iwans* are two storeys high and their light roofs of beams, straw and clay are also supported by a huge wooden column. The tradition of carved wood had existed in Khorezm since time immemorial, and beautifully carved doors, columns etc. can be found almost everywhere, not only in official buildings. In the courtyards of Tash-Hauli there are flat, low circles of bricks that served as bases for *yurts* – the felt tents the inhabitants erected here every winter. The palace had no heating facilities, until some stoves were imported from Russia. The *yurts* were easier to warm by charcoal burners and braziers. The high *iwan*, both in the palace and in ordinary houses, had just the opposite function. It was designed to capture the cool northerly wind and, by turning it into the yard, to reduce the intense summer heat. That is why every *iwan* in Khiva is twice the height of the house and is invariably turned towards the north.

The **Djuma mosque** (Friday, or Cathedral mosque) is a vast structure with a light roof supported by rows of carved wooden columns. (See Plate 7.) Twenty-four of them may be considered the peak achievement of local craftsmen between the tenth and the fourteenth centuries. These columns have been analysed by V.L. Voronina, who divided them into three groups with three different ornamental styles. Four of them (now in the Tashkent Museum) can be dated to the end of the tenth or beginning of the eleventh centuries. Seventeen others (four in the museum) belong to the second style, placed by Voronina in the twelfth century, while Rempel is more inclined to place them into the eleventh or twelfth centuries. The last three – the third group – belong to the fourteenth century.

One of the most beautiful buildings in Khiva is the mausoleum of the local hero, the poet and wrestler **Pahlavan Mahmud** (1835). (See Plate 21.) It has an octagonal dome raised over a rectangular ground-plan that represents the latest type of mausoleum to be found, particularly in Persia. Inside, the walls and the ceilings are completely covered with blue and white ornamental tiles with Persian *stanzas* inserted in the ornaments.

In the main room is the tomb of Alla Kuli Khan, the adjacent smaller one holds the tomb of the poet. The *madrasa* of **Alla Kuli Khan** dates from the same year and, like the mausoleum, has a fine decor of painted majolica tiles. Another *madrasa*, that of **Muhammad Amin Khan**, is of a somewhat later date and is now a hotel. The mausoleum of **Khoja Allauddin**, dated 1303, is a simple domed structure with a beautiful tiled cenotaph inside (see p. 85). The skyline of the city is dominated by two minarets: the **Kok-Minar** (Green), also called the **Kalta-Minar** (Short), is remarkable for its unusually large diameter and the predominance of green and yellow in the colour-scheme. (See Plates 6 and 13.) It was begun in 1852, but remained unfinished. The **Khoja Islam** minaret (1908) is the last notable architectural achievement of the Islamic era in Central Asia. Among the city gates, which date from the eighteenth and early nineteenth centuries, the **Palvan Darvaza** is perhaps the oldest and most interesting. (See Plate 8.)

Khiva ornamentation, although a part of the Central Asian tradition, has an individual character that distinguishes it from others. For example, it is different from those of Bukhara and Ferghana. Only one group of the traditional *girikhs*[19] occur – star-shaped figures inscribed within pentagons. By extending the straight lines of these forms, new patterns of *girikhs* arise that are not to be found anywhere else. The vegetal or floral patterns of Khiva represent the crowning achievement of Central Asian ornament. Even if Khiva ornament falls short of

Bukhara ornament from the point of view of technique, it surpasses it in the rich variety of its motifs. That of Bukhara evolves from architecture, while in Khiva ornamentation is an independent feature and its motifs persist equally in majolica, carvings, textiles, metalwork etc.

The country houses in Khorezm, known as *hauli*, form a particular type of domestic architecture. They were traditionally constructed as miniature strongholds for protection against robbers. We have seen this in several periods of local history, when conditions were unsettled and the threat of raids frequent. The actual house, with its small courtyard and *iwan*, is surrounded by high earth ramparts with battlements and massive pillars, and instead of the usual small postern, a strongly fortified gateway. The surrounding wall was often decorated with folk ornaments, some motifs of which can be traced back to the prehistoric patterns of the steppe nomads.

Among other important sites in Khorezm may be listed, on the left bank of the Amu Darya: Kalaly-Gyr, probably Achaemenid, begun in the fifth century B.C., but abandoned in the fourth century; Kiuzeli-Gyr, same period, sixth to fifth centuries B.C. – typical site with wall-dwellings; Shah-Senem, ancient settlement, revived in the twelfth century; Zamakhshar, Daudan-Kala and Kyzylcha-Kala, early medieval settlements; Ak-Kala (Adak), late medieval town, abandoned probably in the fifteenth century. And on the right bank of the river are Angka, Bronze Age settlement, later Kushan fortress Angka-Kala, third to fourth centuries A.D.; Dzhanbas-Kala, Neolithic, Bronze Age, ancient period; Kavat-Kala, Bronze Age site, fortress built in fourth to third centuries B.C., existed until the thirteenth century A.D.; Kuyuk-Kala, fifth-to-eighth-century fortress on the eastern shore of the Aral Sea, probably of Hephthalite origin; Teshik-Kala, seventh-to-eighth-century site; Yakke-Parsan, late Bronze Age, eighth to seventh centuries B.C., a castle of the fourth century B.C., and another of the sixth century A.D.; Guldursun, third-to-fourth-centuries A.D., resettled in tenth to eleventh centuries; Pil-Kala, second to third centuries A.D., probably the ancient fortress al-Fir, sometimes identified with the citadel of the capital as referred to by al-Biruni; Shurakhan and Narindzhan, early medieval sites.

NOTES ON CHAPTER VI
Full details of abbreviations and publications are in the Bibliography

1   B.I. Vainberg puts the life-span of the castle at only 50 years from the second half of the third to the beginning of the fourth centuries. See *Abstracts of Papers...*
2   Frumkin, *CAR* XIII, p. 80.
3   Frumkin, *CAR* XIII, p. 80.
4   The language was local Iranian Khorezmian. See Stavisky, Bongard and Levin in *Abstracts of Papers...*
5   Frumkin, *CAR* XIII, p. 78.
6   Tolstov, S.P., *Po sledam drevnie-khorezmiiskoy tsivilisatisii*, p. 226.
7   Barthold, *Turkestan*, p. 143, says to 392 yards.
8   Quoted by Barthold in *Turkestan*, pp. 144–45.
9   Gibb (tr.), *The Travels of Ibn Battuta*, p. 171.
10 Tolstov, *Po sledam*, p. 284.
11 Hookham, *Tamburlaine*, p. 33.
12 Rempel, *Ornament*, p. 262
13 Hookham, *Tamburlaine*, p. 92.
14 Hookham, *Tamburlaine*, p. 93.
15 Jenkinson, A.M., *In Early Voyages and Travels*, p. 71.
16 Ibn Arabshah, quoted by Hookham in *Tamburlaine*, p. 94.
17 Jenkinson, *Early Voyages*, p. 70.
18 This view is now being challenged by some archaeologists.
19 Literally, 'the knot', used to describe geometrical ornamental pattern constructed on a grid. Geometrical arabesque.

VII

THE ZARAFSHAN
VALLEY

THE VALLEY OF THE RIVER ZARAFSHAN has always been the most fertile and populous part of Transoxania. Its biggest city, **Samarkand**, was always the most important city in the country, even in times when Bukhara was the capital, as it was under the Samanids in the tenth century and under the Uzbek khans from the sixteenth century onwards. This was due mainly to the fortunate position of the city at the crossroads of several main trade-routes; the Great Silk Route from China split into two at Samarkand, one branch going west to Persia, the other south to India. There was also important trade with the north, where the steppe nomads supplied furs, cattle hides and slaves in exchange for the more sophisticated products of the city craftsmen. The neighbourhood of Samarkand was and still is extremely fertile, and the fields and orchards of the oasis were able to support a very dense population.

According to the Roman historian Quintus Curtius Rufus, the walls of Marakanda, as Samarkand was then called, had a circumference of 70 *stadia*, which is about 10 miles,[1] or at least more than 6 miles.[2] This may well be exaggerated because according to another source, the Chinese traveller Suen-Tsang, it was only 20 *li*, which is something between 4 and 5 miles. There are, of course, no statistics about the number of inhabitants, but Barthold, who based his guess upon the city area described fairly accurately by the Arab geographers, estimates the population in the tenth century to have been more than 500,000.

The city in those days, however, was not quite identical with present-day Samarkand. It lay further to the north and closer to the river, where the cemetery and the excavation site of Afrasiyab are now situated. The mound of **Afrasiyab** was the site of Samarkand up to the Mongol destruction. After that catastrophe the city centre was never rebuilt and the new town grew up from and around what were previously the outer suburbs on the southern perimeter. The reason for this was undoubtedly irrigation, as it was in many other cases. The city depended on the water from the Zarafshan, and an elaborate system of *aryks* (canals) had existed here from time immemorial. For this purpose a dam had been constructed several miles upstream from the city, and the river was divided into four streams, two of them navigable, probably by raft only. The longest of them flowed past Samarkand, and the *aryks* in the town were derived from it. The others irrigated the surrounding fields. This system naturally made the city extremely vulnerable in time of war, and it is worth noting that in the eighth century the Arab commander Asad ben Abdullah used exactly the same method as the Russian general Kaufman in 1868 – he cut off the water supply to the city by building a dam, thus forcing the city to surrender. The Mongols destroyed beyond repair the irrigation network within the city precinct, and most probably also the main canal, and the surviving population quite naturally shifted to areas where some water supply was available.

The post-Mongol city south of Afrasiyab thus became the capital of Timur, which Clavijo described, in 1403, in the following words:

> Samarkand stands in a plain and is surrounded by a rampart or wall of earth, with a very deep ditch. The city itself is rather larger than Seville, but lying outside Samarkand are great numbers of houses which form extensive suburbs… The township is surrounded by orchards and vineyards, extending in some cases to a league and a half or even two leagues beyond Samarkand which stands in the centre. In between these orchards pass streets with open squares. These are all densely populated and here all kinds of goods are on sale with bread-stuffs and meat… The population without the city is more numerous than the population within the walls. Among these orchards outside Samarkand are found the most noble and beautiful houses and here Timur has his many palaces and pleasure grounds… Through the streets of Samarkand, as through its gardens outside and inside, pass many water-conduits and in these gardens are the melon-beds and cotton-growing lands.

Trade has always been fostered by Timur with the view of making his capital the noblest of cities, and during all his conquests wheresoever he came, he carried off the best men of the population to people Samarkand, bringing thither together the master craftsmen of all nations… so great therefore was the population now of all nationalities gathered together in Samarkand that of men with their families the number they said must amount to 150,000 souls… The population of Samarkand was so vast that lodging for them all could not be found in the city limits, nor in the streets and open spaces in the suburbs and villages outside, and hence they were to be found quartered temporarily for lodgement even in caves and in tents under the trees of the gardens, which was a matter very wonderful to see… Throughout the city of Samarkand there are open squares where butchers' meat ready cooked, roasted or in stews, is sold with fowls and game suitably prepared for eating, also bread and excellent fruit both are on sale. All these viands and victuals are there set out in a decent cleanly manner, namely in all those open space and squares, and their traffic goes on all day and even all through the night time. Butchers' shops are numerous, also those booths where fowls, pheasants and partridges are on sale; and these shops are kept open by night as by day.

On the one part of Samarkand stands the Castle which is not built on a height, but is protected by deep ravines on all its sides; and through these water flows which makes the position of the Castle impregnable... Within its walls Timur holds in durance and captivity upwards of a thousand workmen: these labour at making plate-armour and helms, with bows and arrows, and to this business they are kept at work throughout the whole of their time in the service of his Highness.[3]

Barthold, on the other hand, gives the description for the pre-Mongol time (tenth to eleventh centuries) as follows: 'The old palace of the Arab Amirs, in the citadel, was still intact in the time of Istakhri (c.951), but Ibn Haukal (c.976) found it already in a ruinous condition'. Among other buildings there was a prison (also in the citadel), the cathedral mosque nearby (west of the citadel in Afrasiyab), and another castle.

The streets were, with few exceptions, paved with stone; the buildings, as now, were for the most part constructed of clay and wood... In the town and in the *rabad* (suburb), there were as many as 2,000 places where it was possible to obtain iced water gratis, the means for this being supplied by benefactors. The water was kept in fountains or was put in copper cisterns and earthenware vessels.

Remarkable were some 'astonishing figures cut out of cypresses, of horses, oxen, camels and wild beasts; they stand one opposite the other, as though surveying each other on the eve of engaging in a struggle or combat'.[4]

Excavations on the mound of Afrasiyab extend to several layers: the Graeco-Bactrian period has been found in two of them, known as Afrasiyab II and III. Pottery production reached its highest level in Afrasiyab III, and the products are remarkable for the purity of the clay, the fineness and density of their texture, and their elegance of form.

The palace of Afrasiyab was found in 1912, and excavations began the following year. In 1919, Professor Masson found several ornamental panels, dating from the ninth to the tenth centuries. A further set of decorative panels was found by Vyatkin in 1925, but all were destroyed during transport. On those now kept in the Afrasiyab Museum, the ornament is divided into several fields, square and rectangular. Inside the square ones are circles with inscribed hexagonal and octagonal stars of various kinds, and some minor decorative elements filling up the space. In others there are intersecting circles and crosses of circular ornaments, as well as interwoven squares and octagons.

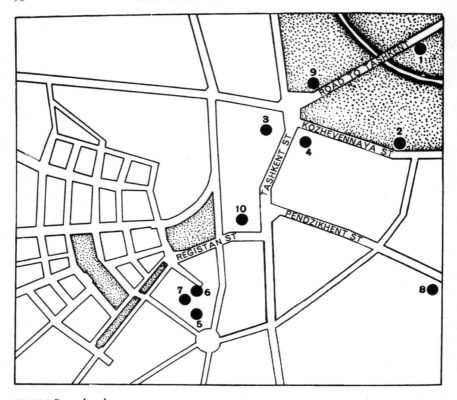

PLAN 2 Samarkand
1 Observatory of Ulugh-beg; 2 The Shah-i Zinda group; 3 Mosque Bibi Khanum;
4 Mausoleum Bibi Khanum; 5 Mausoleum Ak-Saray; 6 Mausoleum Rukhabad;
7 Mausoleum Gur Emir; 8 Mausoleum Ishrat-Khana; 9 Mosque Hazret-i Hizr; 10 Registan

The massive walls of the palace, built of *pakhsa* (beaten clay) bricks, probably
in the sixth to seventh centuries, have been preserved up to the height of 10 feet.
The layout shows large halls alternating with smaller rooms, auxiliary premises,
corridors etc. In one of the halls, which was apparently destroyed by fire, remnants
of wooden ceiling-beams were found with ornamental carving, together with
fragments of several supporting caryatids. In another there was a richly carved
alabaster panel, and in another the walls were profusely decorated with fresco
paintings. These frescoes can now be seen in the Afrasiyab Museum. They are
'without doubt masterpieces of Soghdian art, outstripping even the famous wall-
paintings of Pendzhikent'. Apparently the walls were divided into three horizontal
bands; the lowest one, just above the benches which lined the walls, consisted of

ornaments displaying stylised leaves with ancient acanthus motifs; in the middle was the main field, a monumental pictorial composition with, scattered about, tiny Soghdian inscriptions accompanying some of the figures. The top was formed by a stucco frieze. On the southern wall there is a splendid caravan, led by an elephant carrying a palanquin with a princess, followed by three ladies on horseback, an old man, another old man with a black beard on a camel, and a rider on a dun horse. The caravan brings gifts to the ruler – a herd of horses, some strange white birds that could be swans, but the main gift is the princess herself. On the western wall are the members of an embassy in ceremonial attire, holding gifts in their hands. Above them are figures of armed women with swords and *kinzhals* (short swords or daggers), obviously some warrior Amazons, whose legend was well known in Central Asia. The uncovering of the eastern wall was hardly begun, but spiral-shaped waves can already be seen with fishes, tortoises and figures of naked children.

The colour-scale of these paintings is rather limited: white, black, red, pale blue, brown and yellow, with a background usually painted in bright pale blue. Human figures are drawn very accurately, with all their ethnic and even personal characteristics; however, age is indicated only by the colour of the beard, and there are no individual features or any emotional expressions. The style of the Samarkand paintings clearly shows that they are contemporary with those of Varakhsha and Pendzhikent, and also with those of Kucha in Eastern Turkestan; they can all be dated between the sixth and the eighth centuries, thus representing the peak period of Soghdian art.

The eighth century, the time of the Arab occupation of Soghd, represents on the whole a period of decay, or at least a position of stalemate in the development of Samarkand. Intensive building activity was resumed in the ninth century, when the rule of the Abbasid caliphs became firmly established in Transoxania. It continued throughout the tenth and eleventh centuries, under the rule of the Samanid and Karakhanid dynasties.

The ornamental panels, described above, were found in the ruins of the Samanid palaces. New houses were built on top of the ruined buildings of the pre-Arab period; remnants were found, for instance, of a Karakhanid mausoleum from the twelfth century, decorated with beautifully incised terracotta – but no building as a whole survived the catastrophe of 1220. It was almost 150 years after the Mongol destruction before Samarkand regained some of its former significance. The heyday of the city came when Timur, himself a native of nearby Kesh, made Samarkand the capital of his vast empire. Building was an integral part of Timur's governmental programme – and mosques, palaces, *madrasas*, mausoleums, caravanserais and bazaars began to grow on a grandiose scale. As Clavijo aptly noticed, master craftsmen were brought from Fars, Azerbaidzhan,

FIG. 4 Alabaster carving (*girikh*) from the palace of Afrasiyab (tenth to eleventh centuries) in the Samarkand Museum

Iraq, Syria, Khorezm, India and Khorassan. Huge buildings of an unprecedented size and complexity were built here with a speed that was possible only under a despotism with unlimited power and resources. This feverish activity continued under Timur's successors, especially under his grandson Ulugh-beg, for the greater part of the fifteenth century.

In 1989 a Franco-Uzbek archaeological team reopened the excavations on the Afrasiyab site centred on its northern part where stood the citadel, the palace and the temples. Among the finds so far may be listed the remnants of a temple of the goddess Nana destroyed by the Arabs in 712 and, surprisingly, two palaces with floors paved with fired bricks, dated to the years 740–50 which may be considered the earliest monuments in Central Asia built since the Islamic conquest. Some frescoes have also been found, approximately from the mid-seventh century, showing a reception of foreign ambassadors, a Chinese emperor and empress and a New-Year procession led by the king to the tombs of his ancestors.

In pre-Mongol times the foremost among the sanctuaries of Samarkand was the tomb of Kussam ben Abbas. He, allegedly, was a cousin of the Prophet, and is supposed to have arrived in Samarkand in the year 676; according to one source he was killed, according to another he died a natural death. His tomb, or what is believed to be his tomb, became the object of a cult and a place of pilgrimage. It is now known as **Shah-i Zinda** (The Living Prince). There is a legend that he was not killed, but in saving himself from the infidels entered a cliff that opened miraculously before him and closed again after him.[5] Already in the twelfth century people of importance were buried near his tomb. A detailed description is given by Ibn Battuta (1333):

> Outside Samarkand is the tomb of Kussam ben Abbas. The inhabitants of Samarkand come out to visit it every Sunday and Thursday night. The Tartars also come to visit it, pay vows to it and bring cows, sheep, dirhams and dinars. All this is used for the benefit of visitors and the servants of the hospital and the blessed tomb. Above it is a square edifice with a cupola. At each corner are two marble columns, green, black, white and red in colour. The walls... are of different coloured marble and the roof is made of lead. The tomb is covered with black wood adorned with precious stones... Above it burn three silver lamps. Outside the building flows a large canal... on both banks there are trees, grape vines and jasmine.

Evidently, the architectural complex of the 'Old' Shah-i Zinda did not survive the Mongol destruction. In Ibn Battuta's description we find nothing about the other tombs and religious buildings that formed the complex in the twelfth century. It seems probable that the Mongols destroyed everything but the actual shrine of Kussam – although it is not quite certain if what Ibn Battuta described was the original edifice, or one already rebuilt. Nevertheless, in the fourteenth

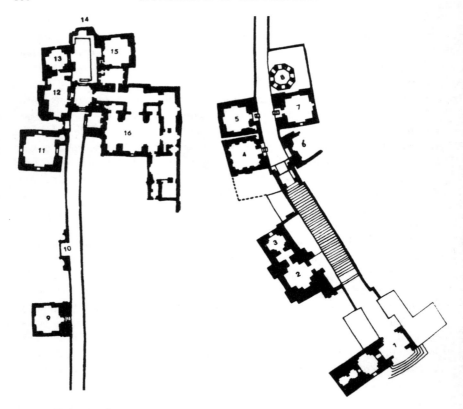

PLAN 3 Shah-i Zinda

century the building began of what is now known as the 'New' Shah-i Zinda, extending south of the shrine of Kussam and across the remnants of a former city wall. The majority of the buildings date from the Timurid period – the reigns of Timur and of Ulugh-beg.

The oldest surviving building of the present complex is the mausoleum and the adjacent mosque of Kussam. They are dated 1334–35 and described by Cohn-Wiener as follows:

> The building is characterised by the severity of its ornamental décor which consists almost exclusively of arabesques, and by the sharpness with which the squinches are cut into the walls. It was in the interior of this building, where a special technique of gilding, imitating local brocade embroideries and known as *kundal*, was used for the first time.[6]

In the mosque of Kussam, the *mihrab* in the western wall is especially interesting, decorated with incised mosaics in the brightest blue and with religious inscriptions executed in fine white letters framed with soft-lined and colourful floral ornaments. In the dark and narrow corridor leading to the mosque, some remnants of a pre-Mongol building have been found – a smallish minaret walled into the later structure, with simple patterns of small bricks.[7]

The whole complex of Shah-i Zinda consists of sixteen buildings clustered along an alley 225 feet long. Some of them are in a bad state of preservation – a good deal of restoration work has been carried out, but at least two or three of the buildings are obviously beyond repair. Moreover, the absence of informative inscriptions on some of them has led to a divergence of views on the dates and chronology of these buildings. In the plan opposite, the buildings are numbered 1–16, beginning with the entrance portico (1) and ending with Kussam's mausoleum (16). Building 14, the mausoleum of Khoja Ahmad, is after Kussam's the oldest, also built in the first half of the fourteenth century. Mausoleum 15 is dated 1360. Under Timur (1375–1405) were built mausoleums 4–7 (central group I), 9–11 (central group II) and, in the northern group, beyond the central portico, buildings 12 and 13. Central group II is in the worst state. It seems as if only members of Timur's family, including women, were buried here. Dating from the reign of Ulugh-beg (1409–49) are the main entrance portico (1) and the southern group of mausoleums (2 and 3), as well as building 8, an open octagon that probably served as a minaret. (See Plates 25, 26, 31, 32 and 33.)

The buildings of the central and northern groups are quite small, and were all built on a rectangular plan, with brick cupolas sometimes raised on a drum and with magnificently articulated and ornamented porticoes. The *iwan* in most cases has a honeycomb or stalactite vaulting, with a rich ceramic tiling. Neither of the mausoleums of the southern (bottom) group has a portico with an *iwan*. But both their domes are raised on high drums. During the excavations a crypt was discovered underneath the mausoleum of Khoja Ahmad, with fragments of several marble tombstones painted in gold and blue. This mausoleum and building 15 (1360) were built and decorated in a similar way. It is probable, therefore, that they are contemporary, and perhaps even the work of the same master or masters. One name is actually given – Fakhri Ali, probably of local origin. Both buildings are cube-shaped and domed, with cupolas resting on squinches and with an elevated and prominent portico. Portals and interiors are covered with flat ornamental tiles, mainly of glazed incised terracotta with some specimens of black or blue majolica painted under the glaze. The ornaments are geometrical, imitating the pattern of bricks, floral and textual. Their main colour is turquoise blue. The geometrical *girikh* (knot) in the *iwan* of Khoja Ahmad is complicated, being constructed on a heptagonal grid.

Rempel[8] compares the decor of the mausoleum of Khoja Ahmad with that of the Karakhanid mausoleums in Uzkend (twelfth century). The ornaments of Khoja Ahmad represent a continuation of the Uzkend style, the difference being mainly in the tiling technique, and correspondingly in the treatment of the surface and the colour range. In Uzkend, the terracotta is unglazed, ochre or brownish in colour, and sometimes incised in alabaster. In Samarkand, glazed incised terracotta and sometimes majolica can be found. In Uzkend, monochrome, with light-and-shade effects, prevails. The plastic concept of the carved or incised ornament is of overall importance. In Samarkand, one finds polychrome, with design based exactly on the same principles, but enriched with colour both in the relief and on the flat surfaces. The graphic design, colours and reliefs combine here to give an effect unknown in the architecture of the eleventh and twelfth centuries.

The mausoleum of Tuman Aka, 13 (1404), in contrast to the preceding two, is distinguishable by its violet colouring and exclusively flat design, more graphic and more sophisticated than the other two. Its cupola rests on a high drum. Inside, tiny idealised landscapes (trees, shrubs, flowers etc.) may be seen painted in small rectangular fields underneath the cupola. The cool whiteness of the interior contrasts sharply with the rich mosaics of the portal outside.

Building 11 is believed to be the mausoleum of Emir Burunduk, one of Timur's generals, and can be dated back to 1380. Both the cupola and the arch of the portal have disappeared, but the ornaments of the *iwan* offer some interesting patterns.

The central group I consists of four buildings: 5 (Shadi Mulk, 1372), 4 (Emir Zade, 1386), and on the opposite side, 6 (Emir Husayn, 1376) and 7 (Shirin Bika Aka, 1385). Building 5 (Shadi Mulk) is also known as Turkan Aka. These were two female members of the family, daughter and mother, who were both buried here. Apart from a ribbed cupola, some architectural innovations are immediately apparent. The *iwan* is far more articulated, corner columns are more slender, their capitals and bases finer and more elaborate. The *iwan* is not covered by an arch, but by a half-dome filled with stalactites (honeycomb vault). The same applies to 4 and 6, while 7 (Shirin Bika Aka) is again different and in many aspects more advanced. A sixteen-sided drum resting on a square base, a low cupola, and a highly ornate portico entrance are the main features of this building. Outside decor consists of incised mosaics in bright colours, floral orna-ments, and inscriptions in the Thulth style. Inside are mosaic panels with fine gold painting on the glaze, others with landscapes (flowers, shrubs, rivulets, trees with birds, clouds), showing a remarkable Chinese influence, which may also be found in the stylised dragons and phoenixes in the wall ornaments. The strange octagonal structure next to it (8) is believed by some authorities to be a minaret; others prefer to describe it as a rather unusual type of mausoleum, yet no grave

38. ABOVE. Ark, Bukhara

39. BELOW. Mosque Maghak-i Attari, Bukhara

40. ABOVE. Mausoleum of Hazret Bahauddin Nakshbandi, Bukhara

41. BELOW. A vaulted bazaar, Bukhara

42. ABOVE. Madrasa
Nadir Divan Begi,
Bukhara

43. RIGHT. Mausoleum
of Ismail Samanid,
Bukhara (detail)

44. Mausoleum Hakim al-Termezi, Termez. The cenotaph

45. Northern Mausoleum, Uzkend

46. Southern Mausoleum, Uzkend

47. ABOVE. Southern Mausoleum, Uzkend (detail)

48. BELOW. Northern Mausoleum, Uzkend (detail)

49. Mausoleum of Nasr
ben Ali, Uzkend

50. Mausoleum of Nasr
ben Ali, Uzkend

has been found in it. It is a sober, early-fifteenth-century building, with a tiny cupola and ornaments mainly formed by patterns of glazed bricks.

The southern group is believed to be the burial-site of Ulugh-beg's teacher, the renowned astronomer Kazi Zade Rumi. (Rumi means from Turkey.) It is a whole complex, not a single-room compact structure. Building 2 is the main shrine; there are cells in the corners, some auxiliary premises, and an adjacent room (3). High slender drums, one of them twice as high as the other, carry high bulbous cupolas covered with turquoise tiles.

Inside, the dome is profusely decorated with monochrome *mukarnas*. Outside decoration exists only on the portals and the drums. The portals have no *iwans*. In contrast to the central group I, this complex attracts attention not by the richness of its decoration but by the sobriety and harmony of its architecture. The same principles apply to the main entrance (1), also built during the reign of Ulugh-beg (1434). In the eighteenth century another mosque (not numbered in the plan) was built just behind the main portico.

Next to the Shah-i Zinda group on the southern side of Afrasiyab, stands the mosque of **Hazret-i Hizr**, built in the mid-nineteenth century. (See Plate 22.) This is a modest building, restored in 1915, but quite remarkable for its asymmetrical composition and the harmonious effect achieved by the combination of the smallish portico, the colonnade of wooden columns, the massive bulk of the main mosque building, and the adjacent minaret, which is not very high. The road passes here through a depression, marking the site of the ancient moat, over which the main city gate (Iron Gate) was erected. Having entered the city by this gate, the fifteenth-century traveller could see in front of him two giant buildings – Timur's cathedral mosque now known as Bibi Khanum (The Old Queen) and, opposite, the *madrasa* of Serai-Mulk Khanum. The gate and the *madrasa* are no longer in existence, but a ruined little mausoleum, also called Bibi Khanum, which formed part of its complex, is still there.

The cathedral mosque **Bibi Khanum** is being thoroughly restored. (See Plates 20 and 23.) It is one of the largest buildings of its kind in the Islamic world, with an inner court of 270 by 180 feet, an entrance gateway 120 feet high, a main building 43 feet long on the inside. The cupola, on a high drum, was heavily damaged, as was the main *iwan* and both side buildings. Clavijo was in Samarkand when the mosque was under construction.

The Mosque which Timur had caused to be built... seemed to us the noblest of all those we visited in the city of Samarkand, but no sooner had it been completed than he began to find fault with its entrance gateway, which he now said was much too low and must be forthwith pulled down. Then the workmen began to dig pits to lay the new foundations when, in order that the piers might be rapidly rebuilt his Highness gave out that he himself could take charge to direct the

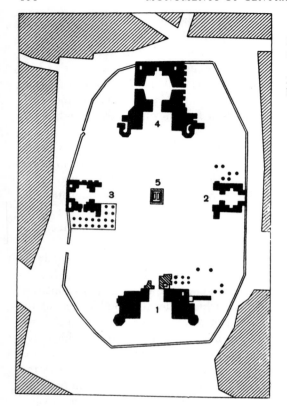

PLAN 4 Mosque Bibi Khanum
(1399–1404)
1 Entrance *iwan* of mosque;
2–3 Small side mosques; 4 Main
building; 5 Pedestal for Koran

labour for the one pier of the new gateway while he laid it on two of the lords of his court, his special favourites, to see to the foundations of the other part. Thus all should see whether it was he or those other lords who first might bring this business to its proper conclusion... Timur was already weak in health, he could no longer stand for long on his feet, or mount his horse... It was therefore in his litter that every morning he had himself brought to the place, and he would stay there the best part of the day urging on the work. He would arrange for much meat to be cooked and brought and then he would order them to throw portions of the same to the workmen in the foundations, as one should cast bones to dogs in a pit... and he even with his own hands did this. Thus the building went on day and night until at last came the time when it had perforce to stop – on account of the winter snows, which began now constantly to fall.[9]

The building was done so hastily that shortly after being completed it began to crumble. Until recently all that could be seen were the ruins of the entrance gate, of three domed buildings – one of them the main mosque – and of one corner minaret. Originally there was an outer wall forming a rectangle 500 by 330 feet, enclosing the inner court with a huge stone pedestal for the Koran in the centre. There were four high vaulted *iwans*, one in the middle of each side of the wall; three of them were entrances to the domed mosques – two minor and one main entrances. There were colonnades on the inside around the courtyard, and in each corner stood a high slender minaret.

Nowadays, the main building again impresses by its colossal dimensions. The diameter of the *iwan* arch is 55 feet; its height is 90. The inner dome has the same diameter and a height of 130 feet. The towers flanking the portal are not round but octagonal and thinning towards the top, which enhances the effect of slenderness. The emphasis on vertical, rather than horizontal, is apparent also in the cylindrical drum that carries a sphero-conical outer dome. The outer decoration consists mainly of brick patterns, either *girikhs* or huge Kufic inscriptions, and of majolica and mosaic ornaments with epigraphic and vegetal motifs used either to fill small spaces or on huge wall panels, arch segments etc.; some incised marble and terracotta may be found here too. Inside there are ornamental paintings on the walls, executed in gold and blue on a white background, and some gold and blue reliefs on papier-mâché on spherical surfaces, such as the dome and the corner arches. Similar architectural principles and decorative techniques were used in the entrance portico and the two lateral buildings. The recent bad condition of the monument can be blamed not only on Timur's haste but mainly on his intention, which he forced upon his architects, to increase the dimensions to surpass all existing buildings in the Islamic world, while disregarding the traditional building modules, the established endurance of the material, and also the seismic character of the area. In spite of this, Bibi Khanum represents a synthesis of the highest achievements of contemporary Eastern architecture and thus anticipates the creation of a new architectural style, the outstanding example of which is Timur's mausoleum, the Gur Emir.[10]

Ten minutes walk away is the main square of the city, the Registan, where once converged six radial thoroughfares leading to the gates in the city wall, as it was built or reconstructed by Timur in 1371.

West from the Registan is the mausoleum **Rukhabad**, tomb of Sheikh Burhanuddin Sagharji, who died in the 1380s. It is a domed building of somewhat archaic construction and recalls the grandiose architecture of the Timurid period mainly by its massive proportions.

The complex of Muhammad Sultan and the mausoleum **Gur Emir** (The Great Prince) originally consisted of a *madrasa* where youngsters of noble family were educated and groomed for honorary state functions, and of a *khaniga*, or guest house, for government guests. Between them was a square yard with high walls, and a minaret in each corner with a high ornamental portico entrance on the north side. Now only this portico and a part of the southern wall are preserved. Both are adorned with flat ornamental mosaic tiles 'of exceptional beauty'. Timur's grandson and successor designate, Muhammad Sultan, died in 1403, allegedly of wounds received in the battle of Angora against the Turks. Timur then ordered a mausoleum to be built for him within the precincts of this ensemble. In 1404 this mausoleum was completed, but Timur had it rebuilt on a more grandiose scale, similar to Bibi Khanum. This restructuring was done within two weeks. Apparently only the drum and the dome were rebuilt. Timur himself died early in 1405 and was buried here while his sons and grandsons fought for the succession. Under Ulugh-beg the mausoleum became a family tomb, where next to Timur and Muhammad Sultan are buried three sons of Timur – Omar Sheikh,[11] Miranshah and Shahrukh; Ulugh-beg himself is also buried here. The only non-relative is the famous sheikh Mir Saiyd Barka, who is buried next to the Conqueror. (See Plates 16, 17 and 18.)

The tombstones on the ground floor are cenotaphs only. All are of white marble; only Timur's tombstone is of one huge slab of dark green jade. This slab was broken down the middle in the eighteenth century when the Persian conqueror Nadir Shah tried to lift and remove it. When the slab broke, Nadir Shah gave up his intention and so left it. The real graves are in a crypt underneath the mausoleum, in exactly the same position as the cenotaphs above. They are all covered with identical flat marble slabs decorated with relief inscriptions. In 1941 Timur's grave was opened by the Soviet Archaeological Commission, who

> found here the skeleton of a man who, though lame in both right limbs, must have been of powerful physique, tall for a Tartar and of a haughty bearing. They examined the skeleton and the remains, which included fragments of muscle and skin, and some hair of the head, eye-brows, red moustache and beard. The skull indicated Mongol features…[12]

It was from the skull revealed at this opening that V. Gerasimov reconstructed the head of Timur.

We find the following description of the building in Pope:[13]

> [Gur Emir] is still a monumental and dramatic structure. Externally it is divided into three equal parts. A bulbous dome, 112 feet high, is enriched with 64 almost round flutes and flanked by minarets 83 feet high. It is set on a high but narrower cylindrical drum which causes a sharp constriction at the base of the dome. This drum, in turn, rises out of a chamber which, on the exterior, is octagonal. Portals pierce each of the major four sides, again reminiscent of ancient Sasanian practice. The dome is covered with bright blue tiles and the high drum, ornamented with a huge inscription of rectangular Kufic, is of golden-buff bricks. The interior is also impressive, with an alabaster dado, grey-green jasper cornice, black limestone niches and a marble balustrade.

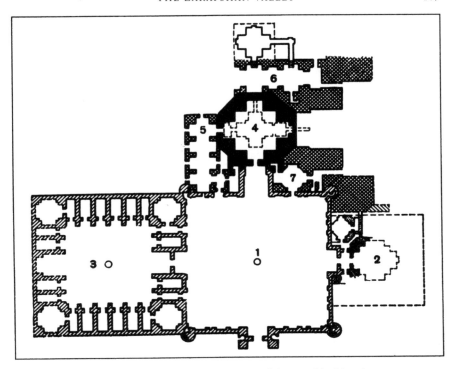

PLAN 5 Mausoleum Gur Emir (with reconstruction of destroyed buildings)
1 Yard of complex of Muhammad Sultan; 2 *Khaniga*; 3 *Madrasa*; 4 Mausoleum Gur Emir; 5
Eastern gallery (1424); 6 Southern group of buildings; 7 Building with cupola

The grandeur of the building is the result not only of its size but also of the simplicity of its component parts – the octagonal base, the cylindrical drum, and the
huge ribbed dome. A big complicated *girikh* adorns the walls of the octagon,
while the drum carries an inscription in Kufic characters which is almost 10 feet
high. In the interior decor we find, among other elements, relief rosettes of papier-
mâché on spherical surfaces. The interior has been recently restored to its former
splendour. The minarets, too, have been rebuilt.

The last of the Samarkand Timurids were buried in the so-called mausoleum
Ak-Saray, south-east of Gur Emir, and built in the 1470s. This modest-sized
building is interesting mainly for its interiors, where new structural elements were
used, such as intersecting arches in the corners replacing the traditional squinch.
Close to it in architectural style and time of construction is another Timurid
tomb, the mausoleum **Ishrat Khana**, where female members of the family were

buried. It was built in 1464 to the east of Registan, on the main road to the Firuzi Gate. It is perhaps the most heavily damaged of all the monuments in Samarkand, and this may be the reason its very purpose remained so long in doubt. It consisted of a central cross-shaped room and two two-storey wings with cells; there was a mosque in one of them and an assembly-room in the other. The central hall was covered with a dome resting on an amazingly high and slender drum that it was possible to build only by making full use of the new structural techniques. The interior decoration, with a profusion of tile ornament, gold paintings, stained-glass windows and rich carpets on the floor, probably once generated such an atmosphere of luxury that local people associated it with a pleasure palace rather than with a house of the dead. Nevertheless, this, like the Ak-Saray, was an intimate type of tomb, quite unlike the grandeur of the Gur Emir.

In a nearby cemetery, the *mazar* complex of **Khoja Abdi Darun** consists of several premises, of which the oldest is probably the mausoleum, dating from the twelfth century. In the fifteenth century a domed structure with a portico was added, while in the nineteenth century a small *madrasa* and a mosque were included. Opposite to this 'Abdi-Inside' is another mausoleum, the **Abdi Birun** (Abdi-Outside), which was built in the seventeenth century outside the city walls.

In **Registan** itself, the intersection of the main arteries was originally covered by a domed bazaar, built either in Timur's time or after. This is how Clavijo saw the beginning of the work.

> Every year to the city of Samarkand much merchandise of all kinds came from Cathay, India, Tartary and from many other quarters, but there was as yet no place within the city where this merchandise might be suitably stored, displayed and offered for sale. Timur therefore now gave orders that a street should be built to pass right through Samarkand, which should have shops on either side of it... and this street was to go from one side of the city through to the other side, traversing the heart of the township. The accomplishment of his orders he laid on two of the great lords of his court, letting them know that if they failed in diligence, their heads would pay the penalty. These nobles therefore began at speed, causing all the houses to be thrown down along the line of the new street. No heed was paid to the complaints of persons to whom the property here might belong and those whose houses thus were demolished suddenly had to quit with no warning, carrying away with them their goods and chattels as best they might. No sooner had all the houses been thrown down than the master builders came and laid out the broad new street, erecting shops on the one side and opposite, placing before each a high stone bench that was topped with white slabs. Each shop had two chambers front and back, and the streetway was arched over with a domed roof in which were windows to let the light through... Thus in the course of twenty days the whole street was carried through: a wonder indeed to behold. But those whose houses had been thus demolished had good cause to complain.[14]

FIG. 5 Portico in the yard of Gur Emir,
Samarkand (end of fourteenth century);
mosaic tiles

Under Ulugh-beg Registan acquired a more solemn function: military parades,
public promulgation of orders, public executions etc. were carried out here. In this
connection it was rebuilt to become one of the most outstanding architectural
ensembles in the Eastern world. First, in the first half of the fifteenth century, the
madrasa of Ulugh-beg was built on the western side, a *khaniga* on the eastern, a
caravanserai on the northern, and two mosques, one large and one small, on the
southern side. Later, when most of these buildings decayed, the square was
rebuilt again. Between 1619 and 1635 another *madrasa*, the Shir-Dor, was built
opposite that of Ulugh-beg. Instead of the caravanserai, yet another *madrasa*, the
Tilla Kari, was constructed between 1646 and 1659. These three monumental

buildings, together with an eighteenth-century domed bazaar, have survived to the present day. The southern side, which was left open, is now occupied with a *son et lumière* podium.

The *madrasa* of **Ulugh-beg** was built to the standard plan: a square courtyard with a two-storey building on each side, housing the students' and masters' cells. (See Plate 24.) In the middle of each wing was a high vaulted *iwan*, and in the corners large domed halls. Opposite the main entrance was a mosque. The main facade facing the square consisted of a monumental *pishtak* (portico), with richly ornamented walls and niches, and two similarly adorned wings. In the corners on the outside were high slender minarets which, however, were not used by muezzins. The *madrasa* had an exceptionally rich architectural decoration – mosaics of coloured tiles, *girikhs* constructed on diagonal grids, and Kufic inscriptions on the walls and minarets. The colours, tilework and patterns were of a very high quality. Unfortunately, the building has been considerably damaged, but was recently thoroughly restored. The present level of the square is some 8–9 feet above the original one. This somewhat distorts the proportions of the buildings.

The *madrasa* **Shir-Dor** was deliberately built as almost a replica of its opposite number. (See Plate 30.) The main differences are the ribbed cupolas on circular drums and, what is quite exceptional, two large panels on the main *pishtak*, each bearing an image of a striped tiger attacking a deer: hence the name Shir-Dor (Bearing Tigers). There is no mosque and no rear halls, and instead of minarets the main facade is flanked by small turrets. As for the decor, the period of decline manifested itself in cruder craftsmanship, larger patterns, over-accentuated lines, exalted floral ornaments and, overall, less harmony in colour.

The third *madrasa*, **Tilla Kari**, was built, like Shir-Dor, by the same ruler, Yallangtush. It combined the functions of a religious college with those of a cathedral mosque. (See Plate 19.) This is why there are covered arcades on the western side of the courtyard, with the domed structure of the mosque dominating in the centre of the front. The main facade is again a replica of the two other buildings previously described. The mosque inside is an interesting building with a big *iwan*, which is nevertheless dwarfed by a huge and heavy cylindrical drum behind, originally designed to carry a dome. This has now been added while the whole building has been thoroughly restored. Inside, the walls are covered with rich carpet-like ornaments with a profusion of gold: hence the name Tilla Kari (Adorned with Gold).

On the north-eastern outskirts of the city there is yet another unusual monument. Here, in the years 1424–28, the prince-scholar Ulugh-beg erected an astronomical **observatory** that was at that time probably the best-equipped establishment of that kind in the world, both East and West. Ulugh-beg himself constructed astronomical tables, and in the seventeenth century the first English

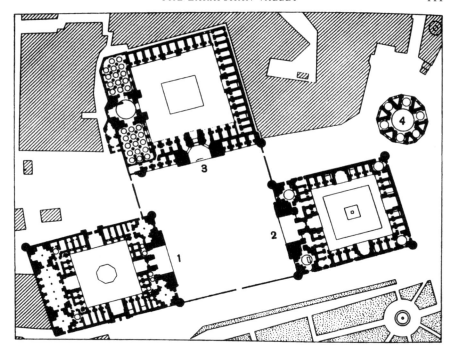

PLAN 6 Registan, Samarkand
1 *Madrasa* of Ulugh-beg; 2 *Madrasa* Shir-Dor; 3 *Madrasa* Tilla-Kari; 4 Vaulted bazaar

Astronomer Royal made extensive use of these.[15] His builders were faced with the difficult task of avoiding disturbances caused by earth tremors, so frequent in this area. This is why they chose this rocky hillock and cut a giant ravine into the rock, which housed the segment of a huge sextant, divided into degrees and minutes and adorned with the signs of the zodiac. Observations and measurements were made by means of an astrolabe, as telescopes were not yet known. The building above the ground was circular, on three storeys, decorated with ornamental tiles. Nothing of it remains today, except a few fragments. According to contemporary description, the walls were decorated with paintings of deserts and steppes, seas, mountains and rivers, as well as those of seven immovable and seven movable celestial bodies. A small circular museum has been built next to the site.

Not far from the observatory stands a fifteenth-century *mazar*, **Chupan-Ata**. This was not a mausoleum (there was no one buried in it), but it was constructed above a grave, mythical or real, to become a place of pilgrimage. The structure is that of a mausoleum, consisting of a simple cube-shaped building, with a high slender drum carrying a dome. Inside, strong intersecting arches may be seen supporting the drum and the dome, which at the time of construction represented a considerable innovation in building technique. Outside, the drum is decorated with a huge Kufic inscription executed in coloured tiles against a background of baked bricks.

Travelling south of Samarkand, we come first to the site of **Tali-Barzu**, four miles from the city. The finds in Tali-Barzu largely consist of clay statuettes, some of which are of the early Kushan period. Others, which include camels, monkeys and other animals, may not be older than the fifth or sixth centuries A.D. Further south, near the village of Aman-Kutan, at the foothills of the Hazret-Sultan range, is a Paleolithic site, where excavations have been going on for several years. The site is in a large limestone cave and belongs to the Middle Paleolithic period. Crossing the range by Aman-Kutan or Takhta-Karacha pass we descend into the valley of the Kashka Darya, and after a few miles we arrive at the village of **Shahrisabz** (Green City). This was the name given to the town of Kesh by Timur, who was born here. At the end of the fourteenth century, he decided to build here his most sumptuous residence, the **Ak-Saray** (White Palace). (See Plates 27, 35 and 36.) This building was even more ambitious than the Samarkand mosque. Intended to overawe all who saw it, the building took twenty years to complete and was not quite finished when Clavijo saw it in 1404.

This palace had an entrance passage constructed to be of considerable length with a high portal before it, and in this entrance gallery to right and to left there were archways of brick work encased and patterned with blue tiles... At the end of this gallery stands another gateway beyond which is a great courtyard paved with white flagstones and surrounded on the four sides by richly wrought arches, and in its centre is a very large water-tank. This courtyard indeed may measure some three hundred paces in its width and beyond it you enter through a very high and spacious gateway the main building of the palace. This gateway is throughout beautifully adorned with very fine work in gold and blue tiles, and over the entrance are seen the figures of the Lion and the Sun, these same figures being repeated over the summit of each of the arches round the courtyard... From this main portal you enter a great reception hall which is a room four square, where the walls are panelled with gold and blue tiles, and the ceiling is entirely of gold work. We saw indeed here so many apartments and separate chambers, all of which were adorned in tilework of blue and gold with many other colours, that it would take long to describe them here, and all was so marvellously wrought that even the craftsmen of Paris, who are so noted for their skill, would hold that which is done here to be of very fine workmanship.[16]

And now the description as given by Pope:[17]

In plan, the building was somewhat novel for the period, with a triple-iwan façade reminiscent of Firuzabad. The portal arch itself was 165 feet high, flanked by a pair of round towers, like minarets, rising out of a twelve-sided base. The centre iwan opened into a huge marble-paved court at right angles to the entrance. On the opposite side, another great iwan led into a large reception hall... The huge rear wall of the reception hall was covered with the finest mosaic faience in quietly fluctuating tones of turquoise, lapis, milk-white, mirror-black, green and aubergine embellished with gold. Such an expanse completely covered with many strong and varied patterns could have been intolerable, but the opulence was organised and controlled by a firmly designed geometrical framework of harmonious proportions. The contribution of each panel is carefully appraised and apportioned with sensitive regards for the total effect... It was a perfect expression of Timur's imperial power and pride, fortunately formulated and controlled by Persian aesthetic genius and experience.

Cohn-Wiener[18] sees Ak-Saray as an important amalgamation of two basic architectural elements, which can be traced back to the origins of Persian art and even beyond, to Assyria. They are the entrance gate flanked by towers, originally designed as a fortification, and the *iwan*, situated inside opposite the entrance, which functioned as an open reception hall. Timur combined these two elements in Ak-Saray, and obtained extraordinary and impressive results. On the other hand, Ak-Saray shows how conservative Islam's architecture was as a whole. While the ornament is continuously developed, the few architectural elements remain virtually unchanged throughout Islamic history. This once proud monument has unfortunately reached us in a very poor state of preservation. All that remains are the two flanking towers of the entrance *iwan* and parts of the richly decorated walls at the base of the big arch. Rempel,[19] who is the leading authority on architectural ornament in Central Asia, emphasises how meticulously the colouring of the tiles was calculated in relation to the lights and shadows on the walls on which they were to appear. The grading of colours for different kinds of design or for various functions of ornaments was developed into a fine art with precisely formulated laws and regulations, and it is mainly in this respect, and in poorer craftsmanship, that the decline of the subsequent period became manifest. South of the Ak-Saray, Clavijo was shown

> a magnificent mosque in which a chapel is seen, where Timur's father was buried and beside this is a second chapel, in which it is intended that Timur himself shall be interred when the time comes... In this same mosque too, is seen the tomb of prince Jahangir, the eldest son of Timur. Here daily by the special order of Timur the meat of twenty sheep is cooked and distributed in alms...[20]

The site of the mausoleum that Timur built for himself has long been unknown. Only recently a domed structure half-buried in the ground has been uncovered and identified. Inside, it is lined with marble and decorated with bands of inscriptions, and houses a sarcophagus of an unknown person. It stood in the centre of a necropolis completely razed by Sheibani Khan. Next to it, the **Dar-al Siyadat** is the mausoleum that Timur had built for his eldest son, Jahangir. According to some, his other son, Omar Sheikh, is also buried here. It is a fortress-like structure with a high portal and conical cupola built by Khorezmian architects in the late fourteenth century. A short distance to the west the Green Mosque, **Kok Gumbaz**, is an imposing edifice with a blue dome built by Ulughbeg in the middle of the fifteenth century and recently restored. (See Plate 37.) Interior walls have painted decoration. Opposite are two mausoleums, **Gumbaz-i Zaidin**, also built by Ulugh-beg for his descendants, has a turquoise dome and tiled decoration. (See Plate 34.) Inside is a number of cenotaphs and, again, tile decoration. Next to it, the *mazar* of **Shams-ad-din Kulal** was built by Timur in the 1370s for his clan, the Barlas. It probably had a dome and tile decoration but now is whitewashed with a plain ceiling: the only outstanding features are two carved columns and a carved door.

To the east of Samarkand, on the territory of Tajikistan, on both banks of the Zarafshan and between the Hissar and Zarafshan ranges, lay the medieval, pre-Arab principality of Ushrusana or Usrushana, the chief town of which was Bunjikath, the present **Pendzhikent**. In the tenth century it had some 10,000 male inhabitants. There was a citadel, a *shahristan* (inner city) and outer suburbs. But it is quite obvious that 200 years previously the city was far more important, and that an earlier settlement was abandoned as a result of the Arab conquest in the eighth century.

This ancient Soghdian city, the ruins of which lie on the outskirts of the present-day town of the same name, became known to the archaeologists following the discovery of the famous collection of Soghdian archives on Mount Mug. These archives, as was established when some of the documents were deciphered, belonged to Divastich, the last ruler of this small princedom,[21] who fled before the victorious Arabs to his castle on Mount Mug, and was subsequently captured and crucified. From this time on, the Soghdians practically disappeared from the history of western Turkestan.

In 1933 a shepherd by chance discovered a manuscript in an almost inaccessible place east of Pendzhikent. This was identified as an old Soghdian document, and it was found that the site, locally called Mount Mug, concealed the ruins of an ancient castle destroyed by the Arabs in the eighth century. The most precious find was a collection of ninety manuscripts, mostly in the Soghdian language. Some of them can be seen in the museum of Pendzhikent.

Pendzhikent came into existence as an urban settlement surrounded by a defensive wall in the fifth or early sixth centuries. It was abandoned at the time of the Arab conquest, and no attempt was made to re-establish it. In consequence, the uppermost building level has remained intact. According to Frumkin,[22] Pendzhikent is not only a great artistic centre, but also provides a key to much of the history and civilisation of pre-Islamic Soghdiana. Excavations began only in 1946 and revealed some significant features of the city's social and economic structure. The chief building materials were rectangular adobe bricks and blocks of *pakhsa* (beaten clay); the walls were built of clay blocks, the vaulted roofs of brick. Domed roofs, too, also of brick, are found occasionally. Stone was not used, except for some column bases. The dwelling-houses were of two storeys. The houses of the wealthier classes had a tetrastyle reception-room, sometimes of considerable size, with benches of beaten clay round the walls. In these rooms walls were usually covered with paintings from top to bottom and decorated with splendid carving. The upper floor consisted mainly of living quarters. The most elaborate houses had facades in the form of *iwans* borne on columns or of loggias with half-domed roofs. The eastern, and even more the southern, part of the city contained houses of a much more modest character, both in layout, number and size of rooms and internal decoration. Unlike elsewhere in this suburban settlement, each house stands by itself and all the houses differ from one another in layout. The citadel was separated from the town by a deep ravine and was only accessible by a bridge.

A local type of temple architecture, which differs from the cult buildings of the Buddhists or Christians and also from fire temples as found in Persia, was revealed here for the first time. The temple consisted of an elaborate complex of separate buildings linked by large courtyards; the main building was erected within the courtyard on a stylobate. It was open to the east, joined by a passage to a cella on the west side, and surrounded on three sides by corridors or open galleries.[23]

In addition to architecture, the major features of the site were the numerous wall-paintings, sculptures and ornaments in clay or plaster, as well as remarkable wood sculptures and carving.

> They offer a fascinating initiation into the history of pre-Muslim Soghdiana, its mythology, language, arts and handicrafts, warfare, religious beliefs, burial rites as well as the mode of living and clothing of the 'upper classes'... They form a bewildering and varied kaleidoscope of fighting warriors, banqueting knights, religious ceremonies, mythological scenes, charming females as well as monsters and demons.[24,25]

The length of one of the best-preserved paintings is over 45 feet.

The pottery of Pendzhikent is remarkable for its elegance of form and variety of decoration. Large numbers of glass objects have been found, mostly of small size. Iron objects include various tools and implements, weapons and pieces of harness, while mainly toilet articles and ornaments, such as bracelets, rings and earrings, mirrors etc., were of bronze. Relatively few articles were made of precious metals, but a great variety of beads and gems made of semi-precious stones were found. Nothing of cloth, wood and leather could be found because, in the loess soil of Pendzhikent, these materials were totally destroyed.

A characteristic feature of Soghdian civilisation was the vast number of religious beliefs, among which were Zoroastrianism, Buddhism and Manichaeism. There were Nestorian bishops in Samarkand and Merv. This multiplicity of influence largely accounts for the still tentative and debatable interpretation of the finds. The widely spread Central Asian cult of seasonally dying and resurgent nature, which stems from other ancient creeds, may underlie the famous painting of the 'scene of mourning'. Other sculptural ensembles reflect fluvial rites. The goddess sitting on a lion and holding emblems of the sun and the moon suggests influences of ancient and remote worship and may be compared with the 'Sasanian' silver dishes from the Hermitage and the British Museum. Similarly, the calendar found in Mount Mug castle enumerates the days of the moon, of Mars, Mercury, Ormuzd, Anahita or Venus. The ancient pre-Soghdian names have survived until our day. In fact, it becomes increasingly evident that in this as in other cases (see p. 217) local worship that stemmed from immemorial tradition and mythology coexisted with other cults.[26]

The road between Samarkand and Bukhara, or 'Royal Road', was always of great importance. In the Middle Ages the distance was reckoned to be six or seven days' journey. Now a scheduled bus service takes about eight hours, with five or six stops on the way. Most of the journey is across the desert. The Samarkand oasis extends as far as Kata-Kurgan, which, according to Chinese sources, became the centre of the district after Marakanda had been destroyed by Alexander. These sources do not mention Samarkand again until the fifth century A.D.

Midway between Samarkand and Bukhara, and near the village of Kermine (Karminiya), we can see from the road the ruins in the desert of an eleventh century caravanserai, the **Rabat-i Malik**, with an impressive wall of ornamental semi-columns. This kind of architectural decor is rare in Central Asia and can be found only on the minaret of Dzhar Kurgan and in the Shahriar ark precinct in Merv. The incised ornament on the portal of the Rabat-i Malik is similar to and contemporary with the ornaments of the palace of Afrasiyab and, in the far west of the country, to those of the carved wooden columns of Khiva (see p. 90). Pope[27] finds Rabat-i Malik, which was built under the Seljuks, one of the most imposing ruins of the Islamic period. Only part of one wall of the caravanserai remains. This fragment alone suffices to show that here was built a massive and forbidding structure of plain brick, simple as becomes a frontier fortress. A row of almost cylindrical piers are connected at the top by arches, the force of which is clearly derived from a squinch, thus relieving the blank walls. A narrow ornamental frieze marks the plain cornices. The total effect of this great wall is an imposing combination of severe simplicity and sheer power.[28] Rempel[29] sees in the columns and arches, as well as in the plain brick tiling covering the wall of sun-baked bricks, a distinct reminder of the ancient Soghdian castles, the *kushks*. On the other hand, the minaret-like towers in the corners and the grandiose portal entrance definitely foreshadow the future style of Islamic architecture. The monument is in danger of complete destruction, the locals using its bricks as building material.

The tenth-century mausoleum **Arab-Ata** at Tim was unknown until recently. It is a cube-shaped dome structure with plain brick decoration in front. An interesting feature of it is the transition from a square base to a round dome. This is done here in two stages: below the corner squinch is another one, decorative rather than structural, flanked with a half squinch on either side. This may be considered the earliest appearance of a rudimentary *mukarnas* (stalactite) decoration.

In Kermine itself the mausoleum **Mir-Saiyd Bahram** was built in the tenth or eleventh centuries, and shares certain characteristics with the famous mausoleum of the Samanids in Bukhara (see p. 119) It is a cube-shaped, domed building with corner columns and wall ornamentation of plain bricks. The portal, on the south side, is flanked by fine three-quarter columns and embellished with a band of ornamental inscriptions in relief Kufic characters.

Before arriving at Bukhara, we have to pass the village of Ghizhduvan, already mentioned in tenth-century sources. A *madrasa* with a typical decor of the Ulugh-beg period was built here in 1433. Another village, Tawawis, is memorable by its name, which in Arabic means 'peacocks'. It was here that the Arabs first saw peacocks in A.D. 710. The top of an extremely high minaret, visible above the trees from a great distance, and romantic, dilapidated walls of clay and sun-baked bricks signal the proximity of Bukhara.

Bukhara, unlike Samarkand, has always occupied its present position. Even the plan of the town, in spite of frequent and devastating nomad invasions, has scarcely changed in a thousand years. In the Samanid period the town was divided, as usual, into citadel, *shahristan*, and *rabad*. The *shahristan* was situated close to the citadel, on rising ground which could not be supplied with running water. It is evident that the *shahristan* occupied the high central part of the present town, which is even now very conspicuous. The old citadel, comprising a palace, a prison, a chancellery, a treasury, and a temple, became the nucleus of a medieval town some time in the sixth or seventh centuries. West of the citadel was the marketplace or Registan. The construction of this citadel was different from the present one. It had two gates, on the west and east, and was presumably built in the seventh century, although nothing remains of the original structure. It was destroyed, probably by the Arabs, and subsequently restored by the Karakhanid ruler Arslan Khan Muhammad in the twelfth century. Following this, the citadel was destroyed and rebuilt at least three times until its final destruction by Chingiz-Khan in 1220.

The streets were remarkable for their width and were paved with stone, as we learn from the Arab geographers of the tenth century. In spite of this, the overcrowding in the town must have been considerable. The lack of space was more evident in Bukhara than in other Samanid towns. For this reason there were frequent outbreaks of fire. The density of population also explains some other disagreeable features of the town: smell, bad water etc., which Makdisi and some poets mention in vigorous terms. In pre-Islamic times there was a bazaar in Bukhara where twice a year fairs were held and idols were sold. Barthold[30] thinks these were probably Buddhist figures, but they may well have been statuettes of the goddess Anahita, used for annual feasts and fertility rites of age-old local tradition. This custom still persisted under the Samanids. The Arabs built the first mosque in the citadel, in 713, on the site where previously there stood a temple of the 'idolators' (Buddhists or fire-worshippers). In the fourteenth century the city did not enjoy the best of reputations.

> This city was formerly the capital of the lands beyond the Oxus. It was destroyed by the accursed Chingiz and all but a few of its mosques, academies and bazaars are now lying in ruins. Its inhabitants are looked down upon because of their reputation for fanaticism, falsehood and denial of truth. There is no one of its inhabitants today who possesses any theological learning or makes any attempt to acquire it.[31]

The city wall encircling the outer *rabads* (suburbs) was first built in the ninth century and, like the present one, had eleven gates. The half-ruined clay walls, which can still be seen in some parts of the city, are of a much later date. They were probably built in the eighteenth century. Several of the gates also exist, with two solid wooden leaves and bastions of baked bricks. It was in the period of prosperity under the Samanids that suburbs of craftsmen and merchants spread all around the city and were subsequently encircled by a second belt of walls which, according to some authorities, was over 100 miles long.

Anthony Jenkinson was obviously not much impressed by Bukhara, although he spent almost three months there, from December 1558 to March 1559.

> This Boghar is situated in the lowest part of all the land, walled about with a high wall of earth, with diuers gates into the same: it deuided into 3. partitions, where of two parts are the kings, and the 3. part is for Merchants and markets, and euery

51. Minaret in Uzkend

52. ABOVE. Erg Kala, Merv

53. LEFT. Buddhist stupa, Gaochang

4. ABOVE. Astana
Tombs (detail of fresco)

5. RIGHT. Excavations
at Nisa. The central
complex

56. ABOVE. Mausoleum of Sultan Sanjar, Merv

57. BELOW. Rock carvings, Tamgaly Tash

58. Mausoleum of Apak Khoja, Kashgar

59. Mausoleum of Sayid Ali Arslan Khan, Kashgar

60. ABOVE. Mausoleum of Apak Khoja, Kashgar (detail)

61. BELOW. Monastery Kyzyl Kara (detail)

62. Dandan Uilik.
Painted wooden panel

science hath their dwelling and market by themselves. The Citie is very great, and the houses for the [most] part of earth, but there are also many houses, temples and monuments of stone sumptuously builded and gilt, and specially bathstones so artificially built that the like thereof is not in the worlde. There is a little Riuer running through the middes of the saide Citie, but the water thereof is most vnholsome, for it breedeth sometimes in men that drinke thereof, and especially in them that be not borne there, a worme of an ell long, which lieth commonly in the legge betwixt the flesh and the skinne, and is pluck out about the ancle with great art and cunning, the Surgeons being much practised therein, and if she breake in plucking out, the partie dieth, and euery day she commeth out about an inche, which is rolled vp, and so worketh till shee be all out. And yet it is there forbidden to drinke any other thing then water and mares milke...

The king of Boghar hath no great power or riches, his reuenues are but small, and he is most maintained by the Citie.[32]

The city was provided with water until the nineteenth century by a large canal from the Zarafshan. In the summer flood season, water was diverted by a system of sluices into locks and beyond the town. In the city there were, and still are, large open reservoirs used indiscriminately for drinking, washing and ritual ablutions. Pugachenkova[33] compares Bukhara to a huge museum of Central Asian architecture, a living museum with no dummies but real monuments. While in Samarkand all main buildings date from the fourteenth to seventieth centuries, the range of monumental building activities in Bukhara covers virtually a thousand years of history. It is one of the rare places where several buildings have survived undamaged from pre-Mongol times.

The oldest among them, and the oldest in Central Asia, is the mausoleum of the Samanids, sometimes described as the tomb of **Ismail Samanid**, who ruled Bukhara from the end of the ninth century to the beginning of the tenth. According to Pugachenkova[34] this building is linked by all its principal elements to the pre-Islamic Soghdian traditions when architecture still had to make use of less solid and less durable materials – wood and sun-baked bricks. (See Plates 43 and 66.)

Pope[35] finds this mausoleum an edifice of imposing force and originality. Built some time before Ismail's death in 907, it exerted a strong influence on subsequent Islamic architecture both in structural development and in the decorative deployment of material. It is almost cubic, roughly 31 feet on each side, with a low hemispherical dome and, at the corners, four small ovoid domes of Sasanian derivation. An open-arcade gallery, just below the cornice, surrounds the building. The walls, which slope slightly inward, are fortified at the four corners by huge, three-quarter inset columns, made more emphatic by dark shadows. In form and emphasis the building has a time-defying solidity, appropriate for a memorial.

The problem of setting a dome over a square chamber is here carried beyond the simple solution of Parthian and Sasanian times. Consisting of three supporting arches which curve down from the crown of the arch to the walls, the squinch carries the thrust of the dome downward – rather like a Gothic flying buttress.[36] The outer surfaces of the walls are covered with brick ornaments, which Rempel[37] considers to be skilfully executed. The brick was used with a vivacity and intensity that had no precedent.[38] The deeply shadowed texture of the walls veils the harsh reflected glare of sunlight. Much of the ornament seems to be derived from techniques in evidence in carved wood – in which Pope sees confirmation that a good deal of wood was used to build the early mosques of this region. The entrance arches show a distinct tendency towards the articulated portico of later times. Rempel[39] sees two trends in the architectural decor of this mausoleum: a transition from an outer layer of bricks on a wall towards an ornamental brick tiling; and the stylising of some ancient motifs while preserving on the whole the ancient architectural tradition. About 250 years later we find the same principles in the Karakhanid mausoleums in Uzkend, with the notable addition of incised (carved) terracotta. The mausoleum has been thoroughly (and successfully) restored and its surroundings turned into a park.

The new citadel, the **Ark** (from the Persian 'Arg') dating from the eighteenth century, was built on an artificial hillock, the site of the medieval citadel, with a high front wall facing the Registan square and reinforced with a layer of baked bricks. (See Plate 38.) Access to the interior is by a narrow winding tunnel with a gate on either side. On top is the palace of the former emir, a simple brick structure, now housing a local museum. Next to it is a mosque with carved columns, built in 1712, but the *iwan* with the columns is from the early twentieth century, as is the adjacent short minaret. Opposite the Ark, at a small pond, is the **Bala Hauz** mosque built in 1712; a richly decorated *iwan* was added early this century. The colours and carvings on the columns and the coffered ceiling are remarkable.

Another interesting monument is the nearby mausoleum **Chashma Ayub** (Well of Job). (See Plate 28.) By its style it belongs to the twelfth century, but an inscription above the entrance gives the date of a reconstruction as 1380, or 1384. There is something crude in the outline of the building, with its elongated walls and conical cupola on a high drum, in the bareness of its structural elements, which are without any architectural decor whatsoever.[40] The conical shape of the cupola, in contrast to the usual bulbous one, is an element alien to Transoxania, ascribed by some to the influence of Khorezmian builders brought in by Timur after the destruction of Gurganj. It has, however, certain similarities to the group of mausoleums in Kasan, in north Ferghana (see p. 155), which date from 1340 and point therefore rather to a general decline of architectural and decorative art in a period immediately preceding the Timurid renaissance. The interior decor

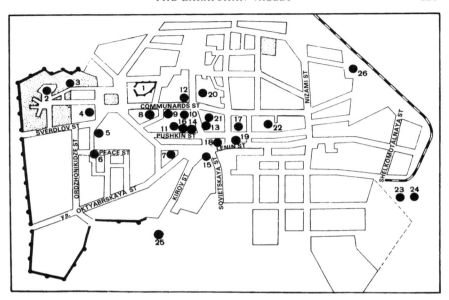

PLAN 7 **Bukhara**
1 Ark; 2 Mausoleum of Ismail Samanid; 3 Chashma Ayub; 4 *Madrasa* of Abdullah-Khan;
5 *Madrasa* Madar-i Khan; 6 Mosque Baland; 7 *Madrasa* Gaukushan; 8 *Khaniga* Khoja
Zainuddin; 9 Mosque Kalan; *Madrasa* Mir-i Arab; 11 Minaret Kalan; 12–15 Vaulted
bazaars; 16 Mosque Maghak-i Attari; 17 *Madrasa* Kukeltash; 18 *Khaniga* Nadir Divan Begi;
19 *Madrasa* Nadir Divan Begi; 20 *Madrasa* of Ulugh-beg; 21 *Madrasa* of Abdulaziz Khan;
22 Char Minar; 23 Mausoleum Saifuddin Bokharzi; 24 Mausoleum Buyan-Kuli Khan;
25 Mosque Namazga; 26 *Khaniga* Faisabad.

is interesting and unusual, consisting of alabaster stalactites in triple rows in the
corners, constructed on a pattern of twelve-sided stars.

South-west of Registan we find the complex called **Kosh-madrasa** (the
Coupled Madrasas). As the name indicates, it consists of two *madrasas* facing
each other, both built in the second half of the sixteenth century, under the rule
of Abdullah Khan. Both were recently restored. The first, **Madar-i Khan** (Khan's
Mother), was dedicated to the ruler's mother and was built in 1566. The other,
built in 1588, bears the name of **Abdullah Khan** himself. The *madrasa* Madar-i
Khan is interesting only as an indication of the general artistic decline of the
period. There is hardly any decoration at all, except for a few tile ornaments on
and inside the portico. Instead of incised mosaics, polychrome majolica and
other laborious techniques, we find only very simple three-colour majolica in
blue, white and turquoise; the patterns are inexact and unsophisticated, and their
contours lack sharpness.

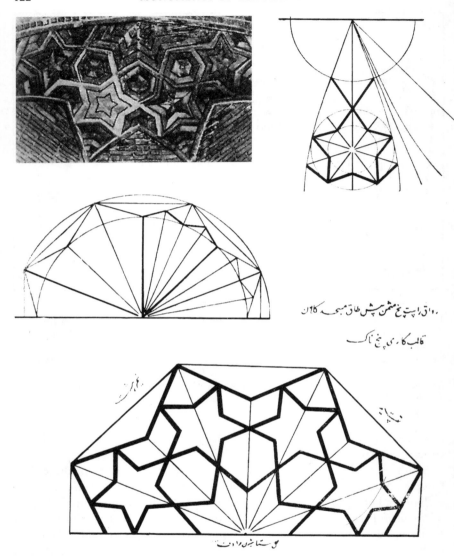

FIG. 6 *Girikhs* on spherical surfaces; main facade of the Masjid-i Kalan, Bukhara

Its opposite is far richer in both architectural and ornamental decoration, but the craftsmanship is equally poor. Only the entrance door, which has a complicated *girikh* ornament with carvings of vegetal motifs inside the geometrical pattern, has a touch of artistic genius. The mosque inside the courtyard is not orientated exactly towards Mecca, but strictly on the four cardinal points, which may suggest that its sponsor, the ageing khan, perhaps contemplated having it as his mausoleum. The interior design of the large halls of this mosque shows some architectural innovations. The system of supporting constructions, owing to the large size of these halls, become so complicated that the structure almost becomes an ornament in itself, thus giving the building a unique individuality.[41]

South of here, and completely insignificant from the outside, is the **Masjid-i Baland**, or High Mosque, built in the sixteenth century. Its main attraction is the interior decoration, which consists of painted vegetal ornaments, religious inscriptions and a superbly decorated *mihrab* niche with patterns of incised mosaics, as well as a beautifully carved and painted wooden ceiling. This was a local mosque not designed for solemn services and gatherings like the cathedral mosques, but for day-to-day services, contemplation and refuge from busy everyday life; the emphasis of its architecture is therefore on cosiness rather than overall grandeur, soft lines and light materials rather than grandiose proportions in a cold or heavy style.

Another similar early-sixteenth-century structure is the **Khaniga of Khoja Zainuddin**. This was simultaneously a district mosque, a *khaniga* (hostel), and a tomb of the khoja, which was situated in a niche in the western facade. The building, seen from the yard, is flanked by two rows of wooden columns supporting a wooden roof. The main hall is rectangular, large and high, and covered with a dome, the lower part of which consists of a belt of stalactites. The dome is divided into sections by means of ribs, and the whole system is decorated with polychrome paintings in gold, blue, red and especially turquoise, to symbolise the heavenly dome.

In the very centre of the city is a group of monuments called **Poy Kalan**, consisting of a minaret, a mosque, and a *madrasa,* which in spite of being from different periods form a remarkable and harmonious complex for which the city is rightly famous.

The **Minar-i Kalan**, or Great Minaret, is an impressive tower, 170 feet high, with a diameter at the bottom of 40 feet. (See Plate 68.) It is a cylindrical structure of baked bricks, narrowing toward the top and culminating in a brick lantern with a circular terrace with sixteen narrow openings. It is decorated with parallel bands of ornamental friezes, with geometrical patterns entirely made of bricks. These patterns are different in each band and never repeat themselves. Below the lantern was a band of tiled relief inscriptions with a glaze in turquoise. This is one of the earliest known examples in Central Asia of colours used in architectural decoration. Originally, in the eleventh century, the lantern was of wood and the minaret stood closer to the citadel; during a siege it was burned down and the Karakhanid Arslan Khan then had it rebuilt a little further away and entirely of brick. The work was completed in 1127.

The adjacent mosque, **Masjid-i Kalan**, connected with the minaret by a bridge on the first floor, was built in the fifteenth century on the site of an older, twelfth-century, mosque. After reconstruction in the early sixteenth century under the Sheybanid khans, the mosque received its present appearance. In size, this cathedral mosque of Bukhara almost equals its counterparts in Samarkand and Herat, but it can hardly compete with them for sophistication of architectural design or harmony of ornamental decor. There is the traditional rectangular yard, 430 by 270 feet, with four *iwans* on the axes. On the longer axis lies the main building, opening into the yard with a monumental arched *iwan*. Squared at the base, the building continues as an octagon with a further transition into a cylindrical drum supporting a double dome, the outer one covered with turquoise ceramic tiles. Domed arcades surround the yard; there are 288 small cupolas supported by mighty columns. Cohn-Wiener[42] assumes that two ornamental panels in the outer wall are remnants of the original twelfth-century mosque, which, he deduces, therefore had the same dimensions. One of these ornaments is exactly the same as on the minaret, the other is typical of the period. Some of the columns may also have survived from that time.

Exactly opposite the main entrance, on the 'twin' principle, is the portal of another monumental building – the **Mir-i Arab** *madrasa*, built in 1535. Among the numerous *madrasas* built in this area in that period of religious zeal, Mir-i Arab is without doubt one of the best. Significant of the period is the fact that the then ruler, Ubaydullah Khan, who provided the builder, Sheikh Mir-i Arab, with money gained from the sale of several thousand Shi'ite Persians into slavery, himself lies buried in one of the corner rooms, alongside the sheikh and among numerous tombs; there is no longer a special mausoleum for the ruler. The style is again horizontal, a rectangular yard with four *iwans* surrounded by four two-storey wings of cells. There are two domed halls, right and left of the main portal. Next to this portal are the two domes, one for the assembly hall, the other for the mosque, supported by cylindrical drums. The architectural decoration still remains within the traditions of the late Timurid period. Incised mosaics, mainly blue and white, decorate the *pishtak*, the *iwans* in the yard and the walls of the tomb hall and the mosque. Inscriptions in elaborate Thulth character, stylised *islimi* (vegetal) motifs, and patterns of coloured glazed bricks appear on walls, arches, columns and ceilings. Mir-i Arab is the only *madrasa* in Central Asia that has served the same purpose for more than 400

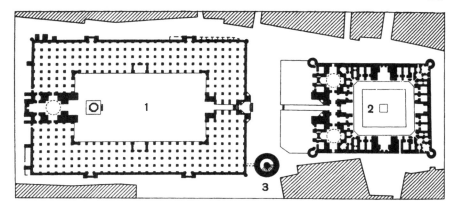

PLAN 8 Poy-Kalan complex
1 Mosque Kalan; 2 *Madrasa* Mir-i Arab; 3 Minaret Kalan

years – it was one of the only two Muslim colleges allowed to operate in the Soviet Union.

A feature of sixteenth-century Bukhara was a number of domed **bazaars** built usually over an intersection of two busy streets. (See Plate 41.) Several of these bazaars have survived, still retaining their original names derived from their function – the Cupola of Jewellers, of Cap-Makers, of Money-Changers. Usually there is the main dome over the actual crossroads and around it a group of smaller and lower cupolas covering the shop premises. Some of them were built over an intersection of several streets that converged from various angles and this, of course, made the design more complicated. All of these structures are highly utilitarian, with no decoration, but with an undeniable architectural character of their own.

Near one of these bazaars is the oldest surviving mosque in Central Asia – the **Maghak-i Attari**, dating from the twelfth century and built on a site where there was already a temple in Soghdian times.[43] (See Plate 39.) Excavations revealed some fragments of alabaster decoration and brickwork from the tenth century. The main twelfth-century facade, now almost 15 feet below ground level, was uncovered and restored in 1930. It represents the most important architectural and artistic feature of the mosque. The rest was completely swallowed by later reconstructions. Pugachenkova[44] sees in the two quarter-columns, paired together on each side of the *pishtak* (portico), a motif reminiscent of pre-Islamic style. The slightly receding *pishtak* is covered by a broken arch and flanked by two corner columns and two sets of ornamental panels in incised terracotta, with geometrical motifs. There are two types of *girikhs* in the upper and lower panels, and one in the middle panel on each side. Rempel[45] connects some elements in the decoration

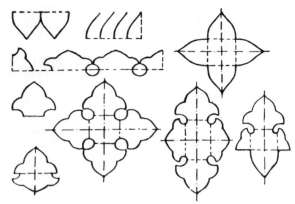

FIG. 7 Medallions; details
from the western *iwan*,
madrasa Mir-i Arab, Bukhara

with the roughly contemporary twelfth-century mausoleums in Uzkend, where, however, the technique of incised terracotta seems to have reached a higher degree of perfection.

Around the water reservoir Labi-hauz is another important architectural complex of central Bukhara. The **Kukeltash** *madrasa* (1568) is yet another typical building of the Abdullah Khan period. It contains 160 cells and is therefore one of the biggest of its kind. In the corners are octagonal vestibules around which the cells are grouped radially. Inside, the ceiling of the vestibule is formed by tiny bricks separated by thin lines of white alabaster which give a very impressive decoration.

On the east side, the **Nadir Divan Begi** *madrasa* (1622) was originally designed as a caravanserai, but was soon converted for a more pious purpose. (See Plate 42.) A rather crude mosaic depicting imaginary birds of paradise decorates the entrance *iwan*, lined with an inscription frieze in ornamental Kufic. Niches and tympans around the courtyard show tile mosaics, mostly in blue and white, with floral motifs.

Ulugh-beg also built a *madrasa* in Bukhara in 1417, and the khan Abdulaziz added its opposite number, across a narrow lane, in 1652. Compared with the Samarkand *madrasa*, the one in Bukhara, a few years older, is much smaller, simpler and altogether more modest. The dome of the assembly room rests not on traditional squinches, but on a system of strong semi-vaults, a type of structural stalactites which demonstrates contemporary effort to seek constructional innovation and improvement.

The *madrasa* of **Abdulaziz Khan** dwarfs its counterpart in all respects but one. It is bigger, richer, more sophisticated, but it somehow lacks the harmony of proportion that marks the older building. There are some new motifs in the decoration, perhaps deliberately introduced to break the straitjacket of tradition:

FIG. 8 Mosque Maghak-i Attari, Bukhara; brick pattern with background filling in alabaster

phoenixes and birds with snake heads among flowers now liven up the mosaic; stylised landscapes appear in wall-paintings, resembling Indian miniatures of the Moghul period; the alabaster ceilings of both the assembly rooms and the mosque have an extremely complicated geometrical pattern. But the decoration, especially the paintings with their profusion of gold and blue, does not harmonise with the geometry of the structure, and these two elements seem to be in permanent conflict. Pugachenkova[46] sees in this building the last effort of Central Asian architecture in the late feudal period 'to break free onto the path of progress by rejecting the restricting traditions of the past, but it could not find enough strength for such an active step'.

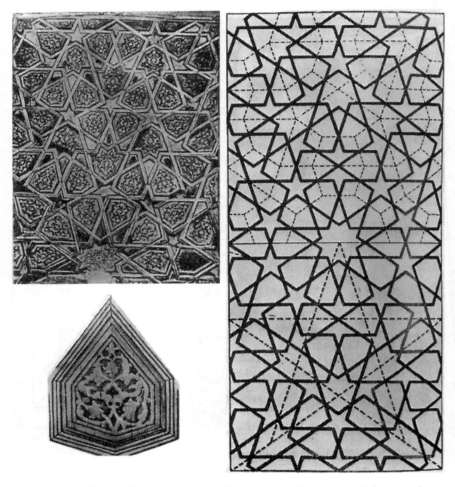

FIG. 9 *Madrasa* Kukeltash, Bukhara (sixteenth century); *girikh* on a carved door-panel

The so-called **Char-Minar** (Four Minarets), built in 1807, is a little building full of character. (See Plate 67.) It consists of four turrets with small turquoise cupolas and a square domed house between them. Originally, it was a gatehouse to a *madrasa*, built by a wealthy merchant, Khalif Niyazkul. The *madrasa* disappeared almost entirely, but this little structure ranks among the most original monuments of late Muslim Bukhara. One of the turrets recently collapsed and is being restored.

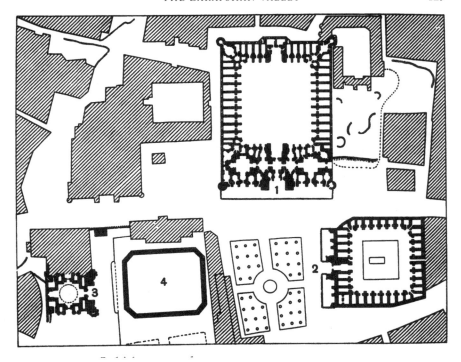

PLAN 9 Labi-hauz complex
1 *Madrasa* Kukeltash; 2 *Madrasa* Nadir Divan Begi; 3 *Khaniga* Nadir Divan Begi; 4 Labi-hauz reservoir

To conclude, we must mention five more buildings on the outskirts of the city. First, to the east, two mausoleums: that of **Saifuddin Bokharzi**, built in the fourteenth century, with a portico added in the fifteenth or sixteenth centuries. It is remarkable for its massive size, its simplicity, and the clarity of its architecture. Two egg-shaped cupolas cover the two rooms inside, and this indicates a considerable evolution from the older style and tradition of single-room structures. Inside, the highly decorated wooden cenotaph with a profusion of carved ornaments ranks among the best works of its kind in medieval Bukhara. Next to Saifuddin Bokharzi, another mausoleum, that of **Buyan-Kuli Khan** (1358), also has two rooms, but they form with the high portico a much more integrated structure than the former. The contrast is not only in size (Buyan-Kuli is much smaller), but also in the emphasis on decoration, intimacy, refinement and subdued lighting. Glazed incised terracotta was the main technique of interior decoration, and this represents an enormous step forward since the preceding period, not to mention the astonishing variety of motifs. Some ornamental panels are now in the Victoria and Albert Museum in London.

South of Bukhara the mosque called **Namazga** dates from the early twelfth-century Karakhanid period and consisted first only of a brick wall with a *mihrab* niche. This *mihrab*, with delicate embellishments of incised terracotta, has survived to the present day. The glazed polychrome tiles were added during restoration in the fifteenth century. Namazga was a type of out-of-town mosque, where on the great Islamic feast days gathered the entire male population of the city and its wider environs. Designed to accommodate such huge popular gatherings, the Namazga mosque had no walls and no arcades, just a light fence to indicate its border and the *mihrab* wall to show the direction of ritual bows and prayers and to provide the imam with a place to conduct the ceremony.

West of the city, a large necropolis called **Char Bakr** was the burial-ground of the Jabari clan. There are two large seventeenth-century *khanigas* (one serving as a mosque), a small minaret, a cemetery and a small mausoleum of Khoja Islam, also built c.1660. North of the city, the mausoleum of **Hazret Baha'ud din Nakshbendi**, dating from the mid-fourteenth century, was converted under the Soviets into a museum of atheism. (See Plate 40.) It is now an important pilgrim place of the Nakshbendi order. **Sitorai Mohi Khosa** is the palace of the last emir and now houses a small museum.

The minaret in **Vabkent**, in the vicinity of Bukhara, was built in 1196–98, and is very similar to the minaret Kalan. The difference is mainly in the decorative bands. There are not so many motifs, flat ornaments are more emphasised than relief, which seems to be the tendency of the period, and there is considerable progress in the use of glazed tiles.

Travelling further beyond Vabkent on the old road to Khorezm, we come to a strange place on the fringe of the Kyzyl Kum desert. Here an 'artificial' saxaul forest was planted some decades ago to prevent the sands from moving; by now the forest has completely covered the ruins of an ancient town, Vardana, or **Vardanzi**, which was swallowed by the desert about a hundred years ago.

The rulers of Wardana bore the title of Wardan-Khudats and were until the eighth century the rivals of the Bukhar-Khudats. Wardana was even considered to be older than Bukhara. The village was of great importance strategically as a frontier point against the Turkish nomads, commercially and industrially. In later times, this locality was the tümen or district of Vardanzi, a considerable portion of which was buried by sand in 1868.[47]

There is no life now at Vardanzi, only the strong scent and silent movements of the leafless saxauls and tamarisks.

On the same road to Khorezm, one day's journey into the desert but still within the great wall of Bukhara, was the castle and village of **Varaksha**. This was, from very ancient times, the private property of the Bukhar-Khudats, and was reckoned to be a more ancient town than Bukhara. Here was the old palace of the Bukhar-Khudats, which had existed, according to tradition, for more than a thousand years. In the eighth century it was restored, but was later confiscated by the Samanids, who intended to convert the palace into a mosque. It was finally destroyed by order of one of the last Samanids, who wanted material for the construction of a palace in Bukhara.[48] The site can now be found about 19 miles north-west of Bukhara, in the eastern Kyzyl Kum. Archaeological investigation has shown that in ancient times the whole area, covering 200 square miles, was densely populated, and that it fell into its present state of desolation between the eleventh and twelfth centuries. This therefore confirms the written sources quoted by Barthold. The surface of the desert is dotted with numerous *tepes* that conceal the remains of towns and villages or of large isolated buildings, forts, or castles. Traces of an elaborate irrigation system can still be detected. Varakhsha is the largest site in the area, covering about 22 acres. In some places it rises to a height of 60 feet above the surrounding plain. It was the object of several expeditions led by Professor V.A. Shishkin, begun in 1938 and continued after the war. The site is composed of several layers ranging from the first centuries B.C. or A.D. until the tenth or eleventh centuries. There was a citadel, a large palace and the city. The citadel, built probably in the fourth or fifth centuries on an artificial mound, was reconstructed several times. It was surrounded by a triangular wall. The palace, too, was built about the fifth century. It seems it had three stories and its walls were lined with alabaster and stucco. The lower layers of the city go back to the Kushan period.

The most important results were produced by the excavation of the palace. Particularly interesting among these results is a series of wall-paintings found in three rooms, described as Red Room, East Room and West Room. The style of both the architecture and the paintings strongly resembles those of Samarkand, Afrasiyab and Pendzhikent. Here again we find fairly large rooms (for example 39 by 26 feet), with benches running along the walls and with paintings covering the walls from these benches right up to the roof. They were preserved, however, only up to between 6 to 7 feet. The figures are painted against a red background and are divided into two bands. The lower band consists of a series of hunting scenes, with hunters mounted on elephants and dressed in loose cloaks fluttering in the wind. Their headdresses are richly ornamented. The elephants are being attacked by large cats and fantastic animals (winged griffins). The principal wall of the second room was occupied by a large and crowded scene representing a state ceremonial reception. The room (56 by 38 feet) was obviously the throne-room, and the centre of the picture is also occupied by a high throne. Similar in this respect to Pendzhikent and to Balalyk-Tepe, the Varakhsha paintings do not appear to be focused on one single creed. Although reminiscent of India, Buddhism appears to be absent from them, and with one exception the paintings may be considered secular.[49] They can be seen in the museums of Bukhara and Tashkent.

The excavation also yielded striking specimens of decorative stucco work, of which a great mass of fragments was found. Originally the stucco panels had covered the upper parts of the walls. There were a great number of geometrical and vegetal ornaments, but also many other subjects, such as animals, birds and hunting scenes. Shishkin noticed in this alabaster decoration the absence of meticulous finish, a rather sketchy manner 'which puts it into a completely different category from later examples of this kind', and he explicitly points out the design of human faces. 'The mouth is sketched in with a few strokes of knife; the eyes are often represented only by almond-shaped convexities...' This may well require comment. The kind of representation, the same strange expressiveness, can be found in several small statuettes, now kept in the museum of Samarkand and ascribed to the Hephthalite Huns of the fifth and sixth centuries. One of them, a striking example reproduced in Plate 2, has a necklace of nine beads; it is known that nine was a sacred number to the Mongols and most probably also to their predecessors, the Huns. On the other hand, several animals from the alabaster friezes of Varakhsha have a distinct note of the 'animal style', of the steppe art, which was traditional with the nomads since early Scythian times. This may indicate that, some time in the fifth to sixth centuries, Varakhsha was a residence of the Hephthalite king and reverted to the Bukhar-Khudats only after the fall of the Hephthalite Empire. Only then did this type of architectural decoration acquire 'the painstaking, scrupulous finish of each trifling detail carried to a pitch of extreme virtuosity'.[50] On the external walls the decoration consists of paired half-columns, the tops of each pair being linked by a small arch. This is exactly the same decoration which we saw, for instance, at Rabat-i Malik, from the eleventh century. On the whole, the palace of Varakhsha was a typical large Soghdian *kushk* (castle), as was admirably shown by the reconstruction of V.A. Nilsen.

NOTES ON CHAPTER VII
Full details of abbreviations and publications are in the Bibliography

1   Barthold, *Turkestan*, p. 84.
2   Belenistsky, *The Ancient Civilisation of Central Asia*, p. 53.
3   Le Strange (tr.) *Clavijo, Embassy to Tamerlane*, pp. 285–86, 289–90.
4   Ibn Haukal, quoted by Barthold in *Turkestan*, p. 91.
5   Barthold, *Turkestan*, p. 91.
6   Cohn-Wiener, *Turan*, p. 233.
7   The mosque has recently collapsed and is now being restored. A beautifully carved door with an inscription in Thulth opens the corridor leading to the mosque.
8   Rempel, *Ornament*, p. 270.
9   Le Strange, *Clavijo*, p. 280.
10 Pugachenkova, G.A., *Pamyatniki arkhitektury Srednei Azii*, p. 75.
11 There is some confusion about the identity of Omar Sheikh. This one is believed by some to have been a holy man while Timur's son of the same name may have been buried in Shahrisabz next to his brother, Jahangir.
12 Hookham, *Tamburlaine*, pp. 9, 83.
13 Pope, *Architecture*, p. 197.
14 Le Strange, *Clavijo*, p. 279.
15 Hookham, *Tamburlaine*, p. 7.
16 Le Strange, *Clavijo*, p. 209.
17 Pope, *Architecture*, p. 193.
18 Cohn-Wiener, *Turan*, p. 28.
19 Rempel, *Ornament*, p. 276.
20 Le Strange, *Clavijo*, p. 207.
21 Belenitsky, *Civilisation*, p. 155.
22 Frumkin, *CAR* XII, p. 177.
23 Belenitsky, *Civilisation*, p. 158.
24 Frumkin, *CAR* XII, p. 177.
25 Now in the Museum of Pendzhikent.
26 Frumkin, *CAR* XII p. 178.
27 Pope, *Architecture*, p. 129.
28 Pope, *Architecture*, p. 238.
29 Rempel, *Ornament*, p. 154.
30 Barthold, *Turkestan*, p. 103.
31 Gibb, *Ibn Battuta*, pp. 171–72.
32 Jenkinson, *Voyages*, p. 83.
33 Pugachenkova, *Pamyatniki*, p. 115.
34 Pugachenkova, *Pamyatniki*, p. 121.
35 Pope, *Architecture*, p. 81.
36 Pope, *Architecture*, p. 85.
37 Rempel, *Ornament*, p. 148.

38 Pope, *Architecture*, p. 85.
39 Rempel, *Ornament*, p. 152.
40 Pugachenkova, *Pamyatniki*, p. 124.
41 Pugachenkova, *Pamyatniki*, p. 135.
42 Cohn-Wiener, *Turan*, p. 13.
43 It is supposed that this was the site of a bazaar, Mogh, or Moon Bazaar, where pictures of folk deities were sold on certain feast-days (see Pugachenkova, *Pamyatniki*, p. 167).
44 Pugachenkova, *Pamyatniki*, p. 168.
45 Rempel, *Ornament*, p. 164.
46 Pugachenkova, *Pamyatniki*, p. 180.
47 Barthold, *Turkestan*, p. 113.
48 Barthold, *Turkestan*, p. 115.
49 Frumkin, *CAR* XIII, p. 249.
50 Shishkin, *Goroda Uzbekistana*, p. 167.

63. Mausoleum Hakim al-Termezi, Termez (interior)

65. Kirk Kyz

66. Mausoleum of Ismail Samanid, Bukhara

67. Char Minar, Bukhara

68. Minar-i Kalan, Bukhara

69. Minaret Imin, Turfan

70. The Green Mosque, Balkh

VIII
TURKMENISTAN

THE ANCIENT CARAVAN ROUTE, roughly followed by the present railway line, brings us south-west of Bukhara to the Amu Darya and to the important crossing at Chardzhou, the medieval Amul. On the way lie the ruins of **Paykend**, which, in pre-Muslim times, was a large trading centre and also a garrison town. It was called The Copper City or The City of Merchants. The local merchants engaged in trade with China, and even engaged in maritime trade, probably with the trans-Caspian provinces. Each village in the province of Bukhara possessed a *rabat*, or caravanserai, near the gate of Paykend. There were more than a thousand such barracks, and in them were kept detachments for the purpose of countering Turkish assaults. In the ninth century, when the country became more secure, circumstances changed; the barracks were abandoned and fell in ruins, although the town itself flourished. Paykend, which was surrounded by a strong wall with only one gate, was on the edge of the steppes, and there were no villages in the neighbourhood.[1] After the fall of the Samanid Empire, Paykend was virtually extinct, and Barthold tells us the following story of an attempt to revive Paykend in the twelfth century:

> Arslan Khan (the Karakhanid ruler of Bukhara) built himself a palace here and wished to dig a new *aryk* (irrigation canal) for the town. The town was situated on a hill but not a high one. The Khan ordered it be cut through to provide a channel for the water. But it turned out that the hill was composed of stony strata and after vain attempts which swallowed much money and cost many lives, the enterprise was abandoned. Shortly afterwards, the palace was in ruins, and some Turkmen families were living there.

The tiny oasis of Karakul is the last place to be watered by the Zarafshan. Beyond it the river disappears in marshes. A stretch of desert separates the River Zarafshan

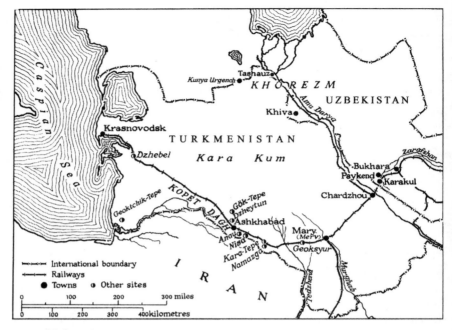

MAP 5 Turkmenistan

from its ancient confluent, the Amu Darya. Following the railway south-west from Chardzhou into Turkmenistan, the first oasis is the small township of Mary on the River Murghab, in medieval times the splendid city of Merv, 'the Pearl of the East', one of the four important cities of Khorassan, and for centuries the seat of the caliph's governor-general. In Achaemenid times the province of Merv was called Margiana. Politically, Merv was always part of Khorassan, which, apart from Merv, comprised also the provinces of Balkh, Herat and Nishapur, had close links with Persia, but was never an integral part of it. Khorassan ceased to exist as a political unit in the mid-eighteenth century, when it was divided between Persia, which retained the province of Nishapur, and Afghanistan, which took the province of Balkh. The province of Herat was divided between the two countries, with the city of Herat in Afghan territory. The province of Merv became a kind of no-man's-land; it was in the hands of warlike nomad Turkmen tribes until the Russian conquest, which culminated in the battle of Gök-Tepe in 1881 and the occupation of Merv in 1884.

Merv has always been one of the most important Central Asian cities, and a cultural centre of the lands west of the Oxus. We find early testimonies of its

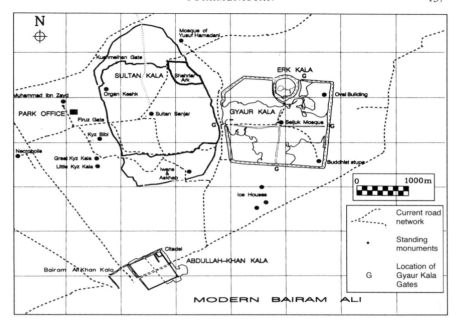

PLAN 10 The site of Merv

importance in the *Zend-Avesta*, at a time when Bukhara did not even exist. The present ruins, which cover a total area of 50 square miles, are the remains of five walled cities, dating from five different periods.

The oldest, in the north, is called **Erg-Kala**. (See Plate 52.) It was an Achaemenid city with a huge citadel in the centre. It was conquered by Alexander the Great and subsequently called Alexandria Margiana. The Parthians added a fortress on its southern perimeter. It is entirely surrounded by a square Sasanian city, called by the Arabs **Giaur Kala** (The City of the Infidels). After the Arab conquest Merv became for a time the principal city of the Eastern Caliphate and second only to Baghdad. It was described in considerable detail by Istakhri. The Seljuks in the eleventh century added another city on the western side, called **Sultan Kala**, which was described by Yakut. The Mongols destroyed it completely, and it was not repopulated until the beginning of the fifteenth century when Shahrukh, the son of Timur, founded on its southern edge another city called **Abdullah Khan Kala**. This was much smaller, and never regained the fame and splendour of its predecessors. However, it was still dependent for its water on the huge dam and canal built by the Seljukid sultan Sanjar on the River Murghab. The dam was in existence until 1795, when it was destroyed by the Emir of Bukhara, after which the city was soon reduced to a sandy mound in the Kara Kum desert.

Erg Kala was circular in shape and surrounded by high ramparts with no obvious access. It is believed that access was by a drawbridge across a moat. There are many marks of excavations on the citadel mound, as well as in the area between the citadel and the walls. The walls of Giaur Kala had towers at regular distances and enclosed a space of some 1.5 square miles. The whole complex of Erg Kala probably served as its citadel. In the north-eastern corner of Giaur Kala is an unidentified oval-shaped building consisting of thirty-three rooms constructed around a courtyard on a raised platform and dated to the Sasanian period. Its purpose remains to be found. In the south-eastern corner an unexpected discovery in 1962 revealed the remnants of a Buddhist monastery with a red-coloured *stupa* and a gigantic statue of Buddha of which only the head was found. This is especially interesting because Margiana was believed to have been outside the Buddhist sphere of influence. Kushan coins from the second century A.D. were also found here.

In the centre of Giaur Kala can be seen remnants of a seventh-century mosque over which the Seljuks built a somewhat larger mosque in the eleventh or twelfth centuries. Next to it was a *sardoba* (cistern) which had a diameter of some 18 feet and a depth of over 25 feet. A metallurgical workshop was recently uncovered, surrounded by small heaps of slag and with an interestingly patterned floor.

In the north-eastern corner of Sultan Kala is a complex of buildings called **Shahriar Ark**, separated from the city by a wall. This was most probably a fortified palace built on two floors around a courtyard with an *iwan* on each side. The ruin of a *kushk* can be seen nearby. In the very centre of Sultan Kala stands an 80 foot high building, partly preserved, which on the basis of Yakut's description can be identified as the mausoleum of **Sultan Sanjar**, who died in 1157. It is one of the most significant monuments in Central Asia and even now, seen in the bleak sandy environment, makes an extremely strong impression. (See Plate 56.)

Apparently, the mausoleum was not an isolated structure but formed part of a larger religious complex described by Yakut in 1219. It is a classic example of a Central Asian *mazar*, which Pope describes as

> a ponderous and solemn cubical chamber, about 90 feet square, which was sur-mounted by a blue-tiled dome (this was restored in 1911) also about 90 feet high. The interlocking framework of the ribs seen on the interior seems to carry the weight of the dome, but in reality it is probably more decorative than structural. The crucial transition from sanctuary block to dome above was beautifully achieved by means of corner galleries which concealed the squinch, so awkwardly exposed on the exterior of earlier Seljuk domes. The circular drum of the dome is similarly arcaded and the galleries, decorated with pierced brick in ornamental

lays, mitigate the severity of the mass without compromising the simplicity of the structure as a whole... The main entrance is on the east facing the rising sun. A comparable opening on the west was closed by a grill. The other two sides are blank. The plain walls are enriched with a typical Seljuk plaster coating marked out in simulated brick bonding with decorative insets of terra-cotta. This mausoleum is the last, and one of the finest, examples of Seljuk architecture.[2]

The tomb inside is not that of Sultan Sanjar but a nineteenth-century cenotaph. A short distance from the mausoleum are two *kushks* (castles or fortified manor houses), the **Great** and **Little Kyz Kala**. The walls of the Great Kyz Kala are made of a series of octagonal half-columns, a decorative element already seen at Rabat-i Malik and also at the small *kushk* at Shahriar Ark. A barrel-vaulted corridor or staircase can be seen in the Little Kyz Kala. (See Plate 64.)

The mausoleum of **Muhammad Ibn Zayid** is a twelfth-century structure standing next to the main entrance to the site. The complex consists of the mausoleum itself, a mosque and an anteroom, all domed. The dome over the mausoleum is the tallest. Four arched squinches provide the transition from the square chamber to the dome with an intermediate zone of small corbelled niches completing the transition from octagon to dome. In the centre of the room is a black marble cenotaph and a band of floral Kufic runs around the walls giving the date as 1112. Nearby is a restored *sardoba* and a cemetery where remains of Seljuk potters' kilns can be seen.

There is not much to be seen in the Abdullah Khan Kala. It is a rectangular site with circular corner towers and a citadel mound in the northern corner, within which was the ruler's palace. Also in the northern part were a large mosque and a *madrasa*. The palace was still in existence in the nineteenth century. The site was first explored and described by V.A. Zhukovsky in 1890.

Excavations on the Merv site are still going on. The International Merv Project, a joint venture of the Archaeological Institute of University College London, and YUTAKE, the Academy of Sciences of Turkmenistan, has been working there every year since 1992.

The second most important site in Turkmenistan is **Anau**, seven miles southeast of the modern capital, Ashkhabad. A settlement already existed here in the Neolithic Age, and some excavations were carried out in 1904–5 by R. Pumpelly. Pumpelly's views that Anau may perhaps have been the oldest farming culture in the world, and southern Turkmenistan the oldest cultivated area, were later corrected, when in the 1930s and after World War II a systematic study of this culture was undertaken, here as well as on other sites in Turkmenistan. The next period of Anau is in evidence at the Hellenistic site of **Nisa**. There are two separate sites of that name not far from one another, Old and New Nisa. New Nisa was a town that continued to exist until the Middle Ages. Old Nisa was a royal residence,

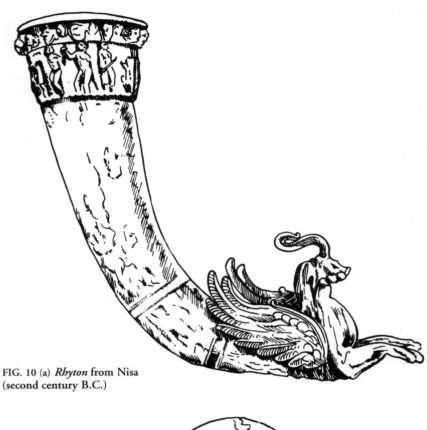

FIG. 10 (a) *Rhyton* from Nisa
(second century B.C.)

FIG. 10 (b) Seals and gems
(first to second century A.D.)

containing within its walls palaces, temples and tombs of the Parthian kings. It was abandoned by the end of the Parthian period at the beginning of the third century A.D. The original name of the town was Mihrdatkart. Its layout differed from that of a normal Hellenistic town, being pentagonal in shape. The ramparts were built of *pakhsa* (beaten clay), and were enormously thick (25–30 feet), and reinforced by towers. The palaces and temples whose architectural structure was revealed by the excavations were of remarkably large size. In one of the buildings, the 'square room' measured 65 feet each way, and the 'round room' had a diameter of 55. Dwelling houses had large store rooms, some of them even wine cellars. The wine was kept in big pottery jars, buried in the ground.[3] The sculptures found at Nisa consisted mainly of monumental clay statues of human figures larger than life. Also, the first marble sculptures found in Central Asia were excavated here. An extremely important discovery was a group of *rhytons* carved from ivory. (See Plates 55 and 97.) They were very badly damaged, but most of them, some forty in number, have now been restored. Their pointed ends are decorated with sculptured figures of centaurs, winged horses, lions, griffins and other fantastic creatures. Round the broad upper ends are bands of ornaments in relief, representing scenes connected with the cult of Dionysus and other favourite themes of Hellenistic art.[4] Finally, 2500 sherds (*ostraca*) with inscriptions were found here. All inscriptions are in the Parthian language, the script is Aramaic, and the contents are mainly records of deliveries of wine etc. The dating is exact, from the second century to the first century B.C.

Rempel has the following to say about the art of Old Nisa:

> The architectural forms of Parthian Nisa, compared with their Hellenistic decoration, seem heavy and ponderous. The décor of the Round and Square Rooms was arranged in two rows, one above the other. Clay polychromed statues were placed in niches in the upper row. The upper part of the Square Room was painted bright red, and some painted wall ornaments could be reconstructed.[5]

Philostratos, writing in the second to third centuries A.D., gives the following description of the royal palace:

> Its roof was covered with copper and shone brightly. Inside were rooms for men and rooms for women and porticos shining with silver and gold ornaments. Plates of pure gold were inserted in the walls like pictures. There were embroideries using motifs from Greek mythology and Graeco-Persian wars. One men's room had a domed ceiling imitating the sky. It was completely covered with blue tiles the colour and brilliance of which resembled the skies.[6]

In Anau, a domed mosque dating from the Timurid period and now heavily damaged was built, according to Cohn-Wiener, in 1446 by a local ruler, **Abdul Kasim Babur**. The mosque was built inside a fortress and both were destroyed at an unknown date that may be as late as 1795. The *pishtak* (portico) of the mosque shows two dragons above the entrance, stylised in the Chinese way, white on blue background with black contours. Ornaments in the corners are white, yellow and black. The characters of the Koranic inscription are in Naskhi script, also white on blue background. Inside the *mihrab* is glazed in several colours. The *pishtak* is about 63 feet high; on either side was a wing with octagonal rooms on three storeys. The rear side of the building was fortified with round towers and connected with the fortifications of the citadel. Other sources, however,[7] identify this building as a mausoleum, and give the date of its construction as 1455.

Among other places of interest in Turkmenistan some prehistoric sites should be mentioned. The **Dzhebel Cave** near Krasnovodsk is a late Mesolithic–early Neolithic site where the age of the latest phase was fixed, with the help of radiocarbon dating, within the fifth and sixth millennia B.C. The material found here has therefore provided a standard for the dating of other sites belonging to the same periods. The excavations at the Dzhebel Cave provided the opportunity to establish the relationship between the Mesolithic and early Neolithic cultures of Turkmenistan, and similar cultures in the Caspian area of Persia and as far afield as Palestine.

At **Dzheytun**, 20 miles north-west of Ashkhabad in the Kara Kum desert, the remains of thirty-five separate dwelling houses were excavated, built of round blocks of sun-dried clay, the forerunners of the adobe bricks that became the principal building material in Central Asia for many centuries to come. The houses were small in size, each consisting of a single room of up to 215 square feet. Neolithic flint industry still prevailed here. Blades were found consisting of flakes sharpened on one side and inserted into bone sickles. Stone querns were also found that were used for grinding corn into meal or flour. The pottery was made by hand, without the use of a wheel, but it already showed some primitive decoration, usually several parallel lines painted in ochre. The animal bones found here were of great interest, showing that the process of domesticating certain animals, such as sheep, had already begun. Dzheytun is now recognised as the oldest evidence of an agricultural civilisation in Central Asia, comparable with Jarmo in north-western Persia and Al-Ubaid in Mesopotamia, for example.

South-east of Ashkhabad is a large hill, **Namazga-Tepe**, with layers of six periods (Namazga I–VI), ranging from the third to the late second millennium B.C., which yielded, among other material, interesting pottery and a layout of a large house. Two further sites, dating from the fourth to the middle of the third millennium B.C., are **Kara-Tepe**, near Ashkhabad, and **Geoksyur**, 60 miles east, near the River Tedzhend.

At Geoksyur, nine sites were uncovered in the years 1956–59, dating approximately from the late fourth to the early third millennium B.C., corresponding roughly to the layers of Namazga I–III, with the site of Dashlidzhin, with one-room houses, corresponding to Namazga II and Geoksyur, where houses already had several rooms, being of the period of Namazga III. Pottery with polychrome geometrical decoration was found here, as were traces of some earliest irrigated agriculture.

At **Ak-Tepe**, some 2 miles from Artyk, remains of a Sasanian palace were excavated in 1964–65. Two citadels, eastern and western, a walled *shahristan* and *rabads* were discovered at **Shahr-Islam** in 1947 and excavated in 1961–64.

In 1990, a Bronze Age settlement was discovered at **Gonur-Tepe** near Merv and at **Altyn-Tepe**. A proto-Zoroastrian temple was found at **Togoluk**, capital of the oasis of Margush in 1250–1000 B.C. A twelfth-century mosque decorated with incised terracotta can be seen at **Dendanakan**, a fortified medieval town some 41 miles from Merv.

In the south-western corner of the country, between the Kopet Dagh mountains and the Caspian, which was the ancient province of Hyrcania, a number of sites should be mentioned situated along an 81-mile canal dating probably from the Iron Age period. O. Lecomte lists more than a hundred sites, some excavated, others merely identified and catalogued. Most recent work has been carried out on the site of **Geoktchik-Tepe** (Sasanian and early Islamic period).

Ashkhabad itself is a relatively modern town. The oldest part of it is a ruined fortress, built by the Russians in 1881. Lord Curzon, who visited Ashkhabad in 1888, referred to it as a flourishing town with a considerable population. The population was made up of many diverse nationalities – Russians, Persians, Polish exiles, Armenians, Tartars and many others. They came from all four corners of the Russian Empire – artisans, former soldiers, craftsmen, workers from the Trans-Caspian Railway – all seeking to make their fortune in this thriving spot. Unlike Bukhara, or even Tashkent, Ashkhabad never comprised an old and a new town. The main reason for this was that the native nomad population had no wish to change their way of life for an alien one in a town. Thus, in 1901 43.1 percent of the town's population were Russians and even today the town remains predominantly Russian. In 1948 a severe earthquake shook the town and caused great damage. Most of it was demolished and the areas around the railway station and the city centre suffered more than others.

Some 30 miles to the north-west lies the old Turkmen fortress **Gök-Tepe**; it was here in 1881 that the last stronghold of Central Asian independence fell before the advancing Russians. The Turkmen defenders, after more than three weeks of heroic resistance, were defeated by the Tsarist army under General Skobelev.

The sites at Kunya-Urgench in the Tashauz Region of northern Turkmenistan are described in Chapter VI.

CHAPTER VIII
Full details of abbreviations and publications are in the Bibliography

1 Barthold, *Turkestan*, p. 117
2 Pope, *Architecture*, p. 131.
3 Belenitsky, *Civilisation*, p. 78.
4 There is a disagreement among archaeologists whether the main temple belonged to a Zoroastrian or a dynastic cult. The *rhytons* can be seen in the museum of Mary and the Hermitage in St Petersburg.
5 Rempel, *Ornament*, p. 41.
6 Philostratos, one of a family of Greek writers. Philostratos the Lemnian (end of the second century A.D.) is the author of two books called *Imagines*, an important source for the knowledge of Hellenistic art. His grandson, Philostratos the Younger (late third century) wrote a second series of seventeen *Imagines*. All *Imagines* were translated by A. Fairbanks and published in 1931.
7 *Cities of Central Asia*, p. 16

IX

THE AMU DARYA
VALLEY AND
SOUTHERN TAJIKISTAN

IN UZBEKISTAN ON THE AMU DARYA, not far from the mouth of the Surkhan Darya, lie the ruins of the important medieval city and fortress **Termez**, sometimes transcribed from Persian as Tirmidh. There are three different sites of the city. Old Termez, situated immediately on the river-bank, was destroyed by Chingiz-Khan. A settlement was already on this site in ancient times, mainly because an island in the river and a shallow bed offered an easy crossing.

> We reached Termez, a large town with fine buildings and bazaars and traversed by canals. It abounds in grapes and quinces of an exquisite flavour as well as in flesh-meats and milk... The old Termez was built on the bank of the Oxus, and when it was laid in ruins by Chingiz, this new town was built two miles from the river.[1]

This town still existed under the Uzbeks. In Timur's time the ford was so important that a permanent floating bridge was kept here and tolls were levied from caravans and travellers who crossed it. The third site is that of the present city, which lies on the intersection of the Bukhara (Kagan)–Dushanbe railway line and the highway from Samarkand to Afghanistan. A modern bridge, a few miles upstream, paradoxically called the 'Bridge of Friendship' served the Russian army in its invasion of Afghanistan in 1979.

Clavijo, the Spanish envoy to Timur, has this to say about Termez:

> We crossed the Oxus and in the evening of the same day we entered the big city of Termez. Previously it was part of Lesser India [i.e. Afghanistan], but Timur made it part of Samarkand. The country of Samarkand is called Mongolia and the language here is Mongolian. Some of the Oxus people speak Persian and cannot understand it. These two languages have hardly anything in common. Even the script used by the Samarkandians is different from Persian and those on the south bank cannot read it currently.

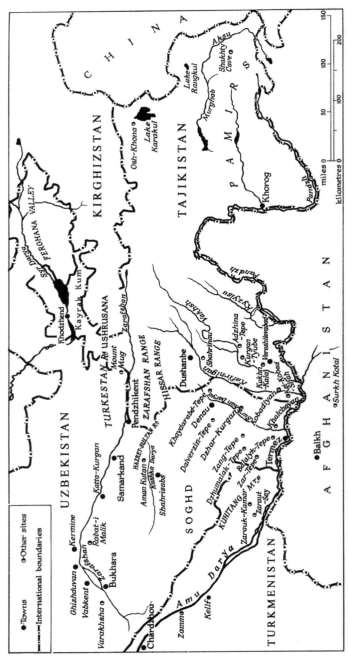

MAP 6 Amu Darya and Zarafshan

By this Clavijo means the Uighur script, which the Mongols took on after their victory over the Uighurs. It was of Syriac origin and was brought to the Uighur country, east of the Tien-Shan and south-west of Lake Baikal, by the Nestorian monks. The Persians at that time used Arabic script, as they still do.

Clavijo also noticed one extremely interesting detail when crossing the river.

Nobody may cross the Oxus from north to south without a special permit or laissez-passer. In this must be stated who he is, where he comes from and where he goes. Even a free man who was born in Samarkand must have such a permit. On the contrary everyone who wants to enter Samarkand, may cross the river freely and does not need anything.

The reason for this ingenious arrangement was obviously to keep people in the country and prevent them from escaping abroad.

The city of Tirmiz is vast and very populous; it has no walls and is not fortified. And it is enough to say, that the inn where they accommodated us was so far from the entrance of the city, that we were quite tired before we arrived there.[2]

Belenitsky[3] regards the name Termez as a distortion of the name of a Graeco-Bactrian king, Demetrius. The existence of the city in the Graeco-Bactrian period seems to be confirmed by many coins and other objects from that time which were found in the ruins. A thorough excavation of levels belonging to the period has so far not been possible, because they lie at a considerable depth under later levels.

However, an important discovery must be mentioned here, although it was made 8 miles upstream from the town, near the village of **Ayrtam**. In 1932 a carved slab of limestone was found in the water, and in 1936 seven other fragments were unearthed during excavations of a Buddhist shrine. All fragments, now in the Hermitage, belong to a frieze that dates from the Kushan period (first or second centuries A.D.) and shows, in high relief, figures of male and female musicians and bearers of offerings. Each figure is framed in acanthus leaves. The site was excavated in 1964–66. It seems that in the second century B.C. there was a fortified Greek outpost, while in the first and second centuries A.D. a Buddhist cult complex was built with a sanctuary, a *stupa*, and some auxiliary buildings. A burial-site nearby dates from the second to the first centuries B.C.

Much valuable material belonging to the Kushan period was discovered in Termez itself, in particular a Buddhist cave-monastery on the hill of Kara-Tepe, in the north-western corner of the ancient city. The distinctive feature of this short-lived building complex of the early Kushan era is that it was mostly hewn out of rock, an Indian characteristic quite exceptional in these areas. It is, in fact, the only site of this kind so far discovered in Transoxania. In addition to badly preserved wall-paintings there were plaster reliefs and statues and also fine thin pottery with numerous inscriptions in ancient Brahmi and Kharosthi scripts. Similar inscriptions were found in Balkh and Surkh Kotal in Afghanistan.[4]

In the ruins of the medieval, pre-Mongol, city we find the group of buildings around the mausoleum of Abu Abdullah Muhammad ben Ali Tirmidhi, called **Hakim al-Termezi**, who died in the year 869. (See Plates 44 and 63.) The mausoleum itself was built towards the end of the ninth century. The present building dates mostly from the twelfth century and is built of unbaked bricks; baked bricks were used as tiles on the outer walls only. On the western and southern walls some ornaments in incised stucco were preserved. Above the cenotaph, a domed ceiling is decorated by some Zoroastrian motifs, circles with symbols of the sun and ornamental vases between them. The cenotaph itself is of white marble or of limestone resembling marble, richly carved. It was donated by Ulugh-beg in the fifteenth century. Next to the mausoleum is a small mosque which, in the eleventh century, was merely a wall with a cylindrical *mihrab*. This, too, was originally covered with ornamented bricks, but after a reconstruction received a much more elaborate decoration, both architectural and ornamental. The entrance to the mosque is through a *khaniga*, a domed brick building dating from the Timurid period.

The palace of the rulers of Termez, of which only a number of decorated slabs and panels have survived, was built perhaps in the eleventh century, but not before 1035. The original decoration, again mainly of bricks, was thoroughly altered at the turn of the twelfth century. The palace consisted of a number of buildings round a courtyard; opposite the entrance was an *iwan*, a large open reception hall with three walls, open on the fourth side; on the walls were three parallel rows, or bands, of ornamental panels, one above the other. The bottom one consisted mainly of medallions in small arches and the middle one of *girikhs*. In the top one we find both *girikhs* and medallions on the columns, and on the walls, between the curves of the arches some pictures of fantastic animals. Incised alabaster was applied also inside the arches, on their fronts, on the corner columns, and on the stalactites. The variety of ornamental motifs is enormous. Some fragments of wall-paintings have also been found. The colour-scheme and the design was most probably similar to that of the alabaster stucco.[5] The outer walls of Termez date probably from the beginning of our era. In the ruins of the medieval, pre-Mongol, city the archaeologists have recently uncovered a house from the tenth and eleventh centuries built of unbaked bricks with column bases of stone in the central room or patio.

Ten miles north of Termez lies the site of **Balalyk-Tepe**, a Soghdian fortress, which existed probably until the Arab occupation. It was a small building, 100 feet square, standing on a mound some 20 feet high and containing fifteen rooms. Most interesting of these is a square reception room in the centre, approximately

16 feet square, with benches all round. Some interesting paintings were found on the walls, dating from the sixth to the seventh centuries.

All paintings are devoted to the same theme – a ceremonial banquet in which a large number of people are taking part. The paintings on three walls contain 47 figures of men and women, wearing splendid garments patterned in many colours. In the foreground are the banqueters in a variety of attitudes, either sitting with crossed legs or in a semi-reclining position. Behind them on a smaller scale are the serving girls. The clothing and various articles they hold in their hands are painted with astonishing care and delicacy. The men wear closely fitting caftans with a broad lapel on the right breast; the women wear sleeveless cloaks thrown loosely over their shoulders. These garments are made of brightly patterned fabrics which show great variety of design.[6]

The paintings of Balalyk-Tepe and carved wood and clay reliefs from **Dzhumalak-Tepe** are considered by Rempel to be the most outstanding art specimens of that period (sixth and seventh centuries). He sees, for instance, in the ornaments on the garments some important motifs, little palmettes, hearts, crosses and circles enclosing human and animal heads that later played a significant role in European and Middle Eastern heraldry. In spite of some Buddhist elements, the wall-paintings and the objects found in Balalyk-Tepe do not seem to relate to Buddhism but more probably to a blend of various creeds and forms of worship.[7]

Sixteen miles north-west of Termez is **Zar-Tepe**, where coins from Greek Bactria to the Hephthalites, as well as pottery from the third century B.C. to the fifth or sixth century A.D. were found. The site was excavated in 1979–81; a walled citadel was constructed on top of a Kushan one that was apparently abandoned at the time of the general decline of Kushan settlements at the end of the fifth and the beginning of the sixth century A.D. **Zang-Tepe**, 20 miles north from the city, was a fortified castle founded in the first century B.C. and rebuilt at the end of the fifth century A.D. Among other interesting finds, like glassware and pottery of the seventh and eighth centuries, were numerous Buddhist texts written in Sanskrit on birch bark a millimetre thick, in a variant of the Brahmi script. Dzhumalak-Tepe and Zang-Tepe are Soghdian forts of a similar type to Balalyk-Tepe. They were basically the dwelling and farmstead of a feudal landowner and were built, for security reasons, on an artificial mound or podium (stylobate). Such castles, or *kushks* as they were called, were the most typical feature of Central Asian architecture of the Soghdian period. They usually stood in the centre or on one side of a rectangular platform on top of an artificial mound of clay. The *kushk* itself contained either a number of rooms alongside each other on both sides of a narrow corridor, or grouped around a central hall with a cupola, which later became known as the *mehman-khana*, or reception room. In the walls were usually some narrow loopholes. From the outside, the *kushk* looked like a massive rectangular fortress. The walls were reinforced with half-columns or half-turrets and towered high above the truncated pyramid of the base.[8]

A typical example of a Soghdian *kushk* is **Kirk Kyz**, a few miles north of Termez. (See Plate 65.) The so-called **Zurmala Tower**, 51 feet high, is believed to have been a Buddhist *stupa* dating from the first century B.C. or the first century A.D. **Fayaz-Tepe**, also north of Termez and recently excavated by L. Albaum, was a late Kushan Buddhist monastery. A courtyard, the monastery buildings around it and the remnants of a *stupa* can be seen.

The two mausoleums of **Sultan-Saadat** near Termez also date from the eleventh or twelfth centuries. They stand alongside each other, built on a square plan, and are joined by a fifteenth-century *iwan* (portico) with a high frontal wall. The northern mausoleum (eleventh century) is better preserved. Its decoration is strictly architectural, both outside and inside, but some ornamental details may be found on the corner columns and in the arches. They are engraved and incised in simple baked bricks, and mark an important step towards the technique of incised terracotta later widely used all over Central Asia.

West of Termez, in the region of the Kuhitang mountains, are several Paleolithic sites containing rock engravings (Zaraut-Say, Zarauk-Kamar etc.).

Following the road west from Termez along the Amu Darya, we come to the town of Kelif. This, according to Arab geographers, was about two days' journey from Termez. In the tenth century, Kelif was situated on both banks of the river and was thereby distinguished from all the other towns along the banks of the Amu Darya. The main portion of the town, with the mosque, was on the left bank. The road from here to Bukhara ran, as it still does, through the Kashka Darya valley. Below Kelif was the town of Zamm, and from here, along the left bank, the waters of the river were used for artificial irrigation. The uniformly cultivated tract began, according to Barthold,[9] from Amul, the present-day Chardzhou. This town, now an important railway junction on the line from Tashkent to Ashkhabad and Khorezm, was, in the Middle Ages, situated on the caravan-route from Transoxania to Khorassan (which the present railway line roughly follows). Where now there is a railway bridge there used to be the most important ferry across the Amu Darya, more important in some periods than the Termez ferry.

East of Termez, on the Kafirnigan River, on the territory of Tajikistan, lies the small town of **Kobadiyan**, near which was found in the late 1870s one of the most famous treasures of all time, the so-called *treasure of Oxus*. This was a considerable hoard of objects dating mostly from the Achaemenid period, now in the British Museum. Unfortunately nothing is known of the circumstances in which it was found, and experts hold different views about its origin. Some

71. The Musalla, Herat. Minaret

72. Guldara stupa

73. Citadel Bala Hissar, Herat

74. Shahr-i Zohak

75. Shahr-i Zohak

76. ABOVE. The stupa, Haibak

77. BELOW. Remains of central sanctuary, Surkh Kotal

78. The 'large' Buddha, Bamiyan

79. Mosque No Gumbad (detail)

archaeologists believe that this was not a hoard of golden objects imported from Persia, having all been found in one place, but the result of continuous looting. Moreover, it cannot be ascertained that the present collection includes everything that originally belonged to it. In 1877 most of these objects appeared on the markets of Bukhara, from where they gradually found their way to the bazaars of Peshawar and Rawalpindi and finally to London.

The site of Kobadiyan itself became a centre of archaeological interest in the 1950s. Two sites were found on which ancient settlements existed and land was extensively irrigated from the seventh to the fifth centuries B.C. The level called Kobadiyan I (seventh to fourth centuries B.C.) was mostly found at Kala-i Mir, and Kobadiyan II (third to second centuries B.C.) at Kei-Kobad-Shah. Kobadiyan III (first century B.C. to first century A.D.) coincided with the period of the Graeco-Bactrian Empire, and Kobadiyan IV (second century A.D.) was contemporary with the reign of the Kushan king Kanishka. Grey-ware pottery and small human and animal figures are characteristic of Kobadiyan III, while red-ware pottery prevailed in Kobadiyan IV. In the last period (third to fourth centuries A.D.) not only pottery but also some coins were found.

In **Kala-i Mir**, an ancient Bactrian dwelling from the seventh to the sixth centuries B.C. was discovered; the pottery here was similar to that of Giaur-Kala (Merv), Samarkand-Afrasiyab and Bactra-Balkh. **Kei-Kobad-Shah** was a fortified place, inhabited continuously from the third or second centuries B.C. until the fourth or fifth centuries A.D. Bases of columns and Corinthian capitals with clear Hellenistic influence were found here.

Of the *kurgans* in the Kobadiyan region it is possible to distinguish between the tombs of the nomadic tribes responsible for the collapse of the Graeco-Bactrian Empire, those of the Kushan period, and finally the post-Kushan tombs. In contrast to the usual practice of burying the corpses, some tombs indicate that the corpses were incinerated. This suggests that some later tribes, possibly the Huns, crossed the region in the fourth and fifth centuries A.D. on their way to Afghanistan.[10]

Still further east, on the Vakhsh River, the biggest tributary of the Amu Darya, eleven miles from the town of Kurgan-Tyube, is the site of the Buddhist monastery of **Adzhina-Tepe**. This is the most important Buddhist monastery so far discovered in Central Asia. Excavations of this mound (approximately 33 by 150 feet) have been going on since 1960. As described by Belenitsky,[11] the monastery consisted of two equal halves, each 150 feet square, joined by a gangway. Each half was built on a four-*iwan* plan. In the south-eastern half there was a courtyard, in the north-western half was a *stupa*, while the monastery proper was in the south-eastern part. In this were the temple buildings, cells for the monks, a large hall or auditorium with an area of over 1000 square feet, and various offices. The different parts of the structure were linked by corridors running round the inside of the perimeter. The *stupa* was surrounded by an outer structure consisting of corridors, small shrines and a number of small chapels, each with an *iwan* opening towards the *stupa*. The entrance, in the middle of the south-east side, consisted of a double *iwan* facing in opposite directions, linked by an arched opening. The whole structure was built in large blocks of *pakhsa* and adobe bricks; the long buildings and the corridors had vaulted roofs; yet the square buildings had domed roofs and the auditorium and temple apparently flat wooden roofs. Here, too, remains of paintings and sculptures were found. The walls and ceilings of the buildings round the *stupa* were probably decorated with paintings, and those in the monastery half of the complex too, but only negligible fragments were preserved on the walls; most fragments of painted stucco-work were found in the rubble on the floors. The clay sculpture was better preserved; all the paintings and sculpture were on religious themes (pictures of Buddha, bodhisattvas, monks, demonic beings etc.). The largest piece is a figure of a reclining Buddha, 40 feet long. All the statues were moulded from clay without any reinforcement, and remains of original colouring can be seen.

In 1954 the fortified building compound of **Kukhn-Kala**, of the Graeco-Bactrian period, was found near the town of Voroshilovabad. Bronze objects and high-grade pottery dating approximately from the end of the second and the beginning of the first millennia B.C. were found in tombs in the lower Vakhsh region, where the Rivers Vakhsh and Kyzylsu join the River Pandzh (upper Amu Darya).

Stone Age and Bronze Age sites were found in abundance in the Pamir mountains in the region of Upper Badakhshan. The area is accessible by road only in the summer months, either from Osh in the north or from Khorog in the west. Paleolithic and Neolithic industries appear to have frequently coexisted here, and distinguishing between them is sometimes difficult.[12] The Paleolithic finds in the eastern Pamirs comprise the **Shakhty Cave**, with interesting rock-carvings, among which was a human figure with a bird's head. The rich Neolithic finds were near Lake Rangkul, north of the Murghab and Aksu Rivers, in Markansu (the Death Valley), north-west of Lake Karakul, and at Osh-Khona, which yielded the richest collection of Neolithic tools found so far in Central Asia.[13]

A great many *kurgans* were explored after 1946, the oldest of them being the Saka tombs in the eastern Pamirs. They yielded a mass of information on the burial rites of the population, which was most probably nomadic. The finds date mainly from the sixth to the second centuries B.C., and contain bronze objects, ornaments, jewellery in bronze with semi-precious stones, and also rather clumsy bronze figures of animals reminiscent of the Scythian animal style.

The valley of the Surkhan Darya, north of Termez, represents another region rich in finds of all archaeological periods. In the extreme north, in the Hissar Range, Neolithic finds have enabled the so-called Hissar culture to be named. The material here is entirely of stone, a grey conglomerate, with a small amount of flint. Floorings have been discovered made of a mixture of plaster and ashes, with the bases of large pots or jars set into the ground. The main occupation of the inhabitants was hunting, but some traces of primitive agriculture were also found.[14] Near the town of Denau there are two sites dating from the Graeco-Bactrian period: a large town site, **Dalverzin-Tepe**, and a smaller one, **Khaydarabad-Tepe**. At the village of Shahrinau, near Dushanbe, the capital of Tajikistan, a site with an area of 860 acres has been discovered. None of these three sites has so far been systematically explored.

Near the mouth of the river lies one of the most important sites of the Kushan period. It consists of a group of separate mounds near the village of **Khalchayan** and dates from the first century B.C. to the second century A.D. A small, well-preserved building discovered in one of these mounds was rectangular in plan. It consisted of a five-bay hexastyle *iwan*, an oblong hall behind it, another room with two columns and several adjoining apartments with linking corridors – a total of eight rooms.[15] Stone bases were found here for the wooden columns that had supported the roof beams, and also fire-baked tiles, antefixes and stepped merlons from the roof. Apart from pottery, various utensils and coins, there were some interesting fragments of clay sculptures representing an important stage in the development of local art. There were several subjects – a frieze with gods, goddesses, girls, musicians and dancers; a group of statues consisting of a seated king and queen surrounded by their family; and yet another group of figures that suggest that they were portraits of particular persons. Horsemen form a separate group, with horses in full gallop and riders clad in closely fitting belted tunics, trousers and soft-soled boots, and probably armed with bows and arrows. Some of them were in bas-relief, but most in high-relief or almost fully in the round. These horsemen recall the figures of Parthian *cataphracts* (cavalry) in Dura Europos, and also fit into Plutarch's description of the Parthians who fought against the Romans at Carrhae in 63 B.C.[16] As for style, the sculptures of Khalchayan represent an early stage of the so-called 'dynastic style' – as opposed to the temple art of Buddhism – and are closely connected with the Parthian art of Nisa.

Also in the Surkhan Darya region, there is an interesting minaret in the village of **Dzhar Kurgan**. It is dated 1108–9, built on an octagonal base, and formed of 24 half-columns or ribs, larger at the base and narrower at the top. Originally, the minaret was much higher, but the top part, just above the band of ornamental inscriptions, has disappeared. The half-columns are decorated with simple brick ornaments that belong to the same style and same architectural school as other outstanding minarets from that period (Kalan in Bukhara, Vabkent) in Central Asia and, somewhat later, in Delhi, Khorassan and elsewhere.

CHAPTER IX
Full details of abbreviations and publications are in the Bibliography

1   Gibb, *Ibn Battuta*, pp. 174–75.
2   Le Strange, *Clavijo*, pp. 201–2.
3   Belenitsky, *Civilisation*, p. 74.
4   Frumkin, *CAR* XIII, p. 242.
5   The sites of the palace and of Kara Tepe lie within a military area and are not accessible.
6   Belenitsky, *Civilisation*, pp. 116–37.
7   Frumkin, *CAR* XIII, p. 245.
8   Rempel, *Ornament*, p. 72; see also above, pp. 39, 51, 117.
9   Barthold, *Turkestan*, p. 81.
10   Frumkin, *CAR* XII, p. 176.
11   Belenitsky, *Civilisation*, pp. 140–42.
12   Frumkin, *CAR* XII, p. 173.
13   Frumkin, *CAR* XII, p. 171.
14   Belenitsky, *Civilisation*, p. 46.
15   Belenitsky, *Civilisation*, p. 100.
16   Belenitsky, *Civilisation*, p. 101.

X

THE SYR DARYA AND FERGHANA VALLEYS

THE COURSE OF THE SYR DARYA has always formed a frontier between the settled civilised territories to the south and the steppeland of the nomads to the north. Moreover, the upper reaches, the Ferghana valley and the valleys of the two confluents, Kara Darya and Naryn, represented at times a sort of enclave, the furthest outpost of civilisation sandwiched between the inhospitable mountains of the Alai, Transalai and Pamirs to the south, the Tien Shan to the north, the bare plains and deserts to the east, and connected with the west only by a narrow gorge, the Ferghana Gate.

Barthold, in his *Geographical Survey of Medieval Transoxania,* gives several names of towns and settlements in the eastern parts of this region, next to the Turkish territories. This hilly, barren country, now part of the republic of Kirghizstan, was not conquered by the Arabs until the tenth century. In fact, it was always a border area, as it is now, between the eastern and the western parts of Turkestan. Near the town of Uzgen (Uzkend) was the passage 'into the country of the Turks', and an important road connecting Kashgar and Kucha with Kokand and Tashkent passed through here. Barthold mentions Osh and Uzkend as the two principal towns on the Turkish frontier.

Taking the road west from Uzkend, we come to the town of Andizhan, on the confluence of the Naryn and the Kara Darya. This was the most important centre of eastern Ferghana, but was completely rebuilt after a catastrophic earthquake in 1902 destroyed all its interesting buildings.

The medieval capital of the province was Aksikath, a city on the right bank of the Syr Darya below Andizhan, on the road to Khodzhend. There is a description of it in Makdisi and Ibn Haukal, according to which it must have been a large and lively place, but nothing of it has survived. Five miles north of the site of

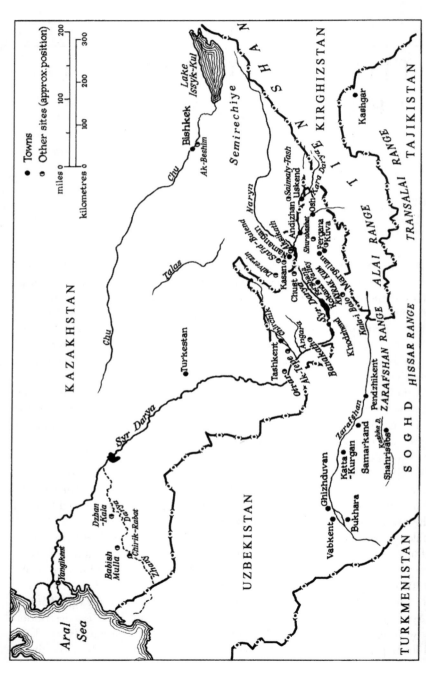

MAP 7 Syr Darya and Zarafshan

Aksikath is the village of Kasan, with ruins of an old town of the same name. Here, at the turn of the eighth century, was the capital of the princes of Ferghana. Nearby is the site of Mug-Kurgan, a fortress and probably a temple of fire-worshippers. All around are scores of black tombstones typical of pre-Islamic civilisation. A few miles east, in the barren country, is a place called Ispid-Bulan, sometimes referred to as **Safid-Bulend**, with a twelfth-century mausoleum, **Shah Fasil**. An Arab commander, Muhammad ben Jarir, died here in battle against the infidels with some 2700 of his followers. The mausoleum is a conical building of unusual design, with a steep cupola set on an octagonal base. The outer walls are completely without decoration, while the inside displays what some experts consider the richest decor in the whole Turan. Every inch of the walls are covered with fine ornaments and there is an amazing variety of motifs. Some of them do not appear anywhere else in Central Asia. This lonely and almost inaccessible monument, which almost miraculously escaped destruction by the Mongols, has therefore a definite place in the history of art in this area.

How deep the barbarisation of the country must have gone may be seen on a group of three mausoleums in **Kasan** itself, built in the early fourteenth century, when Transoxania began to recover from the Mongol devastation. The mausoleum of **Fakhreddin Tuman** (1340–41) is inferior to Shah Fasil in every respect. It is badly built, crudely decorated, and the script used here is rather primitive: 'Barbarously arranged,' says Cohn-Wiener.[1] Elsewhere in the town is another mausoleum, of **Sultan Malik Serbakhsh**, heavily damaged, with a mighty conical cupola and some remains of a terracotta frieze around the entrance. Inside, the transition to the cupola is not achieved by means of a squinch, but by a steep triangle of masonry in each corner of the socle. This technique appears in Turkey, but nowhere else in Central Asia.

The towns of Namangan and Kokand are not mentioned in Barthold's survey, apparently because they were of more recent origin. In **Namangan**, which is a district capital north of the Syr Darya, the mausoleum of **Khojamny Kabri** is a good specimen of seventeenth to eighteenth-century architecture. The same applies to the architectural monuments of nineteenth-century **Kokand**, the mausoleums **Madar-i Khan** and **Dahman Shahkhan** (the latter stands inside the old cemetery), as well as to the palace of **Khudoyar Khan**, built in 1871. It should be mentioned that a member of the Sheybanid dynasty succeeded in 1710 in establishing an independent khanate in Ferghana with Kokand as capital. In 1758 the khan had to recognise the suzerainty of China when a Chinese army appeared on his border. In the early 1800s the Khan of Kokand annexed Tashkent and later also the city of Turkestan, wrested from the Emir of Bukhara. A further expansion brought Kokand some territorial gains in Semirechiye until, in 1876, the whole khanate was annexed by Russia.

The palace of Kokand is probably the last truly monumental building in Central Asia. The impressive facade, recently restored, displays bright colours and good ornaments in the local, Ferghana, style. An expert might even say that too many colours have been used and the eye gets tired. The architecture of the building is not very sophisticated, and inside perhaps only the painted wooden ceiling of the main reception hall is worth mentioning. Also in Kokand, best-quality ornamental tiles can be found on the gate of the **Kamal Kazi** *madrasa* (1913).

In the southern part of Ferghana, a number of rivers flowing from glaciers of the 16,000 feet Alai range were once tributaries of the Syr Darya, but now none of them reaches it, their water all being taken by the irrigation canals. The administrative centre founded by the Russians after the annexation of Kokand is the town of Fergana,[2] originally a garrison town called Skobelevo. The nearby village of Margellan has a long history and was mentioned by the Arabs in the ninth and tenth centuries. However, the only outstanding buildings in present-day Margellan are three mosques dating from the early twentieth century with interesting *iwans* decorated with incised alabaster stucco.

Seven miles west of Osh, in the south-east of Ferghana, a large medieval site is now being excavated near the village of **Kuva**. In pre-Mongol times Kuva (or Quba) was the capital of an isolated district, and was reckoned to be the second city in Ferghana after Aksikath. In quantity of water and number of gardens it even exceeded it. It stood on a stream of the same name, which at that time still reached the Syr Darya. In Babur's time (late fifteenth century) it was only a village. In 1957 a Buddhist temple was discovered and excavated there. The walls had been destroyed by fire, but numerous fragments of clay sculpture were found in a fairly good state of preservation. The most interesting items were a large figure of Buddha or bodhisattva, and a large number of heads and fragments of torsos of gods and goddesses, demons and other figures, typical of Mahayana Buddhist art. Some of the figures still retained traces of the original paint. The temple was decorated with wall-paintings, of which only a few small fragments had survived.[3] This site is, from a cultural point of view, closely related to **Ak-Beshim** in Semirechiye, west of Bishkek in Kirghizstan (see p. 165). Here, too, a Buddhist temple was discovered, the walls of which were very well preserved, standing intact up to 10 feet high, and the architecture of the building could be established almost in every detail. A considerable part of the area was occupied by a large courtyard (105 by 60 feet), surrounded by massive walls. Along the longer side was a continuous line of cloisters in *iwan* form, apparently supported on wooden pillars. The temple on the west side of the courtyard stood on a stylobate and consisted of a rectangular hall 60 by 33 feet; a wide entrance passage was in the east wall and three other openings in the west wall. All the temple buildings were decorated with paintings and stucco reliefs, and there were statues standing on pedestals, some of them of gilded bronze.

Another Buddhist temple found at Ak-Beshim was smaller in size and square in plan. The shrine was cruciform and there were two ambulatories running around it. The pottery sculpture found here was in a better state of preservation than in the first temple, and here too were traces of painting on the walls. Inside the town of Ak-Beshim a small Christian church of a Nestorian community was discovered. It was built on a cruciform plan 17 by 16 feet, conforming with the early Syrian architectural canons. Traces of polychrome frescoes on the walls were unfortunately too small to distinguish their subjects.[4]

In the Ferghana Gate, which separates the valley from the Hunger Steppe, lies the medieval town of Khodzhend. This was in Alexander's time his easternmost outpost, called Alexandreia Eskhate. In the tenth century it was an independent administrative unit, ranking among the large towns of Transoxania, with a citadel, inner and outer suburbs, a cathedral mosque and a palace. The town was famed for its vineyards and gardens. The population was so large that the produce of the neighbouring fields did not suffice for its needs, and corn had to be imported from Ferghana and Ushrusana.[5] During the Mongol invasion, Khodzhend was one of the places that put up the strongest and most determined resistance.

Almost the whole area between Khodzhend and Samarkand (about 200 miles) formed part of the province of Ushrusana or, previously, a Soghdian principality of the same name. It has been discussed in detail in Chapter VII.

On the right bank of the Syr Darya, as we approach Tashkent, near the mouth of the River Angara, lie the ruins of the pre-Mongol town of **Banakath**, and next to it the post-Mongol ruins of Shahrukhiya, which in fact was Banakath rebuilt by Timur. The capital of this province, Shash, was a place called Binkath, not far from the River Chirchik, of which the Arab geographers give the following description:

> The town of Binkath was surrounded by two lines of walls, of which the outer line had seven gates and the interior line ten gates. The shahristan had three and the citadel two gates. The palace and the prison were in the citadel, the cathedral mosque outside but close to it. In the town and its neighbourhood were many gardens and vineyards.[6]

The name Shash or Chach may be found in ancient Chinese chronicles, and the town of Binkath is probably none other than the present **Tashkent**. When, in the middle of the nineteenth century, the Russians were pushing south their 'open frontier' in the Kazakh steppe, towards Tashkent and the Syr Darya, Tashkent was, like other contemporary towns in Central Asia, a walled city surrounded by a moat. The walls were crenellated, 16 miles in circumference and in places up to 15 feet high. There were twelve gates and two passages. Outside, luxuriant orchards and walled gardens stretched for several miles in each direction, so that the traveller approaching the city saw only a vast belt of trees in which no building was visible. The population, some sixty to eighty thousand, consisted mainly of sedentary Uzbeks, but there were also a number of Tajiks and some Tartars, Kazakhs and Indians. There were numerous worships of various kinds, but the great passion of the inhabitants was commerce. Trade with Russia, which had been developing since the seventeenth century, had assumed a dominant position, and Tashkent merchants were regular visitors to the fairs at Orenbug, Troitsk and Nizhniy Novgorod.[7]

Tashkent, although the biggest and by far the most important city of Central Asia, has in fact very little to offer from the artistic and archaeological point of view, especially after the earthquake in 1966. The only relatively old buildings were the sixteenth-century *madrasas* of **Barak Khan** and **Kukeltash** and the fifteenth-century mausoleum of **Qaffal Shashi**, all in the Old Town. Rempel[8] mentions also the mausoleum of a Suyunij Khan, built in 1531–32, with some interesting interior decorations. The mausoleum of Yunus Khan, who died in 1486, built at the end of the fifteenth century, had no special architectural or ornamental features, and it was used, when the author visited it, as an architect's office. The new large museum houses an excellent collection of antiquities from the whole area.

A huge archaeological site is offered by the unexplored ruins of **Otrar**, an important town on the Syr Darya not far from Tashkent. It was in Otrar that a caravan of Muslim merchants friendly to the Mongols was put to death by the local governor, thus giving Chingiz-Khan the reason for his devastating raid on the Khorezmian Empire. The city of Otrar was never rebuilt after the Mongol destruction and it was near its ruins that Timur died in 1405, just after he had launched his campaign against China. The site, known as Otrar-Tyube, covers some 49 acres, and has walls dating from the eleventh and twelfth centuries, with some later reconstructions. Excavations on a large scale have begun recently.

Down the river, below Otrar, the steppe on both banks was the territory of the Turkish Ghuzz, or Oghuz. Their capital, situated two days' journey from the estuary, was Yangikent (New Town), which corresponds to the site of **Dzhankent-Kala**. Nearby began the Khorezmian, or Khivan, territory with the border fortress of **Dzhan-Kala**. A caravan-route connected this district with central Khorezm, roughly following the eastern shore of the Aral Sea.

On the Zhany Darya, which was the ancient river-bed of the Syr Darya, is the site of **Chirik Rabat**, a fortified Scythian settlement of the seventh to second centuries B.C. **Babish Mulla**, 25 miles north-east, was a fortress of the fourth to second centuries with a necropolis where many gold and silver objects were found. These two, and some other sites in the same area, are believed to have been inhabited by the Apasiaks (Water Saka, or Massagetae).

The site of Uigarak, in the delta of the Syr Darya, comprises some eighty kurgans, several of which were excavated in 1961–65.

As for the prehistoric cultures, many sites have been found on the left bank of the Syr Darya, on the western boundaries of Ferghana, belonging to the so-called Kayrak Kum culture. This is a Bronze Age culture related to the Hissar culture south of the mountains. In some cases the settlements occupied a very large area, up to 25 acres, but most of them ranged between quarter of an acre and seven-and-a-half acres. The houses sometimes reached a length of 65 feet with a width of 55 feet. Farming and stock rearing were the main occupations, but hunting and fishing also played a part in the economy. Domestic animals included cattle, sheep and horses. A large number of querns found here shows that grain was grown as well. Bronze-working techniques were highly developed and a considerable part of the population was obviously engaged in mining, exploiting the nearby deposits of copper ore. Remarkably fine casting moulds and bronze articles of a very high standard were found in this area. Their pottery was often moulded round a cloth bag filled with sand, traces of which were found on the inner surface of the vessels.[9] Also from the Bronze Age is the large settlement named after the village of Chust. The pottery found here includes some magnificent tableware covered with a red slip and decorated, after glazing, with a pattern in black.

The settlement of **Dalverzin** was already surrounded by a strong defensive wall, partly constructed of adobe bricks. The houses were built at ground level, but their layout has not been fully established.[10]

In eastern Ferghana, the large site of **Shurabashat** dates from the Achaemenid period, while **Kala-i Bolo** on the border of Tajikistan is the site of a Soghdian *kushk*, similar to Ak-Tepe, mentioned above. Frumkin[11] dates this site mainly from the eleventh to twelfth centuries, with only some wooden sculptures belonging to the pre-Arab, seventh-to-eighth-century, period.

As for the ancient period, it is worth quoting Rempel,[12] who says that in the Tashkent oasis, in Ferghana, and also in the lowlands of the Syr Darya, which remained virtually unaffected by Hellenism, older art forms were preserved much longer, as may be judged by the pottery. These forms are linked partly with cultures of the Anau type (see p. 139), partly with the culture of the steppe nomads. On the Syr Darya there emerged, in the course of time, the so-called 'culture of marshland villages' with its original ornament – geometrical, floral and animal – which is linked to the ancient culture of the 'steppe bronze', and to that of the early nomads, and which developed its own independent motifs, related to the culture of the peasant population of Khorezm and Soghd.

NOTES ON CHAPTER X
Full details of abbreviations and publications are in the Bibliography

1   Cohn-Wiener, *Turan*, p. 22.
2   Not to be confused with Ferghana the region.
3   Belenitsky, *Civilisation*, p. 139.
4   Belenitsky, *Civilisation*, p. 139.
5   Barthold, *Turkestan*, p. 165.
6   Quoted by Barthold in *Turkestan*, p. 171.
7   *CAR* XIII, p. 104.
8   Rempel, *Ornament*, p. 34.
9   Belenitsky, *Civilisation*, p. 47.
10 Belenitsky, *Civilisation*, p. 48.
11 Frumkin, *CAR* XII, p. 176.
12 Rempel, *Ornament*, pp. 62–64.

XI

KAZAKHSTAN AND KIRGHIZSTAN

NORTH OF TASHKENT, on the territory of Kazakhstan and on the railway line linking Central Asia with European Russia, is the town of **Turkestan**, previously called Yassi. Timur built here, at the same time as the palace in Shahrisabz, a mosque above the grave of a local saint, **Hazret Ahmad Yassevi**, which is one of the most outstanding specimens of Timurid architecture. Built by a Persian architect, it has a monumental *iwan* flanked by towers. Behind it is the actual mosque with a stalactite vault, and further behind the tomb of the saint and auxiliary premises. Both the mosque and the tomb have fine domes – the ribbed dome over the tomb is the first of this kind – but on the outside the complex is heavily damaged. Only some of the mosaics in the rear and some large brick ornaments have been preserved. Inside, however, is a remarkable collection of handicrafts: implements of bronze, wonderfully carved doors etc., all most probably of Persian origin. The museum of Almaty (formerly Alma-Ata) houses a complete model of the building.

Osh, which in Arab times had a citadel with a palace and a prison, an inner town and outer suburbs with three gates in the city walls, and a fine cathedral mosque, is now an insignificant provincial town of which the only interesting features are the nearby oilfields and the high mountain road that starts here and traverses the Alai and the Transalai to the Pamirs.

Uzkend, on the other hand, although very small, has more character. The valley of the Kara Darya narrows considerably here, so that the road that passed through it could be easily controlled and tolls levied. This was most probably the reason for the town's past importance. In the eleventh century it even became the seat of the Karakhanid dynasty, which ruled Transoxania for a while. From this time there remains a group of three mausoleums and a minaret dating from the twelfth century, which represent an important example of Islamic architecture of that period. They form a significant stage in the development of wall ornament and a step towards the superb monuments of the Timurid period, 200 years later.

All three mausoleums had imposing porticoes; at that time this was a new feature for this type of building. The central mausoleum of **Nasr ben Ali**, who died in about 1012–13, dates from the eleventh century and is now in ruins. (See Plates 49 and 50.) Discernible on the remains of the facade is a simple terracotta ornament – one of the earliest *girikhs* – and inside, a band of remarkably fine carved plaques with what are clearly pre-Islamic motifs. Of the dome, only one corner remains. Inside was a room 26 feet square, with a niche in each wall. Below the band of plaques some remains of an inscription frieze were still visible in the late 1950s. Cohn-Wiener described the buildings in the mid-1920s, when it was in a slightly better condition.

The **minaret** of Uzkend dates most probably from the same period. It stands north of the mausoleums, near the present-day mosque. (See Plate 51.) Its diameter at the bottom is 30 feet, height only about 65 feet, but the upper part is missing. The ornament is geometrical, composed of smaller and larger bricks alternating in sequence. The style is the same as that of the mausoleum mentioned above. This was most probably a model for the still existing monumental minarets in Bukhara and Vabkent, both built under Karakhanid rule.

The northern mausoleum, **Jalal ad-Din al Husayn**, built in 1152, is one of the best surviving specimens of early Islamic art. (See Plates 45 and 48.) Here, perhaps for the first time, the facade of the building is accentuated. Hitherto, all Islamic buildings were oriented towards the inside and tended to neglect the outer appearance. The portico is beautifully decorated with incised terracotta ornaments, on the flanking columns, inside the portico, and on the soffit of the arch. A band of inscriptions on the arch is in the flowery Naskhi script, while above the entrance a plaited Kufic has been used. The **southern** mausoleum, built in 1186, is even more decorative than the northern one. (See Plates 46 and 47.) The elements on the inner side of the *iwan*, which were later used on the famous Shah-i Zinda in Samarkand, can be characterised as follows: the corner column; an inscription band; a concave segment also filled with inscriptions; an outer column with inscriptions and geometrical ornaments. They are separated from each other by brick bands and incised ornamented terracotta plaques. Interwoven *islimi* (floral motifs) dominate the ornament completely. This was not the case with the older building, however.

North of Uzkend, in the midst of the Ferghana range and in an almost inaccessible spot, lies the site of **Saimaly-Tash**, almost 10,000 feet above sea level. Here, well over 100,000 rock engravings were found, presenting a unique panorama of wild animals, hunting scenes, domestic animals, vehicles and ploughs, as well as human beings. The chronology is difficult to ascertain and, according to some authorities (Bernshtam for one), they date from the Bronze Age period up to about the third to the eighth centuries A.D. The site was discovered in 1903, but was partly explored by Zima only in 1948. A more thorough exploration by Bernshtam followed in 1950.[1]

Ak-Tepe near Tashkent is the site of a typical Soghdian *kushk* – a square building without any windows, with a corridor all round and a large number of rooms facing into it. The outer corners were reinforced with round towers and the decoration consisted of terracotta plaques in the form of tents and discs.

Buddhist remains were discovered in several places in the Chu valley, both east and west of Bishkek, the capital of Kirghizstan. The most important of these is Ak-Beshim, east of Bishkek, which has already been described (p. 158). Other sites are Dzhul, west of Bishkek, Saryg, and Suyab, east of the city. In other areas, the sites are confined mostly to *kurgans*, or tombs of the nomad tribes, ranging from the Bronze Age to the Turkic tribes of the fifth to seventh centuries A.D.

Many of these *kurgans* are scattered in the steppe between Almaty and the Ala-tau mountains. Some have been excavated. The finds included, among other things, gold jewels and statuettes, one of them highly elaborate. Most of them are in the Almaty Museum.

Some 50 miles west of Almaty, the rock-carvings of **Tamgaly Tash** date from the Saka period (seventh to fifth century B.C.) to the Turkish period (sixth to eighth century A.D.). (See Plate 57.) They are mainly zoomorphic, but there is a curious humanoid figure with an aura probably representing a solar deity.

In this connection a brief mention should be made of the Turkish *balbals*, or stone sculptures found either in some *kurgans* or free-standing in the steppe. They are more or less schematic human figures ranging from flat engravings to reliefs believed to represent enemies killed in battle who, after death, are supposed to serve the man who killed them. They have usually a big head, tiny arms, the right one folded at the waist, sometimes with a cup in the right hand and the left arm resting on a sword. (See Plates 95 and 96.) They were characteristic of western Turks and were found all over southern Siberia, but not in Transoxania.[2]

NOTES ON CHAPTER XI
Full details of abbreviations and publications are in the Bibliography

1   Frumkin, *CAR* XII, pp. 21–25.
2   *Balbals* can be seen in the museums of Almaty and Tashkent.

80. Friday Mosque, Herat (detail)

82. Monastery Kyzyl Kara (general view)

84. Bamiyan (general view)

85. Mausoleum of Gawhar Shad, Herat

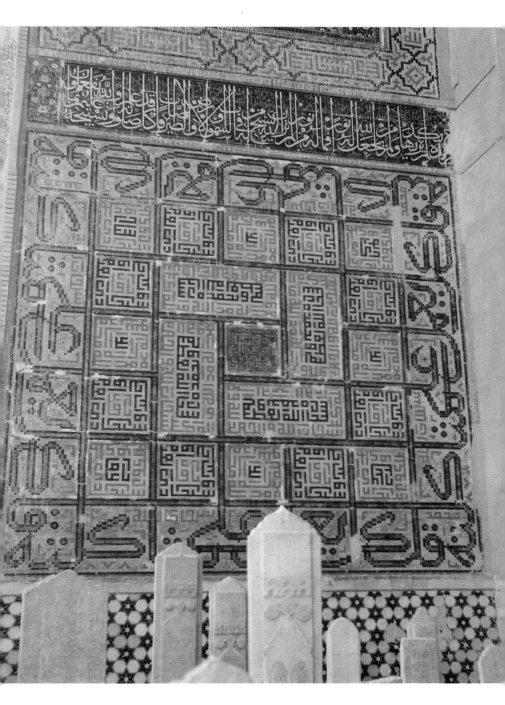

86. Gazurgah, Herat (detail)

87. Tomb of Khoja Abdullah Ansari, Gazurgah, Herat

PART III
XINJIANG, OR EASTERN TURKESTAN

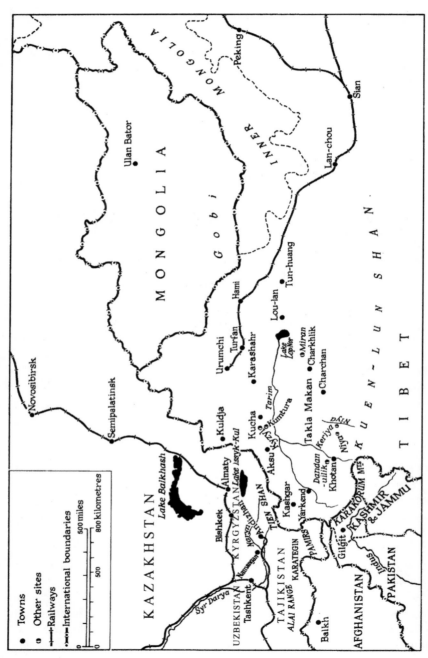

MAP 8 Xinjiang

XII
HISTORY

XINJIANG, OR THE UIGHUR Autonomous Republic of China, consists of the Tarim
Basin, which is mostly desert with a belt of oases in the north and south, and of
the valley of the Ili and the region of Dzungaria west of Urumchi and north of
the mountain range of Tien Shan. The Dzungarian Gate as well as the Ferghana
Gate west of Kashgar were the favourite passages, from time immemorial, for the
nomadic incursions from the Siberian and Mongolian plains into the settled
areas of Turan and Iran.

The oases of the Tarim Basin form a semicircular belt, the northern part of
which consists of Turfan, Karashahr, Kucha, Aksu and Kashgar. The southern
belt includes Lou-lan, Miran, Niya, Keriya, Khotan and Yarkend to name just
the important ones. It thus stretches north of the Kuen-lun Range all the way
from Tun-huang in the east to Kashgar in the west. From Khargalik, near
Khotan, a caravan-route linked Xinjiang with Ladakh and India.

The Chinese first captured eastern Turkestan from the nomadic Huns in the
first century B.C., and thus established their control over the Silk Route. In those
times most of the country was inhabited by Indo-Europeans of Iranian origin in
the south-west (the Asian Scythians, or Saka) and of 'Tokharian' origin in the
north and north-east (the so-called Yue-che). The Huns pushed these Yue-che
westwards and started a big migration movement that finally brought the Saka
to southern Afghanistan, to the province of Sistan (Saka-stan) and the Yue-che
to Bactria, which in some sources is called Tokharistan. This movement marked
the end of the Graeco-Bactrian Empire. Strabo mentions the Tokharoi and the
Sakaraulai among the tribes who defeated the Greek king Heliocles between 140
and 130 B.C. The Kushan dynasty was probably of Yue-che origin and their
empire began as a federation of Yue-che tribes. When this empire reached the

peak of its power, it clashed with the Chinese on the western frontier of Xinjiang, at the end of the first century A.D. By this time, in the later Han period, the dominance of the Tarim was again disputed between the Chinese and the Huns. The famous general Pan-Chao re-established Chinese control over the area. When some oases like Kucha applied for help to the Kushans, their ethnic relatives, Pan-Chao was able to isolate the Kuchan expeditionary force, which perished in the deserts of Kashgaria. In A.D. 97, Pan-Chao dispatched a detachment across the Parthian Empire to meet the Romans. The Chinese, frightened by the hostile reception they got from the Parthians, soon decided to return home, but their venture probably gave grounds to the otherwise unconfirmed legend that Pan-Chao's army pushed as far west as the Aral Sea in pursuit of the Kushans. (Some sources even mention the Caspian Sea.)

Under the Han dynasty, when the Silk Route was firmly in Chinese hands, Buddhist religion, Indian literature and Hellenistic art could take root in the Tarim oases. Indian missionaries followed this route when travelling to China to preach Buddhism. Graeco-Roman art came quite naturally with trade and religion. The southern road was probably used more frequently. Sir Aurel Stein found there, among other things, Roman coins of the Emperor Valens, Graeco-Buddhist bas-reliefs in the purest Gandhara style, Roman caskets, intaglios and Indo-Scythian coins.

The civilisation of Inner Asia at that time may be divided into two distinct longitudinal zones: in the north we encounter the art of the steppe, nomad art *par excellence*, characterised by bronze buckles and parts of harness in animal style, with purely ornamental tendencies; in the south, along the Silk Route, across the double belt of oases around the Tarim Basin, we find the art of sedentary peoples, paintings and sculptures directly inspired by Greek, Persian and Indian art, which was brought in and united by the Buddhist religion.

South of Tarim there is the same mixture of Persian and Buddhist elements, particularly in the paintings on wooden panels found at **Dandan-Uilik**, northeast of Khotan. Female nudes reminiscent of Ajanta, horsemen and camel riders entirely Persian in appearance, and a bearded bodhisattva dressed more like a Persian nobleman all indicate both Persian and Buddhist influence. We may therefore conclude that before the conquest of the country by the Turkic tribes in the second half of the eighth century, the Indo-European oases both north and south of the Tarim derived their culture from the great civilisations of India and Persia, and owed nothing, or very little, to the civilisation of the steppes.[1] (See also p. 180.)

While Kucha was mostly influenced by Persia, Turfan was more exposed to currents from China. Here the Indo-Iranian elements gradually disappeared and merged with the cultural trends of the Tang dynasty. After all, Turfan was ruled by a Chinese dynasty from the beginning of the sixth century, but when the locals rebelled against the suzerainty of the Tang, a Chinese army occupied and annexed the oasis in A.D. 640. The Tang expansion westwards continued, Karashahr and Kucha were defeated in turn, and the Indo-Iranian civilisation was thus destroyed. Kashgar, Khotan and Yarkend also recognised the supremacy of the Tang, and the whole of Xinjiang was once again under Chinese rule. Karashahr, Kucha, Kashgar and Khotan formed a Chinese defence line called the 'Four Garrisons', but after the defeat by the Arabs in 751 the whole of Inner Asia was lost to the empire.[2]

Turkish domination followed in Xinjiang. The Uighurs, originally a Turkic tribe from western Mongolia, appeared on the scene. They intervened in the Chinese Civil War, helping the Emperor Su-tsong, and were able to carve a vast empire of their own on the western fringes of China proper. Manichaeism, an amalgam of Persian Mazdeism and Nestorian Christianity, became their state religion, no doubt imported from Persia when the followers of this sect were persecuted there by the Arabs. Nestorians came to Xinjiang most probably at the same time, and their colonies were the source of the medieval legends of Prester John.

In the ninth and at the beginning of the tenth century the Uighurs were squeezed out of Mongolia and came in great numbers to Xinjiang, where they still represent the main element of the population. With the Manichaean religion the Uighurs also took over the Soghdian alphabet, derived from Syriac, and developed it into the famous Uighur script. This replaced the Turkish runic script of the Orkhon and was subsequently used by the Mongols of Chingiz-Khan and by Timur, 500 years later. Gradually, the influence of the Manichaeans and Nestorians faded and the penetration of Islam began. In the twelfth century the population was already predominantly Muslim by religion and Turkic by ethnic origin, and it has remained so up to the present day.

In the eighteenth century, under the Qing dynasty, the Tarim basin became Chinese once more and the penetration of the Han settlers began. This provoked local discontent, which culminated in an uprising in 1864 when Xinjiang Muslims rebelled against the Manchu dynasty. An officer from Kokand, Yakub Beg, came to Kashgar in 1866, and within months became ruler of a state that was duly recognised by Britain, Russia and Turkey. However, in 1877 he was defeated by the Chinese commander and died shortly afterwards. The centre of his short-lived empire was the oasis of Turfan.

When European explorers and geographers had almost completed the survey of Inner Asia, in the last two decades of the nineteenth century, they heard rumours that somewhere in the deserts of Chinese Turkestan scores of fragmented remains of ancient civilisations had been found preserved, apparently, as well as those in the deserts of Egypt. Following this, numerous archaeological expeditions made for Xinjiang, and in 1907 their efforts were crowned by Sir Aurel Stein's discovery of the 'caves of a thousand Buddhas' near the village of Tun-huang.[3]

Shortly before and after the First World War, several French, German, Russian, Japanese and, of course, British expeditions worked on the Xinjiang sites, but unfortunately their time ran short. In the early 1920s Xinjiang became a contested area between Russia and China, and the Chinese authorities were extremely reluctant to let foreigners in. After a brief spell of fame, Xinjiang fell again into obscurity.

Nevertheless, since the nineteenth-century Great Game, Britain and Russia were in competition in Xinjiang. Both powers opened consulates in Kashgar and there was also a British representation in Urumchi. The Russians, however, gained an advantage when they extended their railway as far as Andizhan in the Ferghana valley, and even more when, under the Soviets, the Turksib (Turkestan-Siberian) line was built, bringing the Russian communication network within easy reach of the Xinjiang border. The trade with India declined sharply and the Russian influence, both commercial and strategic, increased. Xinjiang gradually became a virtual Russian protectorate and remained so until the Chinese Communist victory in 1949. This is how Peter Fleming described the situation in the mid-1930s: 'the only powers in the land are the Russian civil and military advisers. Every department, every regiment, is in effect directed by a Soviet agent occupying a key position; the Province is run from Moscow.'[4]

When the Communists seized power in China, the Russians had to leave, and Xinjiang became more inaccessible than ever. After the Sino-Soviet split in 1960 thousands of nomads crossed the border into the USSR. After the collapse of the Soviet Union the traffic between Xinjiang, Kazakhstan, Kirghizstan and also with Russia became much livelier. New communications were opened such as, for example, the rail link between Urumchi and Semipalatinsk, planned since the 1930s, a rail and road link with Almaty in Kazakhstan etc. Tribal, personal and commercial contacts between the Turkic nations were gradually resumed, and these, in turn, provoked anti-Chinese tensions in Xinjiang resulting, from time to time, in armed clashes and riots of which only sporadic news penetrate abroad.

A railway line from Urumchi to Kashgar was opened in spring 1999.

NOTES ON CHAPTER XII
Full details of abbreviations and publications are in the Bibliography

1   Grousset, *L'Empire*, p. 92; Dabbs, *History*, p. 119.
2   Sir Aurel Stein explored the remains of the Chinese *limes* or border defences in the eastern part of Xinjiang in two expeditions in 1907 and 1916.
3   In one of these caves, walled up for nine hundred years, Stein found a huge library of scrolls written in a number of languages and scripts, dated from the fifth to the tenth centuries A.D.
4   Fleming, P., *News from Tartary*, p. 258.

XIII

URUMCHI, TURFAN
AND KUCHA

ALTHOUGH THE CAPITAL of the province, Urumchi, is not a very interesting city in itself, its local museum has recently acquired certain fame due to the 'discovery' by an American scholar, Professor V.A. Mair, of a number of ancient mummies that he believed to be up to 4000 years old. The mummies, which are in fact desiccated corpses remarkably well preserved thanks to the dry climate, were brought to the museum from Lou-lan and were first believed to date from the early Middle Ages or, at the most, from the Kushan period (first centuries A.D.). This, at any rate, was the opinion of Sir Aurel Stein, who saw them at the site in 1907.

> ... the absolute aridity of the climate since ancient times had assured here a truly remarkable state of conservation of the bodies of men and women found in graves outside what evidently was a look-out post occupied by indigenous Lou-lan people. Several of the bodies were wonderfully well preserved together with their burial deposits... It was a strange sensation to look down on figures which but for the parched skin seemed like those of men asleep... and who, no doubt, were content with this dreary Lop region 2000 years ago. The characteristics of the men's heads showed close affinity to that Homo Alpinus type which... still remains the prevailing element in the racial constitution of the present population of the Tarim basin.[1]

Stein already noticed the 'Alpine character' of their features, but their dating by Professor Mair to as far back as 2000 B.C. may, eventually, transform the established opinion of the ethnic and cultural origins of Xinjiang's earliest population. Another interesting aspect of the 'mummies' is the remarkably good state of preservation of textiles that have been found on them. Their materials and weaving techniques were analysed by E. Wayland Barber.[2]

West of Urumchi, in the valley of the upper Ili, the fifteenth-century mausoleum of **Tughluk Timur Khan** should be mentioned. Situated near the town of Huoch'eng (Khoros), it is a cube-shaped structure domed with a large, Timurid-style *iwan*. Its tiled decoration is rather damaged, but inscription bands in Thulth and Naskhi can still be seen lining the *pishtak* and the pointed arch of the entrance vault. Inside the arch is a geometrical ornament in stylised Kufic. Other decoration consists of vertical bands of tiled geometrical and floral ornaments on the front facade and on the tympan above the entrance arch.

Also west of Urumchi, near the town of Hutupi, the **Kangjiashimenzi** anthropomorphic rock-carvings were explored in 1991 and again in 1997. The low-relief images, dating probably to the second and first millennia B.C., depict human figures engaged in some fertility rituals. As other rock-carvings in Eurasia (see, for example, Tamgaly Tash, p. 165) are mainly zoomorphic, the site of Kangjiashimenzi is, in a way, unique.[3]

The oasis of **Turfan** (Turpan) is, next to Tun-huang, one of the most important sites in Xinjiang. On the outskirts of the town itself, an eighteenth-century minaret is the dominant building of the oasis. Called **Imin minaret** (and sometimes, after its builder, Suleiman Wang), it is decorated with a profusion of simple, geometrical ornaments of monochrome baked bricks. Next to it is a rather plain mosque with a light ceiling supported on wooden columns. (See Plate 69.) Several cemeteries, some with vaulted *mazars*, are in the neighbourhood.

To the west are the spectacular ruins of **Jiao-he** (also called in some sources Kia-ho or Yarkhoto), the capital of the kingdom of Che-Shi-Qian (Kia Che), dating from around 200 B.C. to A.D. 450 and corresponding roughly to the Kushan period in the west. (See Plate 83.) It stands on a promontory between two steep river valleys. The name, in fact, means 'city of joining rivers'. The citadel and the remnants of a *stupa* within the precinct of a Buddhist monastery can be clearly discerned.

After its demise the centre shifted to another site, now called **Gaochang** (or, alternatively, Karakhoja, Kotcho or Idikut Shahri, i.e. the town of Idikut). (See Plate 53.) Its origins go back to around A.D. 110, and it was definitely abandoned in the fourteenth century, having reached its peak in the ninth. A number of buildings can be seen here. Near the top end of the site there is a Buddhist *stupa* with niches where statues used to be and, next to it, a vaulted structure with the dome supported on interesting early squinches. Elsewhere, walls of palaces and temples, the grid of streets and the ramparts with many towers are still partially preserved. There were four gates, and the streets connecting them crossed in the centre where the mausoleum of Uighur Manichaean kings stood. In the seventh and eighth centuries a remarkable series of portraits, now in Berlin, were produced here.

They are described by Talbot-Rice:

> In each case a single sitter was portrayed on a large silk panel in hieratic pose, yet often shown holding a flower in one hand. The paintings combine physical exactitude with real psychological insight. Generally, only kings and soldiers of distinction appeared on these panels... certain items of their armour recall Assyrian models and others Gandharan ones, but those made of solid pieces of metal are obviously of local origin. The portraits foreshadow very similar pictures of far smaller size produced by Islamic painters in Persia.[4]

On the northern fringes of the oasis two sites should be mentioned. **Bezeklik** was a Buddhist cave-monastery where a number of wall-paintings still exist showing Iranian and Soghdian influence as well as that of India and China. (See Plate 81.) In Bezeklik, as well as in other cave-monasteries in the area mentioned below (Kyzyl, Kumtura, Kyzyl Kara), the wall-paintings suffered considerable damage in different periods. Some were damaged after the Islamic conquest, some were taken down, often rather brutally, by Western expeditions, and the Red Guards during the 'Cultural Revolution' did the rest. As a consequence, better preserved are those out of reach, high on the walls and on ceilings.

Astana is a series of underground tombs (Karakhoja tombs) dating from A.D. 273 to 782. Beautifully preserved frescoes with strong Chinese influence can be seen in some; two mummies of tall men are in one of them. (See Plate 54.)

Stein took down some of the Bezeklik frescoes and shipped them to the museum in Delhi. He describes the monastery as

> an extensive series of ruined temple cellas, partly cut in the rock, their walls decorated with paintings in tempera dating from Uighur times and representing scenes of Buddhist legends and worship in considerable variety of style and subject. In richness and artistic merit they surpassed any similar remains in the Turfan region...[5]

Stein also opened some of the Astana tombs, where he found 'neatly worked models of household furniture and utensils as well as many painted stucco figurines intended to represent the attendance to be provided for the dead in another world...'[6]

A number of interesting sites can be found north and south of the town of Kucha, half-way between Turfan and Kashgar. Some 15 miles south of the town, in **Kumtura**, there are about ninety Buddhist caves with some inscriptions in runic or old Turkish script, in old Uighur and Sanskrit. When a house was recently built in Kumtura, a chest full of papers with runic inscriptions was found. It was probably an old Turkish book, but the finders were so scared of charms that they burnt everything. Poucha[7] visited Kumtura, copied some of the inscriptions and also saw the remaining frescoes, which were not taken away by von Le Coq fifty years previously. According to recent reports, the frescoes are increasingly threatened by humidity rising from an artificial lake nearby.

To the north of the modern town, in the foothills of the mountains, are the ruins of **Subashi** believed to be the capital of the kingdom of Qinci. The citadel and the temple mound can be seen, as well as the walls, ruined houses etc. The city dates approximately from the fourth century, the palace probably from the fifth. It was destroyed and abandoned in the twelfth. The palace walls show interesting patterns of layers of unbaked bricks and river-gravel fixed in mortar.

At **Kyzyl**, north-west of Kucha, there was a Buddhist monastery consisting of some 235 caves, cut deep into the rock. Some were monk's cells, some were temples, others served as stores or workshops. Each temple usually had an ante-room and behind it a shrine with a statue. Wall-paintings there date from the fifth to the eighth centuries. Some temples are domed, as in Persia; their paintings are older and show Indo-Iranian influence with some Hellenistic elements. In one of the biggest caves, von Le Coq found a library with manuscripts on palm-leaves, birch-bark, paper and wood, with texts in Sanskrit and Tokharian, all very well preserved.[8]

The first period of wall-paintings at Kyzyl may be dated from A.D. 450 to about 650.[9] It is characterised by precise modelling, subdued and discreet colours, grey, brown-red, dark brown and bright green. Indian influence is dominant, but Sasanian elements may also be found. The second period is dated by Hackin[10] as A.D. 650 to 750. Modelling is less apparent, colours are brighter, and Sasanian influence dominates both in appearance and in dress. In the military scenes, for example, the knights of Kucha wear cone-shaped helmets, armour and long lances reminiscent of Sasanian knights and, at the same time, of Sarmatian horse-men from the frescoes of Panticapaeum in Crimea.[11]

Not far from there, on a promontory between two deep valleys, the monastery of **Kyzyl Kara** also consists of a number of caves decorated with frescoes. (See Plates 61 and 82.) There are rows of paintings of small Buddhas, on the ceiling a band of *apsaras*, with symbols of the sun and the moon, the wind etc. In one place there is an image of a bird with two faces. In another cave, the ceiling has two bands of *apsaras* and musicians in alternating black and white. Fifty other caves are in a place called **Sim-Sim**, 30 miles from Kucha.

East of Kucha, in the oasis of Karashahr, the ruins of what is now called the city of **Shorchuq** are probably those of another ancient capital. The layout was similar to that of Idikut Shahri. It was a city of temples and shrines; some domed structures in Persian style were tombs. Art objects found here by von Le Coq were mostly in Gandhara style. The city was destroyed by fire some time in the second half of the eighth century. Few of the frescoes survived.

At Tumshuq, between Kucha and Karashahr, there are two monasteries, **Toqquz Sarai** and **Tumshuq Tagh**, the frescoes of which show a marked Indo-Iranian influence. It is interesting to compare them with those of Shorchuq, lying east of Karashahr, where Chinese influence is more dominant.

Grousset has words of high praise for the society of Kucha in the seventh century.

This society, as we know it from the texts and frescoes in Kyzyl and Kumtura, seems a strange success, almost a paradox in time and space. It benefited from all the intellectual heritage of India, brought in by the Buddhist civilisation, and on the other side, used caravan links with Iran to copy material civilisation of Sasanian Persia. It seems like a dream, that such an elegant and sophisticated society could develop only a few days' ride from all these Turco-Mongolian hordes, on the border of all that barbarity, on the eve of being submerged by the most uncivilised of all primitives. It is a sheer miracle that it could survive so long on the fringes of the steppe, protected only by stretches of desert and threatened every day by the raids of the nomads.[12]

NOTES ON CHAPTER XIII
Full details of abbreviations and publications are in the Bibliography

1   Stein, A., *On Ancient Central Asian Tracks*, pp. 135–36.
2   Wayland-Barber, E., *The Mummies of Urumchi*.
3   Davis-Kimball, *The Kangjiashimenzi Petroglyphs*.
4   Talbot-Rice, *Ancient Art of Central Asia*, p. 197.
5   Stein, *Ancient Tracks*, p. 230.
6   Stein, *Ancient Tracks*, p. 234.
7   Poucha, P., *Innermost Asia*, p. 151.
8   The Grunwedel-Von le Coq expeditions are referred to by Dabbs in *History...*, p. 125ff.
9   Grousset, *L'Empire*, p. 91.
10 Hackin, J., *Buddhist Art in Central Asia*.
11 Grousset, *L'Empire*, p. 9.
12 Grousset, *L'Empire*, p. 92.

XIV

TUN-HUANG TO
KASHGAR

THE SITE OF TUN-HUANG lies 14 miles south-east of the village and contains 480 caves. There are wall-paintings, statues, painted ceilings and altars from the fourth to the fourteenth centuries, from the Northern Wei to the Yuan dynasties. One of the inscriptions gives the year A.D. 366 as the date when these cave-temples and shrines were founded. The caves of Tun-huang were known to Europe as early as 1879, when a Hungarian traveller visited them and later described them to Stein.[1] Most of the buildings have now crumbled and no decorations from the earliest centuries survive, but in many caves there still stand statues of Buddhas and bodhisattvas modelled out of stucco in Graeco-Bactrian or Gandhara style. However, in scenes depicting the lives of monks and in the floral motifs Chinese style predominates.[2]

The walled-in library was discovered by a Taoist priest in 1900. He was restoring one of the wall-paintings when he noticed that underneath the fresco (in reality tempera) were bricks not rock. He knocked a hole into the wall and found behind a room full of scrolls. Seven years later he met Stein, showed him his treasure, and sold him part of it. The following year, when Paul Pelliot met him, there was still enough left for the French scholar to acquire some 15,000 manuscripts.

There were Buddhist religious texts from the fifth century, written in Chinese and in Brahmi; further Tibetan manuscripts; one of the oldest Tibetan chronicles covering the years 650–763; manuscripts written in the Iranian-Soghdian language and Aramaic script;[3] old Turkish Manichaean texts and also a Turkish book written in the Orkhon-Yenisei runic script etc. The Buddhist paintings in the caves were described in detail by Stein.[4]

In **Lou-lan**, apart from the desiccated corpses, or 'mummies', already mentioned, and now in the Museum of Urumchi, the excavations revealed a number of houses built in the same style as those at Niya, but only one *stupa*, which seems to have been the only religious building there.

In **Miran** a Buddhist temple was found consisting of a cella that was square on the outside and circular on the inside, where there was a *stupa*. It is possible that the whole was vaulted over. Several other monasteries were founded there in the third and fourth centuries A.D. Many of their shrines were set up in caves, the walls and ceilings of which were covered with paintings. Miran's art stemmed from India and Gandhara, but was of a subtler character than either of these and attached importance to figural compositions.[5] Miran's style and iconography were then adopted by Tun-huang and numerous other centres in eastern Xinjiang. From the period of Tibetan occupation (eighth and ninth centuries) Stein noticed a Buddhist *stupa* and scraps of paper and wood inscribed with Tibetan texts. A ruined fort on the same site also yielded a large amount of Tibetan documents.

Niya, further west, is an important site on the river of that name, where in 1901 Stein found wooden tablets and manuscripts in Kharosthi and Sanskrit, as well as seals and figurines with motifs of Greek origin. Stein visited the site again in 1906 and, among other things, found in the ruins of a large building a whole set of Kharosthi records and a cellar with a complete archive.

> Beyond a small room which seemed to have served as an antechamber for attendants, there adjoined a large apartment. It was a room twenty-six feet square with a raised platform of plaster running along three of its sides, very much as in the 'Aiwan' or hall of any modern Turkistan house of some pretension... a raised roof had been arranged to admit light and air just as in large modern houses.[6]

The houses at Niya were decorated with frescoes of which some fragments were found. There was a *stupa* and a temple with a hall where the excavations also yielded fragments of frescoes.

The site of **Endere** was abandoned already around A.D. 645. The fort, or citadel, which dates from the time of the Tibetan invasion, was surrounded by a circular wall within which was a temple and a palace. North of the fort a *stupa* was found built on a square, three-tier base on which stood a cylindrical drum.

North-east of Khotan, the site of **Dandan-Uilik** yielded a number of Chinese documents dating from the years 781–90. (See Plate 62.) Obviously, the Tibetan invasion that marked the end of the Tang domination in the Tarim basin was also the reason for the abandonment of these places. Documents found here were also in Khotanese Saka language, written in the Indian Brahmi alphabet while others were in Sanskrit. The Saka texts were mostly translations from Sanskrit and Tibetan (see also p. 170).

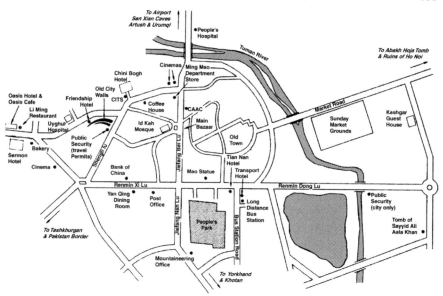

PLAN 11 **Kashgar**

When the small eighth-century temple was excavated, the external walls were found to have been adorned originally with paintings which included figural scenes. One showed a group of youths riding camels and horses. Some riders are Chinese looking, others Persian and more particularly Sasanian. All have haloes to indicate that they are not only legendary but also holy personages. Dandan-Uilik was abandoned in 791, but in Tang times Chinese influence had made itself particularly strongly felt there.[7]

The paintings of Dandan-Uilik are among the most important ones found in Xinjiang. Fragments of frescoes, paintings on wood, stucco and clay were also found on the site of **Farhad-Beg Yailaki**, which was a vast complex containing six temples inside an enclosure with a further one outside it. At **Rawak** there was a monastery with a huge *stupa* built on a three-tier base and accessible by four stairways, a feature also found at Taxila, Pakistan. Among the paintings found at **Balawaste**, east of Khotan, the best known is the Buddha Vairocana, head and upper part of the body with tattooed chest and arms.

Not only was the Khotanese school strongly influenced by China, it was also highly appreciated there, and Chinese artists were in turn influenced by it. It was also greatly esteemed in Tibet. Khotanese artists followed Buddhist monks there, bringing with them styles and traditions that they imposed on the Tibetans.

All communities along the Tunhuang trade-route further east were profoundly influenced by the art of Khotan.

In the city of **Kashgar** (Kashi in Chinese) the most interesting monument is the mausoleum of **Apak Khoja**. (See Plates 58 and 60.) It is an important shrine with a number of tombs, built in the late Timurid style in the seventeenth century. The walls are lined with ceramic tiles of rather inferior quality, the dominant colours being green and yellow, with some blue. With its tiled dome and four minarets it may remind of a miniature, brightly coloured and not-so-magnificent Taj Mahal.

The mausoleum of **Yusuf Kader Khan** is the tomb of an eleventh-century sage. It was also built in the Timurid style, and the original date of the building is not known. It is now in full reconstruction with tiles predominantly blue and white. The Great Mosque (**Id-Kah**) is a nineteenth-century building of limited interest. The mausoleum of **Sayid Ali Arslan Khan** is a modest structure of unbaked bricks, next to a vast cemetery with many vaulted *mazars*. (See Plate 59.)

The old town is a maze of little lanes opposite the Id-Kah Mosque. A short stretch of the old city wall, perhaps late medieval, can still be seen not very far from the old British Consulate building.

The main attraction of present-day Kashgar is its huge Sunday market.

North of Kashgar, on the outskirts of the town of Artush, is the mausoleum of the Karakhanid ruler **Bugra Khan**. Built in the eleventh century, it has undergone several reconstructions and little now remains of its original outlook.

West of Kashgar, the road to the Ferghana valley was first opened in 1935 when the Russian penetration of Xinjiang was on the increase. It was closed again for most of the time after the Second World War and was reopened only recently when the Central Asian republics became independent.

South of Kashgar, on the road to the Pamir, the small town of Tashkurghan (not to be confused with the town of the same name in north Afghanistan) boasts an ancient fort, now in a rather dilapidated state, which is most probably late medieval, but may have more ancient origins. In fact, Ptolemy mentions it as a stop on the road to China.

The road south of Tashkurghan is a modern one leading to the Khunjerab Pass and links with the Karakorum Highway of Pakistan.

The ancient caravan road branched west of it towards the Kilik and Mintaka Passes and from there to Kashmir. Between Kashgar and Tashkurghan two more roads, or rather tracks, branch off to the west, the first one to the former Russian Pamir (which is now Tajikistan's), the second to the Wakhan valley and into Afghanistan.

88. Mausoleum of Hazret Ali, Mazar-i Sharif

89. The citadel walls, Balkh

90. City walls, Ghazni

91. Friday Mosque, Herat. Inner courtyard

92. Friday Mosque, Herat (detail)

93. ABOVE. Tower of Masud III, Ghazni

94. BELOW. Tower of Masud III, Ghazni (detail)

Balbal. Turkish
vestone. Tashkent
useum

Balbal. Turkish
vestone. Tashkent
useum

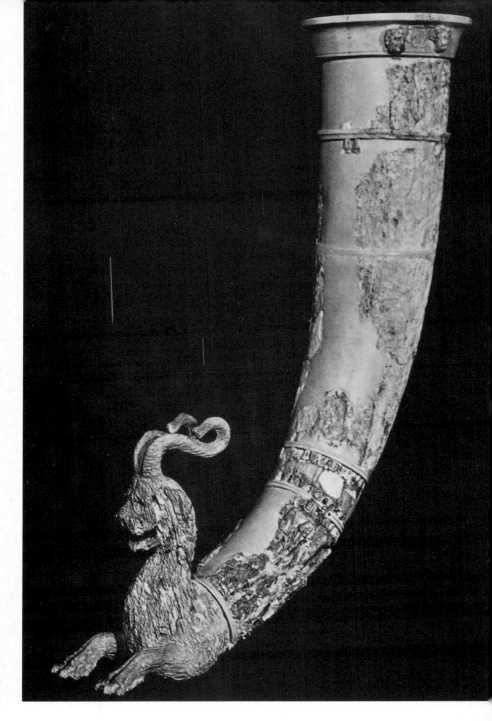

97. Parthian art. Ivory rhyton from Nisa

NOTES ON CHAPTER XIV
Full details of abbreviations and publications are in the Bibliography

1 Professor de Loczy, head of the Hungarian Geological Survey, was a member of Count Szechenyi's expedition and thus a pioneer of modern geographical exploration in Kansu.
2 Talbot-Rice, *Ancient Art*, p. 219.
3 Stavisky, Bongard, Levin, *Abstracts of Papers...*
4 Stein, *Ancient Tracks*, pp. 190–207.
5 Talbot-Rice, *Ancient Art*, p. 214.
6 Stein, *Ancient Tracks*, p. 71.
7 Talbot-Rice, *Ancient Art*, p. 206.

PART IV
AFGHANISTAN

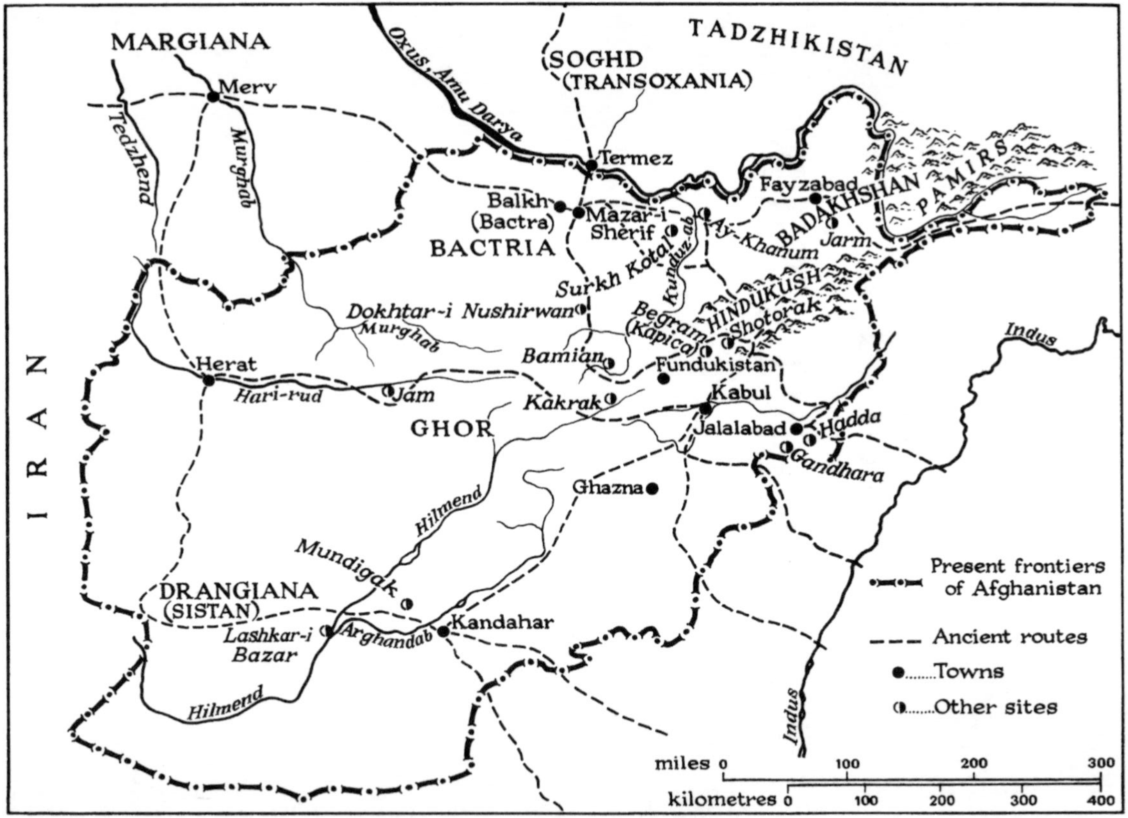

MAP 9 Afghanistan

XV

HISTORY

THE HISTORY OF AFGHANISTAN is so complex that every attempt at simplification must inevitably lead to superficiality and confusion. Perhaps, in view of what has been said in Chapter II it may suffice to say that all the nomadic incursions that affected Central Asia also played their role in the history of Afghanistan. The Saka, the Yue-chi, the Hephthalites, the Turks, the Arabs, the Seljuks, the Mongols – they all left their traces in the economic as well as the cultural pattern of the country. They destroyed irrigation, diverted caravan trade and decimated the population, but they also brought new impetus to the arts, new elements in ornament and design, and provided, broadly speaking, a sort of cross-fertilisation between one area and the other, between the civilisation of the nomads and that of the sedentary peoples.

At the time of the Achaemenids, Afghanistan was a loosely administered set of eastern *satrapies* of the empire. The Greeks brought in an alien element implanted on the Iranian cultural base, which, in its turn, got mixed with Indian influences brought in by the westward expansion of Buddhism. In the Kushan times, the art of Gandhara flourished and expanded north as far as Xinjiang (see p. 37 and Chapter XII). Then, for a century and a half, the Afghan provinces were again part of the Persian Empire under the Sasanians, with a corresponding increase of Iranian cultural influence. Buddhism and Zoroastrianism coexisted peacefully until the Arab invasion produced a new religion and with it a new cultural pattern.

At the court of the Ghaznavid and Ghorid sultans (tenth to twelfth centuries) the settled Iranian culture mingled with the nomadic Turkish one while the repeated raids into the Indian subcontinent inevitably exercised some influence upon the rulers of both dynasties.

After the devastating incursions of the Mongols and of Timur, Afghanistan, or more precisely its western part, experienced a century of prosperity under Timur's successors, Shahrukh and Husayn Baykara.

After a lengthy period of war between principalities, Afghanistan became part of the empire of a Turkish usurper, Nadir Shah, who defeated in turn the Safavid shah of Persia and the Moghul sultan of Delhi. After his assassination, the chief of the Durrani (Abdali) tribe, Ahmad Shah, gained supremacy over other Afghan tribes and in quick succession extended his holdings as far as Khorassan in the west and the Punjab in the east.

In the first half of the nineteenth century Afghanistan became a pawn in the 'Great Game' between the two great powers of the time, Britain advancing into the Punjab and Russia moving into Central Asia. In 1839, the British army moved into Afghan territory while the Russians moved against Khiva. Both expeditions ended in disaster. The Russians became bogged down in the desert without ever reaching their target, while the British, in 1842, had to retreat from Kabul and on the way to Jalalabad were massacred by the Afghans.

While the tug-of-war between Britain and Russia continued for the rest of the century, Afghanistan was, after 1880, reunited under the firm rule of Amir Abdurrahman who, in a series of radical reforms, tried to modernise the country, break the power of local strongmen and introduce an administrative structure based on provinces governed by appointed governors. In 1884 the occupation of Merv brought the Russians into the vicinity of Afghanistan, and both the amir and the British were worried about the possibility of a Russian advance on Herat. The town's defences were hastily strengthened and it was in the course of these works that the remnants of the famous Musalla were destroyed.

In 1893 the boundaries between Afghanistan and India, as well as between Afghanistan and Russia, were fixed by the Durand Commission. The McMahon Commission similarly established, in 1903, the border between Afghanistan and Persia. Nevertheless, a stretch of this border was definitely fixed as late as 1935.

The rivalry between Britain and Russia continued after the First World War, with both sides competing for influence in Kabul. The reforms aimed at western-style modernisation introduced in the late 1920 by King Amanullah provoked an uprising and had to be partially revoked by the king's successor, Nadir Shah. Under King Zahir Shah Afghanistan accepted aid from Germany, Italy and Japan, and prior to World War Two the Germans had become the most important foreign community in Kabul.

After the war the Afghans supported the idea of an independent 'Pushtunistan' comprising also the north-western province of Pakistan. Frustrated by the American aid to Pakistan, the Afghans turned to the Soviet Union, whose aid led to the increased influence of the Soviets in Kabul. In the late 1950s Afghan officers were trained in the USSR and Soviet advisers were active in Afghan military schools. A crisis over 'Pushtunistan' led to the closure of the Pakistani border in 1961 and left Afghanistan wholly dependent on the USSR. In 1973, King Zahir was deposed and the Prime Minister, Muhammad Daoud, proclaimed a republic with himself as President. The Soviet penetration increased under his rule until, in 1978, a group of Moscow-trained officers staged a bloody coup in which Daoud was assassinated. A Communist-led government under Nur Muhammad Taraki took power, but factional strife within the party led to another coup in 1979. After only three months, in December 1979, the Russians invaded Afghanistan and installed a puppet government under Babrak Karmal as President. This sparked off a guerilla war that lasted ten years, without the Russians ever being able to pacify the country. Their ignominious retreat in 1989, after heavy casualties, triggered off the collapse of the Soviet Union. In Afghanistan their retreat provoked a civil war that lasts to this day, with millions of refugees in Iran and Pakistan, and with the risk of militant Islamism spreading over into the newly independent Central Asian republics.

XVI

THE CENTRE
AND THE EAST

ALTHOUGH A VERY ANCIENT CITY, Kabul was overshadowed in the earliest part of its history by Kapisa (Begram), which was the capital and the royal residence in the time of Greek Bactria as well as of the Kushan Empire. Kapisa remained the centre of the area under the Sasanians and the Hephthalites. Suen-Tsang, the Chinese pilgrim of the seventh century A.D., barely mentions Kabul, but describes Kapisa at length and with enthusiasm. Kabul began to play a more important role at the time of the Arab conquest, when the victorious advance of Islam was halted by the stubborn resistance of its rulers, the Turkish, Indianised dynasty of the Kabulshahs or Ratbilshahs, also referred to as the Turk-Shahi. Although Kabul was taken in 644, the Arab occupation did not last long, and the Turk-Shahis survived for another 200 years, until, around 850, they were replaced by the purely Indian Hindushahis. The definitive victory of Islam came only with the Ghaznavids, who captured Kabul in 977.

In the time of the Timurids, **Kabul** was a provincial capital, but the real turning point came when Babur, the young Timurid prince of Ferghana, made it his capital in 1504. It was from here that he departed in 1525 for his celebrated conquest of India, but even after he established his imperial residence in Agra, he kept returning to Kabul. He also wished to be buried in the beautiful gardens that he founded. However, unrest following his death in 1530 prevented the immediate fulfilment of this wish, and it was only nine years later that his wife brought his remains to Kabul.

Bagh-i Babur Shah, Babur's Garden, is the first of the famous Moghul gardens of which a number were built by Babur and his successors in Delhi, Lahore and Srinagar. It follows the traditional Persian principle of the Chahar-Bagh, or Four Gardens, which is a square divided into quarters by channels of running water.

The garden consisted of several such squares laid on sloping terraces. In the centre of one of them usually stood a pavilion.

The **Bala Hissar**, or the citadel, stands on a rocky spur where a fortress is known to have stood already in the seventh century. The walls of Kabul, 18 feet high and almost 12 feet thick, which the Hephthalites are said to have built originally, start here. It was in this citadel that Babur was married and his son and successor Humayun was born. In Moghul times, gardens and palaces were built within the citadel, which probably resembled the forts of Lahore, Delhi or Agra. It became a royal residence again at the end of the eighteenth century under Timur Shah. In the early nineteenth century there was a Lower Fortress with three palaces and, at the top of the hill, the Upper, or Inner, Fortress with the armoury and the prison. The British army was quartered in part of the citadel for a short time in 1839. It was then sporadically occupied by the ruling amirs until the 1870s. In 1879, it was damaged by an explosion of the powder magazine, and in 1880 it was finally demolished by the orders of General Roberts, in retaliation for the massacre of the British mission the previous year.

The Christian cemetery contains the tomb of Sir Aurel Stein, the explorer and archaeologist who died here in 1943 at the age of eighty-two.

Near the village of Begram, some 40 miles north-east of Kabul, at the confluence of the Panjshir and Ghorband Rivers, lies a long mound encircled by high ruined ramparts. This was **Kapisa**, the summer capital of the Kushan kings. It was excavated twice, in the late 1930s and the early 1940s. The stratigraphic sequence established by Ghirshman in 1941–42 shows three major occupation periods. The first was from the second century B.C. to second century A.D., which coincides with the Indo-Parthian level of Taxila. This was perhaps the capital of the last Indo-Greek (Graeco-Buddhist) kingdom. The second was from the second to third centuries A.D., a Kushan city probably destroyed by the Sasanian king Shapur in 241. The third was from the third to fifth centuries A.D., a period up to the Hephthalite invasion. This invasion was, of course, not the end of Kapisa, for Suen-Tsang, when he visited it in the seventh century, found it a very lively place, although a little rough.

> The Kingdom of Kia-pi-che has a circumference of about four thousand li. In the north, it leans on the snowy mountains; on the other three sides it is surrounded by black mountains. The distance around the capital is about ten li. The country is well suited for the cultivation of cereals and wheat; there is a great number of fruit trees… The climate is cold and windy. The character of the inhabitants is cruel and rude. Their language is low and coarse and their marriage is just a shameful mixing of sexes… The inhabitants wear dresses of wool, sometimes lined with fur. In trade they use gold and silver coins and small bits of copper the size and shape of which is different than in other kingdoms. Their king… rules

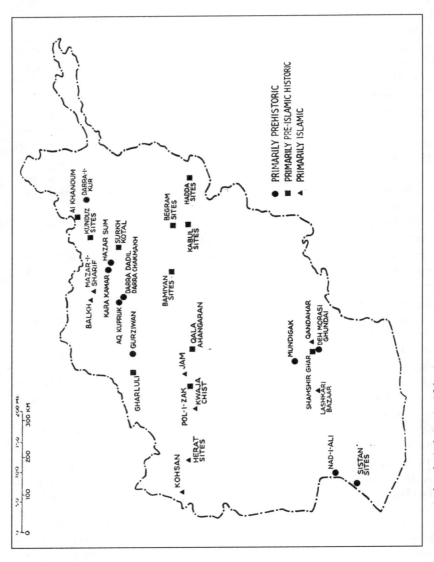

MAP 10 Archaeological sites in Afghanistan

over a dozen kingdoms. He loves and protects his people; he respects and honours the Three Jewels. Every year he has a silver statue of Buddha made, eighteen feet high and then he calls the Grand Assembly in which he dispenses grants to the needy and alms to widowed men and women... There are a good hundred monasteries there with more than six thousand monks who all study the doctrine of the Greater Vehicle (Mahayana)... There are several dozen temples of various deities and a thousand heretics. Some of them go naked, others rub themselves with ashes or make bonnets of skull-bones and wear them on their heads... The princes of various kingdoms in India return in summer to Kia-pi-che; in spring and in autumn they stay in the kingdom of Kien-to-lo (Gandhara). This is why, in each place where these hostages stay for three seasons, there was a monastery built for them. This one, which we describe, has been built as their summer residence. This is why, on all the walls, they have painted the portraits of these hostages whose faces and dress resemble those of the men from the East [sc from China][1]

The excavations of Hackin (1936–40) yielded some of the most spectacular museum pieces found in this century. In the so-called new royal city two rooms were found that were probably a rich merchant's treasure or warehouse. They were filled with luxury goods and rare Buddhist objects, carved ivories from India, vases and lacquerware from China, classical Graeco-Roman bas-reliefs, Graeco-Egyptian bronzes, Phoenician glassware. There was jewellery from India, Rome, Egypt and Central Asia. Some specimens even resembled those found in Sarmatian tombs in the Russian steppe.

Two Buddhist monasteries were excavated to the east of the site of Begram, dating probably from the first to third centuries A.D. One of them, **Shotorak** (Baby Camel), was the monastery built for the Chinese hostages taken by the Kushans.

The most romantic of these dead monasteries is the Shahzade-i Chin, 'The Chinese Princes'. It is, in fact, the place where a clutch of distinguished Chinese hostages was held, in honourable confinement, by the Kushan emperor Kanishka. The emperor is said to have paid his prisoners the compliment of sharing their monastery-prison with them for a month.[2]

These were the 'men from the East' whose portraits on the walls Suen-Tsang saw some five centuries later. It was a large complex consisting of two spacious courtyards and ten *stupas* bearing bas-reliefs in schist depicting scenes from the life of the Buddha. The main *stupa* in the first courtyard measured 27 feet square and was built of stone, whereas the surrounding buildings were built of clay. Inside the *stupa* was found a terracotta vase filled with earth. No other relics were found, and it is assumed that the earth probably came from some holy spot connected with the life of the Buddha, and was itself a relic.

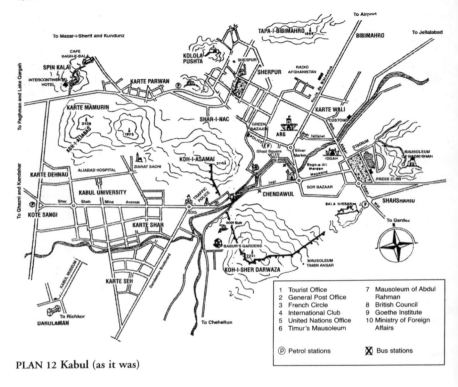

PLAN 12 **Kabul** (as it was)

There were four small *stupas* in front of the main one, some 4.5 feet square. None had a cupola. All show certain similarities with the *stupas* at Mohra Moradu, Jaulian and Takht-i Bhai in north Pakistan. The *sangharama* or monastery, was a two, or possibly three-storey building. Its ceilings were probably made of matting covered with clay and supported by wooden columns. Everywhere, the dome, or cupola, is conspicuous by its absence.

The style of the bas-reliefs belongs to the latest period of Gandharan art, but the reliefs are heavier, more rigid and more schematic. Among other sculptures the most remarkable find was a throne supported by two lions. The other site, **Paitava**, is a *stupa* dating from the third or fourth centuries A.D. with some stucco heads and bas-reliefs in schist.

The **Guldara stupa**, in desolate countryside about 3 miles from the village of the same name, stands on a square platform on a high rocky spur. Below, in a sheltered corner, a spring with a single tree catches the eye, the only refreshing sight in the stony desert. (See Plate 72.) The *stupa* has a square base, a two-tier drum and a dome. The dome has collapsed and only part of it is still in position. The square base is an unusual feature, as most Buddhist *stupas* in Afghanistan have only a high cylindrical drum. The base is decorated on three sides with a row of false columns and a central niche; on the south-west side, a staircase leads to the platform on top of the base. The decoration on the lower part of the drum is fairly simple, but the upper part shows elaborate ornamental ledges, which form a false arcade of alternating half-circles and half-hexagons. In between is a motif symbolising the umbrella mast. According to some authorities,[3] this motif is that of a console carrying ornamental stucco eagles with spread wings, painted gold. The masonry, both on the base and on the drum is of the 'diaper' kind, typical of the Kushan period. The layers of schist that make the wall-facing are interspersed with large blocks of stone of a different colour, thus achieving a pronounced ornamental effect. Gold Kushan coins and several other gold objects were found in the reliquary chamber inside the drum. The *stupa* was part of a monastery complex, the main building of which was excavated in 1963–64.

East of Kabul, the most important site is **Hadda**. It is the modern name of a group of Buddhist monasteries, *stupas* and caravanserais situated on the outskirts of the ancient city of Nagarahara, which corresponds to the present-day Jalalabad. The site is some 5 miles south of Jalalabad on what used to be one of the main caravan roads linking the Punjab and the Kabul area. It dates from the second to seventh centuries A.D., when the Jalalabad area was among the most sacred in the Buddhist world. There were reputedly as many as a thousand *stupas* in the land of Hilo, which is how the Chinese chroniclers referred to Hadda. So far, the French archaeological mission has explored more than five hundred of them.

There are seven main groups of ruins in the area; the most important of them is the site of Tepe Kalan, on which the excavations concentrated. They have yielded a fantastic number of statues in limestone, schist and stucco that show great similarity with the art of Gandhara and Taxila, although with a slightly provincial touch. Between 1923 and 1928, the French expeditions uncovered some 23,000 heads of Buddhas, bodhisattvas, various demons and other figures, such as donators, monks etc. Apart from the heads there were bas-reliefs and other sculptures depicting episodes from the Buddhist legends, scenes of offerings and individual persons. Some fragments of secular scenes were also found in addition to pieces of architectural decor. The art of Hadda comes from two main periods: the second to third centuries A.D. and the fifth century. It is a mixture of Bactrian, Graeco-Roman and Indian elements. The Western influence is particularly visible in the classic profiles, pseudo-Corinthian capitals, vine-scrolls and Roman drapery.

It was in Hadda that the stucco technique reached its peak. The bodies of figures were moulded in mud and covered with decorated gypsum plaster. The heads were made separately from lime plaster mixed with straw and pebbles, and then covered with a shell of stucco, which consisted of lime, sand and marble dust. They were then painted in bright colours, pink and ochre, the hair often blue.[4]

The valley of **Bamiyan**, 146 miles north of Kabul, with its colossal statues and innumerable caves, has attracted the interest of travellers ever since the Buddhist pilgrims Fa-Sien and Suen-Tsang described it in the fifth and seventh centuries A.D. respectively.

The valley, which is some 9 miles long and not more than 2 miles wide lies at an altitude of 8250 feet, but it is well sheltered from winds and has abundant water supplies. (See Plate 84.) It is now as it was in the past, an oasis of intensive cultivation and refreshing greenery amidst the barren mountainous landscape that surrounds it on all sides. It became the home of a colony of Buddhist monks in the early stage of their movement across the Hindu Kush and into northern Afghanistan. It was conveniently situated half-way between the important cities of Balkh and Kapisa, on the caravan-route linking India with Bactria and Transoxania, at a place that, probably for centuries before, had been a natural caravan halt offering a sheltered resting place to traders and pilgrims, well equipped with provisions and repair facilities, grazing grounds and replacement mounts. Its additional attraction, which may well have been decisive for its selection as a place of worship, was a long, sheer vertical cliff-face of soft rock, eminently suitable for digging cave sanctuaries and carving statues. There was an established tradition of such sanctuaries in India, whence Buddhism came, and no doubt Ellora, Ajanta and others provided the models for the first cave sanctuaries at Bamiyan, just as they were to provide them for the similarly situated sites later developed in Xinjiang.

The most striking feature of Bamiyan are the two giant statues of the Buddha, carved in the cliff, one 115 feet and the other 175 feet high. Each is surrounded by a number of man-made caves of various sizes and shapes, some of them in elaborate sanctuary complexes. Between them there were other statues of seated Buddhas.

To the west of the statues was the capital city, its northern flank protected by the cliff. Nothing remains of that city, except perhaps some disused caves. A mound east of the 'small' Buddha, which hides the remnants of a *stupa*, is the only trace of an open-air construction from the Kushan period. The complex of caves surrounding the statue of the smaller Buddha originated as an extension of the monastery into the rock.

The caves were not spread haphazardly over the rock face. They formed organised units serving definite purposes, and they were connected by a wealth of communications, both horizontal and vertical. Steps and staircases were dug in the rock and horizontal galleries linked caves on the same level so that each complex had its own independent access. Unfortunately, many of these communications have been destroyed or blocked, and it is not easy nowadays to reconstruct the original picture.

The niches of the statues and several of the caves were decorated with frescoes of which a fair amount is still discernible. Their style is predominantly Indian with some Iranian elements.

The smaller of the two Bamiyan statues of the Buddha stands in the eastern part of the cliff in a niche 26 feet deep. Its disproportionately large head, wide shoulders and thick-set body betray an artistic primitivism as well as inexperienced craftsmanship. The hair is dressed in Greek fashion, the folds of the garment are stiff and unnatural. The face has been systematically obliterated. The whole statue has been hewn out of solid rock, with the exception of the folds and the forearms, which were made of plaster. The forearms are missing. The statue was covered with a layer of clay mixed with straw on top of which came a layer of mortar which was painted. The body was originally blue, the hands and the face were painted gold. The niche was decorated on the inside with frescoes, some of which are still clearly visible. They formed a vast composition centred around a lunar, or solar, deity surrounded on the right and on the left by two rows of figures, bodhisattvas, donators etc. There are strong indications that the frescoes, which resemble those found at Kyzyl and Kumtura in Xinjiang, are of Iranian origin and were probably executed in the fifth or sixth centuries A.D.

Artistically, the statue of the 'large' Buddha, which stands quarter of a mile farther west inside a trilobate niche, represents a considerable improvement. Its proportions are better balanced and it looks as if the artists modelled their work on certain Hellenistic statues. (See Plate 78.) On the other hand the ornamental folds of the garment are very shallow, and in places barely indicated, being thus closer to the schematic arrangement typical of the Gupta period, which differs considerably from the softer and deeper folds of the Hellenistic style. The face, again, has been completely destroyed; only part of the chin remains. The forearms, which are missing, were not cut out of the rock but were made of plaster carried on wooden beams. The legs were damaged by cannonballs fired by Nadir Shah's troops. The folds were modelled in plaster and fixed to the body by wooden pegs, the holes of which are clearly visible.

The body was probably painted red, while the face and the hands might again have been gold. Being later than its smaller counterpart, it must be assumed to have originated in the fifth or sixth centuries A.D.

The niche of this statue was also decorated with frescoes, the oldest of which can be seen on the lateral surfaces. There is, for example, a series of five medallions with two female and one male figure in each, surrounded by winged demons reminiscent of Gandharan iconography, a series of five Buddhas resembling those of Ajanta – although drawn much more clumsily – seated under the sacred fig tree with a group of royal donators, framed by architectural decoration and floral ornaments. There are female figures with Indian faces, semi-nude or thinly veiled in transparent robes, some dancing and others playing musical instruments. Behind each group can be seen a dome or an umbrella of a *stupa*. The contours of the figures were drawn in ochre, and indigo-blue was used for some surfaces which, again, points to the Indian origin and, in particular, to the Gupta period. Certain details of dress and hairstyle, as well as some decorative elements, show Iranian influence, while the virtuoso brush-stroke and the softness of lines betray a Chinese hand.[5]

In the valley of **Kakrak**, a short distance to the south-east of the main valley, another giant statue of the Buddha stands 23 feet high with its face intact in a niche amidst a group of cave sanctuaries. The niche was decorated with frescoes and sculptured ornaments.

Two other sites in the valley of Bamiyan must be mentioned. East of the township, the spectacular ruins on a high rocky promontory is the **Shahr-i Zohak**, the Town of Zohak, also called the Red City because the colour of its brick wall is reddish-brown. (See Plates 74 and 75.) Zohak, or Zahak, was in Iran's national epic, the *Shahname*, a tyrant reigning a thousand years, in another epic a legitimate king. The rulers of Ghor traced their ancestry to this legendary figure. According to Schlumberger, the fortress was originally a Turkish castle dating from the sixth or seventh centuries A.D. The ruins of the fortress are one of the most dramatic sights in the whole country. Soaring on inaccessible cliffs, perfectly blended with the natural rock, dominating the fertile valleys to the east, north and west with its three-tier ramparts, it was nevertheless conquered and destroyed by the Mongols of Chingiz-Khan. The same destiny befell the strongly fortified Islamic city of Bamiyan, the ruins of which are now known as the **Shahr-i Gholghola**, the City of Murmurs (more exactly, City of Noise). It was built in the eleventh century on a hillock south of the Bamiyan cliff, in the middle of a well-irrigated plain. The patterns of the bazaar, the mosque, the palaces and the caravanserais of this once prosperous city are still discernible in the maze of dilapidated clay walls. From the top a beautiful view extends towards the valley of Bamiyan in the north, the valley of Foladi in the south-west, the Kakrak valley due south and the majestic barrier of the Kuh-i Baba on the horizon behind it.

Almost exactly half-way between Kabul and Bamiyan, about 31 miles from the town of Charikar and 3 miles from the village of Siyahgerd, lies the site of **Fundukistan**, one of the most important monastic sites in the country. Excavations carried out in 1937 revealed a monastery complex consisting of a square courtyard surrounded by a wall with twelve niches, and with a small *stupa* in the centre. The architectural decoration, arcades with foliated scrolls and columns with pseudo-Corinthian capitals is perhaps less remarkable than the magnificent frescoes reflecting both Indian and Sasanian elements, and the sculptures reminiscent of the Indian Gupta school.[6]

NOTES ON CHAPTER XVI
Full details of abbreviations and publications are in the Bibliography

1   Translated from Julien, S., *Hiuan-Tsang*, pp. 40–42.
2   Toynbee, A., *Between Oxus and Jumna*, p. 128.
3   Auboyer, J., *Afghanistan et son art.*
4   Barthoux, J., 'Les fouilles de Hadda', *Mem. DAFA* IV, 1933.
5   Godard, A., Godard, J., Hackin, J., 'Les antiquités bouddhiques de Bamiyan', *Mem. DAFA* II, 1928.
6   Duprée, N., Duprée, L., Motamedi, A.A., *The National Museum of Afghanistan*, p. 99.

XVII

THE WEST

THE OASIS OF HERAT stretches along the right bank of the Hari Rud, between the river and the foothills of the Safid Kuh range, the ancient Paropamisus, in the north. On the left bank, the green belt is confined to the immediate vicinity of the river-bed. The stony and sandy desert begins, abruptly, only a few hundred yards from the river. From the air, it can clearly be seen that the irrigation network extended much further in the past and that the area of cultivated farmland began much higher upstream than now.

Herat is, without doubt, one of the oldest cities on Afghan soil. When Cyrus the Great of Persia conquered it in the sixth century B.C. it was already an important stronghold mentioned in the *Avesta* as Hairava. Alexander took it in 330 B.C., rebuilt and strengthened the fort, and gave it the name of Alexandria Ariana. It was held in succession by the Seleucids, Parthians, Kushans and Sasanians. For a period in the fifth and sixth centuries it was dominated by the Hephthalites, or White Huns, who ruled their empire from the nearby province of Badghiz. At the end of the sixth century it was sacked by the Turks, and in 645 fell to the Arabs. From then on, it remained firmly Muslim, but the story of conquest continued. It was taken by Mahmud of Ghazna in the year 1000, fell to the Seljuks after the defeat of the Ghaznavids in 1040, and to the Ghorids in 1175. Although the Ghorid domination lasted less than half a century, it is the earliest period from which some architectural monuments have been preserved in Herat.

Shortly before the Mongol invasion, Yakut considered Herat to be 'the richest and largest city he had ever seen'.[1] His contemporary, Kazwini, notes that 'here might be seen many mills turned by wind, not by water', for him an uncommon sight.[2] Some of these curious mills, working on the principle of a vertical shaft revolving in a cylindrical tower, still exist.

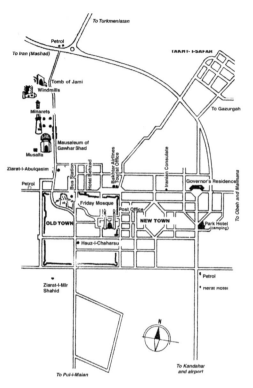

PLAN 13 Herat

The second period of prosperity came in the fifteenth century, under the Timurids, Shahrukh (1405–47) and Husayn Baykara (1469–1506). Shahrukh, Timur's fourth and youngest son became governor of Herat after his father's conquest of the city. When, after a brief interlude following Timur's death in 1405, he established himself as his successor, he made Herat the capital of the Timurid empire. Politically, culturally and commercially, it became the metropolis of Central Asia, competing with and, for a time, surpassing Samarkand.

The citadel (**Arg, Bala Hissar**) is an imposing building constructed in the ninth or tenth centuries on the site of an earlier fortress the origins of which would probably go back to antiquity. (See Plate 73.) No excavations have been carried out here, and the hypothesis that this may be the site of Alexander's fort, Alexandria Ariana, still awaits confirmation. The ramparts and round towers were rebuilt several times, especially by the Kart dynasty after the Mongol onslaught, and by Shahrukh in the wake of Timur's conquest. It forms a rectangle of approximately 4300 by 4600 feet, situated on an artificial mound in the

north-western corner of the city. A bastion built by Shahrukh between the
northern city wall and the north-eastern side of the fortress made the city and
the citadel into a single defensive complex. The ramparts of the fortress were
equipped with semicircular towers; on the bottom part of one of these in the
north-western part, remains of an inscription frieze with geometrical patterns
in glazed bricks could still be seen. This decorative frieze consisted of a wide
ornamental band framed in a curious way with dark and pale blue tiles and filled
in with a sophisticated imitation of Arabic calligraphy in pale blue.

Although after the citadel the Friday mosque was the oldest monumental
building in Herat, medieval texts contain surprisingly little information about it.
As we have seen in Ibn Hawkal, it stood in the midst of the chief market, and
no mosque in all Khorassan or Sistan was its equal in beauty. (See Plates 80, 91
and 92.) Other sources are even more laconic. We would have to wait until the
nineteenth century for a more meaningful description, and by then, of course,
the original aspect of the building might have been altered beyond recognition.
To Byron,

> this morose old mosque inside the walls growls a hoary accompaniment to the
> Timurid pageant of the suburbs... The Friday mosque was old and ruined before
> the Timurids were heard of. It is less ruined now they are not heard of. For seven
> centuries the people of Herat have prayed in it. They still do so, and its history is
> their history.[3]

The layout of the building is that of a traditional Iranian four-*iwan* mosque,
which developed from a combination of the original Arab *hypostyle* mosque and
an Iranian fire temple.[4] On the west side – or the south-west, according to some
sources – of a courtyard measuring approximately 300 by 195 feet is the main
iwan with a prayer hall, flanked by two minarets. Opposite is the entrance *iwan*,
and in the middle of the longer sides of the rectangle, two lateral *iwans*. All the
iwans are unusually deep. Inside the arcaded wings enclosing the courtyard are
halls of columns concealed behind the facade niches. Each of the courtyard
iwans has its counterpart in the outer facade. All outer *iwans* are flanked by two
minarets each, and there is a small turret in each corner.

The present state of the building is the result of restoration carried out since
the mid-1940s.

The general impression may be Timurid, and there are undoubted similarities
with other monuments of the same period, but conspicuous differences point to
earlier origins. For example, the pillars in the passages are remarkably strong, the
iwan vaults have unusual proportions, the points of the arches differ from the
usual Timurid style. Melikian-Chirvani,[5] who has analysed the building,
believed these elements to be closer to twelfth-or-thirteenth-century models.
There are at least three distinct items pointing to this period of origin: right and

left of the western *iwan*, the low vaulting and its brick pattern, in addition to the inscription along the base of the vault in the passage leading south from the *iwan*; a large portal on the south side of the eastern facade, half hidden under a layer of late Timurid decoration; and the remnants, still visible some forty years ago, of a mausoleum incorporated into the northern facade just behind the northern *iwan*.

The portal in the eastern facade was 'discovered' only in 1964, although Byron noticed 'a Kufic legend in fancy brick over an arch in the north-east corner',[6] and Wilber described it – with a photograph – in 1937.[7] Earlier stucco decoration has been found under Timurid tilework. The portal, which originally had a high arch lined with an inscription frieze, was framed by a band of script and flanked with two pillars covered with geometrical ornaments. The medallions decorating the spandrels of the arch and the patterns of the columns were executed in incised terracotta. The Kufic in the portal, likewise in incised terracotta, was more conservative in design than that in the passage, but also of a very high quality. The motifs in the frame are essentially the same as those on the minaret in Dawlatabad,[8] which again dates from the twelfth century.

Thus three separate sections of the mosque, lying west, east and north of the courtyard, date back to the early thirteenth century, to the reign of the successor to Ghiyat-ud-Din, Abu'l-Fath Muhammad ben Sam, or of his son. It can therefore be assumed that the layout of the Ghorid mosque was substantially the same as it is now and that all the subsequent restorations have little affected the inner structure. Only the eastern and western facades show sixteenth-century additions. The outer facades were, of course, completely reshaped. A beautifully decorated bronze cauldron stood until recently in front of the eastern *iwan*.

Walking north from the citadel past the recently restored fifteenth-century mausoleum of Abu'l-Kasim on the right, we arrive at a vast site stretching, on the left of the road, along both sides of an irrigation canal and marked by a number of high elegant minarets that from a distance look rather like a group of factory chimneys. There are six of these at present: four in the middle of an enormous field of rubble on the north side of the canal, the remaining two in the gardens on the south side of it. A beautiful mausoleum with a typical Timurid ribbed dome stands between the two. This is all that remains of what the French traveller, Ferrier, described in 1845 as 'one of the most accomplished, most imposing and most elegant architectural complexes in Asia'. It is the site of the **Musalla**, which, in the fifteenth century, was a vast complex of learning, a 'university district', founded by Queen Gawhar Shad, the wife of Shahrukh, in 1417 and extended and completed by Husayn Baykara at the end of the century. (See Plate 71.) Musalla means 'space (or place) for prayer'. In Arabic, the word originally indicated an open space oriented towards Mecca, the same as the Persian word 'namazgah'. Later, it was used in a wider sense to describe any place destined for religious gatherings.

There is a sketch made by a British officer just before the demolition of 1885. It shows the portal of the *madrasa* in an advanced state of decay, with one minaret out of the two; on the right, the arcades of the *madrasa* court; and behind, the *iwan* and the two domes of the Musalla. It was on this sketch that Byron[9] based his description, in which the Musalla had a monumental portal, a square courtyard with two-storey arcades, and four minarets. Opposite the portal, on the west side, was a single *iwan*, behind which were two circular chambers with saucer-shaped domes. Adjacent to the north side of the Musalla was the *madrasa*, inside which stood the royal mausoleum.

Turning now to the description of the existing buildings: the minaret with one gallery stood in the western corner of the courtyard of the Musalla, which according to a reconstruction measured some 386 by 231 feet. Its octagonal base was once covered with exquisitely carved marble panels. The whole tower was entirely covered with ornaments in mosaic faience and bands of calligraphy, of which only parts remain.

The other minaret, with two galleries, standing to the east of the mausoleum was probably one of the flanking towers of the entrance *iwan* of the *madrasa*. The galleries were supported by lavishly decorated stalactite vaults (*mukarnas*). On the tower itself, brick ornaments alternated with bands of tilework. Both minarets have lost their tops.

The four minarets on the north side of the canal form a square of some 330 feet, which was the area occupied by the *madrasa* of Husayn Baykara. The minarets are between 100 and 130 feet high, but their original height cannot be assessed as their tops, too, have collapsed. Their decoration consisted mainly of geometrical ornaments in mosaic faience, turquoise blue framed with white. Curiously enough, the white mosaic has survived better than the turquoise one, so that in parts bare bricks are laced with a pattern of white tiles.

The mausoleum, commonly ascribed to **Gawhar Shad**, stands in a pine grove not far from the canal. It is a squat square structure with a bulbous dome on a high drum, some 83 feet high. It has been almost entirely restored, and remnants of the original decoration can be found on the west side only. (See Plate 85.) The drum has also been partly restored, but a good deal of the decoration still exists. The dome, on the contrary, is in its original state, with a dilapidated top but with the lower part of the rib decoration still in place. (A damaged part of the top shown in a photograph in Byron has been repaired). The drum bears a high outer dome and itself exceeds the height of the lower, inner dome.

On the outside, the decoration of the dome consists, on the ribs, of geometrical ornaments in turquoise, blue and white tiles. At the bottom is a white-

and-blue band with medallions of rosettes and stylised lettering. The transition between the dome and the drum is made by stalactites, again decorated in blue and white. The upper part of the drum carries a band of rectangular medallions filled with floral ornaments, white on a blue background. In the middle part is an inscription frieze, now largely damaged, whereas the lower part consists again of ornamental rectangles, only much larger than at the top. Dark blue hexagons with stylised golden flowers are separated by natural brickwork with blue and white rectangles above and below.[10]

Inside, there are two zones of transition between the square base and the dome. First, four pointed squinches make the square into an octagon, and then a band of sixteen *mukarnas*-niches transform it into a sixteen-sided figure on which rests the dome. The dome and the transition zones offer one of the most spectacular decorations ever achieved in Islamic architecture. Intersecting pointed arches – which are remotely reminiscent of the gothic arch, but have nothing common with it,[11] divide the sphere into various polygons and *mukarnas* decorated half and quarter-domes bearing painted ornaments in lapis-blue, gold, ochre and white. The lapis-blue pigment was obtained from the genuine lapis-lazuli of Badakhshan.

It is not clear how many tombs were originally in the mausoleum. Some sources mention as many as twenty. Khanikov still saw nine in the 1860s. Yate saw five and Byron only three. There is nothing unusual in this, as the habit of re-using tombstones was widespread. Strangely enough, where Byron saw three, there are now six. According to Wolfe,[12] they belong to Gawhar Shad (d.1457), her son Baisanghur (d.1432 or 1433), his son Ala-ad-daula (d.1459), his grandson Ibrahim (also d.1459) and two other members of the family, Ahmad and Shahrukh ibn Sultan Abu Said (d.1493). As mentioned above, the mausoleum was originally built for Prince Baisanghur, who predeceased his mother; Golombek (and also Saljuqi, *Khiaban*) call it the mausoleum of Baisanghur and Gawhar Shad.[13]

Some 3 miles north-east from the city, and near the village of Gazurgah, stands the shrine also referred to as **Gazurgah**, built around the tomb of a Muslim saint, the Khoja Abdullah Ansari. Best described in an excellent monograph by L. Golombek (*The Timurid Shrine at Gazur Gah*, Toronto, 1968), the shrine is one of the most complex architectural and artistic monuments in the Islamic world. (See Plates 86 and 87.)

Gazurgah means 'bleaching ground', although some authorities would prefer to interpret it as 'site of a battle'. It lies at the foot of the mountain known as Zanghir Gah, which is part of the chain running east to west, along the southern slope of which flows the Hari Rud. Since part of the oasis has been relatively well watered it has always been a favourite site for gardens, palaces and burials of

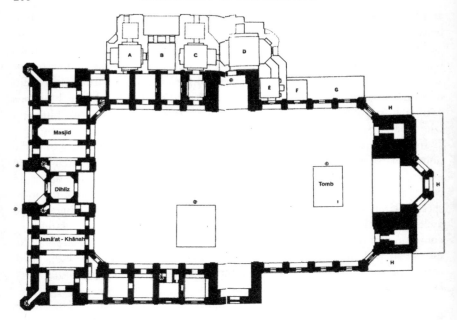

PLAN 14 Gazurgah
A,B,C First additions; D,E Second additions; F,G,H Modern additions

prominent Herati personalities. Already before the tenth century, medieval historians mention a shrine on the slopes of Zanghir Gah.

It was the teacher of Khoja Ansari, Sheikh Amu, who established a *khaniga* (*khanaqah*) at Gazurgah and thereby raised it from a minor sanctuary to a flourishing centre of Muslim learning. Sheikh Amu died in 1049, and Khoja Ansari became, in his turn, the leading personality among the Sufis of north-eastern Khorassan. He was a philosopher and mystic, and soon after his death in 1089 became venerated as a saint.

According to literary sources, a *madrasa* was built at Gazurgah in the Ghorid period, in the late twelfth or early thirteenth centuries, and there was at least one royal burial at the site.

Most of the present shrine goes back to two periods in the fifteenth century. Originally built by Shahrukh in the years 1425–26, it was heavily damaged in a disastrous flood in 1493; Ali Shir Nevai, the *vazir* of Husayn Baykara, repaired and rebuilt it in 1499. Some later additions were made under the Safavids, while the Chinghizid khans in the seventeenth century added some interior decoration and restored and reconstructed parts of the complex.

The shrine itself consists of an entrance *iwan* framed by a high portal screen and flanked on either side by an arcade terminated by a corner turret. Behind it, to the east, is a rectangular courtyard framed, on the north and south sides, by arcaded wings with an *iwan* in the centre of each side. The east side is formed by a monumental *iwan* with a mammoth portal – *pishtak* – in front of which lies the tomb of the khoja. The entire surface of the courtyard is densely covered with tombstones representing 'one of the richest graveyards in the East'.[14]

The west wing of the shrine contains, first and foremost, the entrance complex consisting of the main portal, or *iwan*, facing the forecourt, the vestibule behind it and another *iwan* facing east into the inner courtyard. On each side of the vestibule is a large room, a mosque on the north side and an assembly room on the south side. Each of these two rooms, the proportions of which are similar, has direct access from the outside through lesser portals on the north and south sides of the outer facade.

The entrance portal consists of a five-sided bay covered by a semi-dome joined to a portal screen. The decoration is mainly in turquoise and black glazed tiles, with medallions executed in mosaic faience. The large inscription frieze that frames the portal screen has been added in the seventeenth century.

The interior of both the mosque and the assembly room displays a striking architectural decor. Their ceiling consists of a complex system of plaster vaults, semi-domes and transverse arches with fan-shaped plaster *mukarnas* in the domes between the arches. The entire interior is white, except the lower part of the walls, which are decorated with a wide band of buff-coloured tiles lined with black and blue mosaic faience and set in a simple geometrical pattern.

Seen from the courtyard, the north wing consists of a central *iwan* flanked on either side by a facade with four arcaded recesses, or niches.

The decoration of the *iwan* is preserved mainly on the inside wall, and consists of large geometrical patterns in glazed bricks (*banai*-technique). Parts of an inscription frieze in mosaic faience still exist on the outer wall, and there is a well preserved panel in the same technique above the entrance.

One more room should be mentioned on this side of the courtyard. It is a mud-brick construction added in modern times, which can be entered by a door in the curtain wall east of the *iwan*. Inside is the famous cenotaph of carved black stone known as the Haft Qalam or Seven Feathers. According to Golombek, it is 'one of the most intricate and delicate carvings ever created by the Iranian world'.

Like the north wing, the south wing consists of a central *iwan* and an arcaded facade, the eastern part of which is just a curtain wall, while behind the western part is a series of rooms, the size and layout of which more or less corresponds to its northern counterpart. Generally speaking, the structures on the south side are much more damaged, especially the rooms and roofs nearest to the south-western corner. No interior decoration survives. Most of the decoration on the facade is in a poor state, too. The interiors of some of the rooms were reconstructed to the extent that it is difficult to determine the original layout. There were no later additions on this side.

The eastern *iwan* is the most imposing part of the shrine. The *pishtak*, some 100 feet high, is visible from afar. It was originally completely covered with ornaments of glazed tiles, but unfortunately much of it has disappeared. Inside the *iwan*, however, 'the surfaces have preserved some of the richest and most imaginative glazed tile compositions ever created'.[15] The five-sided bay in the back of the *iwan* is decorated in the lower part with rectangles consisting of an arched panel with a square above it; the middle part is formed by a large inscription frieze in what looks like Kufic script but is, in fact, a 'rare example of Naskhi script executed in *banai*-technique'.[16] The semi-dome above it is filled with stars and polygons, a favourite motif symbolising the dome of heaven.

The vault of the *iwan* is separated from the bay by an arch decorated with an inscription frieze. The inscription, executed in beautiful two-line Thulth, continues horizontally along the sides of the *iwan*. The upper section, or arch, of the *iwan* is covered with a kaleidoscopic design consisting of small geometric units, squares, rhomboids and triangles, centred around a hexagon and fitted together to form a larger design. The hexagons are decorated with floral and arabesque motifs, the rhomboids bear the word 'Allah' in stylised Kufic etc. The lower section is equally remarkable. It consists of squares and rectangles made up of minuscule simulated brick-ends featuring imaginative epigraphic themes in alternating colours. The whole design is framed by a wide band in the same pseudo-Kufic script as in the bay, endlessly repeating the same evocation of God.

The tomb of Khoja Ansari is in front of the eastern *iwan*, hidden behind a latticework structure. North of it stands a 16 feet high ornamental marble column adorned with inscriptions and stucco *mukarnas*, which was erected in 1454. Next to the column is the tomb of Amir Dost Mohammed, who died in Herat in 1863 in the course of a military campaign.

Among the many tombstones in the yard, the most imposing is the large rectangular platform in front of the southern *iwan* known as the Takht or Throne. Built by Husayn Baykara in 1477–78, it is decorated with a pattern of white marble inlaid with black along the sides. On the platform itself are six cenotaphs of black marble belonging to the sultan's family (his father, uncle and brothers). Another black marble stone, elaborately carved but undated, lies opposite the north-western corner of the platform.

Immediately west of the shrine complex two buildings should be mentioned, the Zarnigar-Khana and a pavilion called Namakdan, the Salt Cellar. The main entrance to Zarnigar-Khana is through a large *iwan* on the north side, facing the forecourt, in which remains of elaborate decoration in tinted plaster can be seen. The outer facade is bare. Inside is a large domed hall, some 30 feet square, with a *mihrab* in the western wall. The transition zone between the dome and the walls and the dome itself are covered with gold and blue paintings remarkably well preserved.

Some of the floral motifs in the paintings are similar to those found on the carved tombstones of the 'haft qalam' type executed in Herat toward the end of the fifteenth century. A common inspiration for both is seen by some scholars in carpet designs that go back at least to the beginning of that century, and have as their ultimate source Chinese silks.[17]

The decoration of the Zarnigar-Khana dates in all probability from the very end of the fifteenth century. It is possible that the structure itself was erected somewhat earlier. It now houses a local school. The Namakdan is a garden pavilion twelve-sided on the outside and octagonal on the inside. The central octagon is covered by a star-vault composed of interesting plaster ribs. There is no other decoration. It was probably built in the seventeenth century, and is at present used as a guest house by the administrator of the shrine. There is evidence that a similar pavilion stood some 100 yards farther west.

The covered cistern, Zamzam, was restored in the year 1683 or 1684. An inscription attributes its original foundation to Shahrukh, who is believed to have brought water for it from the holy well in Mecca.

The inscription, which is in the form of a poem, not only compares the cistern with the Zamzam of Mecca but alludes to the shrines of Hebron and of Medina, which also appear in the paintings of the vestibule. It is therefore highly probable that these paintings were executed at the same time as the cistern.

The underground mosque, just west of the cistern, consists of a dome-chamber and deep recesses leading to small meditation cells. The vault of the chamber is probably of the Timurid or Safavid period.

About 60 miles farther east up the valley we come to one of the most famous monuments of Afghanistan and, indeed, of the whole Islamic world, the minaret of Jam. The road is difficult to find, and can only be negotiated by Jeep or Land-Rover. After the village of Shahrak, a track to the left leads to the river, where the minaret stands in complete isolation. It was only discovered in 1957 by a French archaeological expedition, although rumours of its existence had been circulating for some time. With its height of 215 feet it ranks second in the Islamic world, after the Kutub Minar in Delhi (241 feet). It consists of a low octagonal base some 26 feet across, and three cylindrical stages; the first is decorated with geometrical patterns in fired bricks arranged in panels separated by vertical bands of Kufic inscriptions. A wide horizontal band of blue tiles with a Kufic inscription runs around the top of the first stage. In it, a line of Naskhi gives the name of the calligrapher as 'Ali'. The second and third stages are decorated with horizontal bands of inscriptions, again in fired bricks. The stages were originally separated by galleries, which have not survived. The top was closed by a lantern, which has also collapsed. An interior staircase leads up to the second stage. The inscriptions confirm that the minaret was erected by Sultan Ghiyat ud-Din Muhammad ben Sam, the ruler of Ghor. It was built, in all probability, between 1193 and 1202.[18]

NOTES ON CHAPTER XVII
Full details of abbreviations and publications are in the Bibliography

1   Le Strange, G., *The Lands of the Eastern Caliphate*, p. 409.
2   Le Strange, *The Lands*, p. 409.
3   Byron, R., *Road to Oxiana*, p. 103.
4   Lewis, B. (ed.), *Islam*, pp. 66–67.
5   Melikian-Chirvani, A.S., 'Eastern Iranian Architecture', *BSOAS* XXXIII, 1970.
6   Byron, *Oxiana*, p. 85.
7   Wilber, C.N., *The Architecture of Islamic Iran*, p. 35.
8   Sourdel-Thomine, J., 'Deux minarets de l'epoque seljoukide en Afghanistan', *Syria*, XXX, p. 108.
9   Byron, R., 'Timurid Monuments in Afghanistan', *IIIe Congrès International d'art et d'archeologie iraniens*, 1935.
10 Byron, *Oxiana*, p. 96.
11 Renz, A., *Geschichte und Stätten des Islam*, p. 468.
12 Wolfe, N.H., *Herat, a Pictorial Guide*.
13 Golombek, L., *The Timurid Shrine at Gazur Gah*, p. 90.
14 Golombek, *Gazur Gah*, p. 28.
15 Golombek, *Gazur Gah*, p. 45.
16 Golombek, *Gazur Gah*, p. 45.
17 Golombek, *Gazur Gah*, p. 66.
18 Auboyer, J., *Afghanistan*, p. 162.

XVIII

THE NORTH

THE BEST VIEW of the ancient city of **Balkh** is from the air. The huge circular mound of yellow clay is clearly visible among the gardens and fields, ringed with the craggy remnants of once formidable ramparts. This is the Bala Hissar, the 'citadel' covering an area of almost 300 acres, with a hillock in its south-eastern part marking the site of the fort. Its history goes back perhaps to the Achaemenid period or even beyond, for Balkh has traditionally been associated with Bactria, or Bakhdi, the legendary birthplace of Zarathustra and one of the earliest outposts of the Aryan civilisation in the area north of the Hindu Kush. It was the capital of the Persian *satrapy* of Bactria, was taken by Alexander in his pursuit of Bessus, and became not only his base during his four years of campaigning in Transoxania, but also the scene of his marriage to Roxana.

In 1924, the village of Balkh was framed by the old citadel mound in the north, by the ruins of two caravanserais in the east, by the ruined *madrasa* in the south, and by a Jewish quarter in the west. By 1947, this village has disappeared. A reconstruction was undertaken, based on a modern layout with a circular park in the centre, between the Green Mosque and the *madrasa*, and with several large avenues radiating from it. The intention was to rob Mazar-i Sharif of its present position and make Balkh the capital of the province again. This plan misfired, and Balkh remained what it is, a sleepy little town or large village, inhabited mostly by Uzbeks, in which the only life is to be found around the bazaar street.

In the environs of Balkh, as in those of Bukhara and Samarkand, there was a wall, 36 miles long, which surrounded the town and neighbouring villages. It ceased to exist in the ninth century, when both the *shahristan* (inner city) and the suburbs received their own walls. Under Chingiz-Khan, Balkh was completely

211

destroyed following a rising of its inhabitants, and was still lying in ruins in the fourteenth century, when Ibn Battuta passed here.

> We crossed the river Oxus into the land of Khorassan and after a day and a half's march through a sandy uninhabited waste we reached Balkh. It is in utter ruin and uninhabited, but anyone seeing it would think it inhabited on account of the solidity of its construction.[1]

However, it was restored some time later, but did not regain its former importance. This is how Clavijo saw it, in 1404:

> This city is very large and it is surrounded by a broad rampart of earth which along the top measures thirty paces across. The retaining wall flanking the rampart is now breached in many places, but inside this last the city proper is enclosed by two walls one within the other, and these protect the settlement. The area between the outer earthen rampart and the first inner wall is not occupied by any houses and no one lives there, the ground being divided up into fields where cotton is grown. In the space between the second and the innermost wall there are houses, but still this part is not very closely crowded. The innermost circle of the city however is densely populated; and unlike the other towns which we have come to in these parts, the two inner walls of Balkh are extremely strong and as yet well preserved. They treated us with much honour in Balkh, providing us amply with provisions and excellent wine'.[2]

The walls of the city were examined meticulously by two French expeditions. Their findings confirmed that the **Bala Hissar**, the citadel with the fort, was the most ancient part of the city. (See Plate 89.) South of it was a suburb with its own walls, which in one period extended to the east. Later, this eastern extension was abandoned and the city extended to the west. It is not certain how far back the history of the citadel goes. Pottery shards dating from the pre-Kushan period were found here, and some authorities are inclined to believe that the earliest fortifications could be older still. If this is right, then Balkh could indeed have been the legendary Bactra, capital of the Graeco-Bactrian kingdom of the third to second century B.C.

The funeral mosque of Khoja Abu Nasr Parsa, also known as **The Green Mosque** is the most conspicuous monument in present-day Balkh. The khoja, a theological lecturer in Herat in Shahrukh's time, died in Balkh in 1460. (See Plate 70.) The shrine – which is not a mausoleum for it contains no tomb – is a typical Timurid building comprising a large *iwan* flanked by two truncated minarets, with behind it an octagonal structure under a ribbed dome on a high drum. It was built near the saint's tomb at the end of the fifteenth century.

> The colours of the facade are confined to white and dark and light blue, reinforced by discreet touches of black. It is the absence of purple and other warm tints which produces the silvery effect. This effect is continued by the dome,

whose fat round ribs are covered with tiny bricks glazed with greenish turquoise… The building as a whole is unsubstantial and romantic. An unknown force seems to be squeezing it upwards. The result is fantasy, and in some lights, an unearthly beauty.[3]

Byron was certainly a sensitive observer.

The dome has been recently restored, but the tilework on the *iwan* and on the drum is original and rather damaged. The sides and the back of the octagon are bare. There is a band of decorated *mukarnas* forming the transition between the dome and the drum. On the drum are two lines of Kufic inscription in white tiles framed by black on a blue background. Interwoven in these bands are two small bands of highly stylised script in white tiles only. The portal screen of the *iwan* is framed by two vertical bands of elongated Kufic, each terminated at the bottom with a floral medallion. The corners of the screen are formed by two 'corkscrew' pillars (Byron's expression) covered with alternating geometrical and floral ornaments. The bottom ends of these pillars are vase-shaped and richly decorated with floral mosaic faience in white and blue. A wide band of Kufic in the same colours and a band of *mukarnas* form the transition between the 'corkscrew' and the vase. The minarets, of which only the lower parts remain, stood immediately behind the pillars. They were decorated with geometrical ornaments in panels and bands, and with bands of two different varieties of script, a Kufic similar to that on the drum and above the vases, and a 'cursive' Kufic, or rather a special kind of Naskhi similar to that which we have already seen on the eastern *iwan* at Gazurgah in Herat.

The *iwan*-niche has a geometrical decoration on the inside of the arch as well as on the entrance wall. Floral ornaments adorn the spandrels of the arch. Above the entrance is a wide rectangular band of script, again in 'cursive' Kufic, framing a pattern of square panels composed of a stylised angular script-like design around an octagonal medallion.

Five-sided bays on two floors flank the *iwan* on both sides; the lower ones have been restored. The upper ones are covered with a semi-dome and richly decorated with arched floral medallions and spherical floral ornaments in blue and gold.

Inside, where women are not admitted, the *mihrab* niche is embellished with mosaic faience with geometrical and floral motifs. The squinches and the stalactite niches are adorned with inscriptions and floral ornaments. The dome, carried by a triple band of *mukarnas*, is decorated with ribs reproducing those on the outside and painted with repetitive floral motifs.

Some 40 miles from Balkh, on the Akcha road, the mausoleum **Baba Hatem** is a monument from the Ghaznavid period. A cube-shaped, domed building, it has above the entrance an inscription frieze in floral Kufic, in incised terracotta and another inscription in decorative Kufic on the drum. Inside, the dome rests on squinches or quarter-vault pendentives. An interesting decorative element are stylised ibexes.[4]

In the fields south-west of Balkh stands the oldest existing building in the area, and one of the oldest known monuments of Islam. It is the **No Gumbad** (Nine Domes) mosque, also known as the Masjid Hadji Piyade. It is rectangular on the inside, 60 by 51 feet, and almost square on the outside, 66 by 64 feet. As the name indicates, it had nine domes, 13 feet in diameter, supported by massive columns measuring 5 feet in diameter.[5] (See Plate 79.) The domes have collapsed, and the fallen masonry hides the lower parts of the columns, thereby preventing any measurement of their height. Some of the arches supporting the domes still exist. The *mihrab* was in the centre of the south-western wall. The material used was partly baked bricks and partly mud-bricks (*pakhsa*), covered with alabaster stucco. The decoration on the arches and capitals is mostly of incised alabaster, and shows stylised floral motifs divided into geometrical fields and separated either by meanders or by simple straight or circular bands. There are also geometrical ornaments consisting of circles and half-circles, octagons and four-leaf figures.

The dating of this monument poses serious problems. Pugachenkova, who based her dating mainly on architectural analysis, found similarities with certain monuments in Iran and Turkestan dating from the tenth century. Nevertheless, it bears no resemblance to the early Arab type of mosque, and points directly to pre-Islamic models, for example to Sasanian palaces and temples. On the other hand, the decoration, which is 'of exceptionally high quality', points to ninth-century origins.

The architecture reflects aspects of three different forms: the *iwan*, consisting of three barrel-vaulted and arcaded naves; the *apadana*, which was a square with four columns in the centre supporting four cross-beams and thus dividing the whole into nine equal parts; and the Soghdian *kushk*, which was a square building consisting of nine cells covered with cupolas and divided by walls. Thus the architecture represents a mixture of foreign models imported from the West (Mesopotamia and Iran) and of traditional local ones. The fact that local models were used to facilitate the adaptation of the foreign ones would point to a period fairly soon after the conquest of Islam, and yet later than the Samarra monuments. It would seem likely, therefore, that the building originated some time in the first half of the ninth century. At any rate, the No Gumbad mosque belongs to the transitional period of medieval architecture, when it was still linked with pre-Islamic traditions but when new features were already beginning to emerge, foreshadowing the formation of a new architectural style which would reach its peak between the tenth and twelfth centuries.

Half way between Balkh and Mazar-i Sharif is the mosque of **Takht-i Pol** whose three domed halls alongside each other indicate Indian influence. The halls have slightly pointed arches with mukarnas decoration. There is an *iwan* in front of the central hall; this hall is higher than the lateral ones and contains the mihrab. The interior is richly decorated with paintings in a good state of preservation, showing a mixture of late Indian and Islamic traditions.

Mazar-i Sharif, the present provincial capital, is a modern town centred around the shrine of **Hazret Ali**, one of the holiest places of the Shi'a. Tens of thousands of pilgrims flock here, in particular for the New Year celebrations (Now Ruz, 21 or 22 March) to pray to Ali, the son-in-law of the Prophet and the fourth caliph, who was murdered in Kufa in 661. (See Plate 88.) According to legend, his followers put his corpse on a white she-camel and let her loose. She wandered as far as the neighbourhood of Balkh, where, some four centuries later, the body of Ali was found intact. A shrine was built over the tomb in 1136, but was destroyed by Chingiz-Khan. The tomb was re-discovered in 1480, and Husayn Baykara erected a new sumptuous mausoleum over it. The building then underwent numerous restorations and reconstructions, so that hardly anything remains of the original Timurid structure.

The main building, with an imposing *iwan*, stands in a large courtyard. There are three gateways into the yard, on the north, east and south sides; the main gateway, flanked by minarets, is in the south. The west side is taken up by a large mosque. Originally, there was a gateway similar to the others, the dome of which had been incorporated into the mosque. The pattern of the pavement in the yard consists of outlines of innumerable *mihrabs*, which are used by worshippers at prayer time. Non-believers may enter the yard but not the sanctuary.

The building has two pointed domes indicating an inner and outer sanctuary. Inside, there is first a carpeted and decorated anteroom in which, by the door to the inner chamber, stands a huge bronze cauldron similar to that in the mosque in Herat, but with no decoration. The tomb of Hazret Ali is in the inner chamber, surrounded by a railing and covered with embroidered cloth. The walls and ceiling are decorated with painted floral ornaments dating from the second half of the nineteenth century. The entire outer facade is covered with glazed tiles, mostly turquoise and blue, but the ornaments are not of any special interest. On the outside, a number of individual shrines are built against the walls of the sanctuary. Several tombs on the west side belong to the members of Amir Dost Muhammed's family.

By far the most exciting site in the region of Kunduz is **Ay Khanum** (Moon Lady), which was discovered in 1963 by French archaeologists at the confluence of the Amu Darya and the Kokcha. It is the eastern-most genuine Greek city, a proof of the Hellenistic period in Bactria sought by archaeologists for decades.

The site, which can be dated to between the fourth and the second centuries B.C., is situated on the left bank of the Amu Darya, and comprises an upper town with a huge citadel in its northern part and a lower town based on a regular grid of broad straight streets with residential and administrative areas, including a palace with a peristylar courtyard, a Greek-style gymnasium, a large private house, an Oriental temple and other buildings.[6] It had gates and ramparts with rectangular towers more than 66 feet wide. Water was brought by canals from the river.

The ceramics and terracotta roof tiles resemble those found in other Hellenistic cities from the same period in Western Asia and on the Greek mainland. Persian-style column bases and Corinthian capitals provide evidence of the coexistence of the two civilisations. Two important Greek inscriptions in stone have been found here which confirm the overall Greekness of the site.[7]

The city was destroyed by fire, most probably when the area was invaded by the nomads some time at the end of the second century B.C. It has never been reoccupied, the most plausible reason being that the destruction of the irrigation system rendered the region uninhabitable.

In 1946, at Khisht-Tepe, some 56 miles from Kunduz on the bank of the Amu Darya, the frontier guards from the district of Kala-i Zal found an earthenware vase full of coins when digging foundations for a new stable. There were 628 Bactrian coins of various sizes and denominations with the names, in Greek, of twenty-two rulers. This find, which became known as the 'hoard of Kunduz', provided some useful information for the dating and history of the last decades of the Bactrian kingdom. It is now accepted that these coins date from the second century B.C.; the latest of them come from the last two decades of that century, from the period immediately preceding the invasion of the Yue-che and the establishment of the Kushan Empire.

Some 9 miles north of Pul-i Khumri, within sight of the main road to Mazar-i Sharif, **Surkh Kotal** is the site of a Kushan temple from the second century A.D. that provided 'the first definite evidence of an indigenous Bactrian art, possible inspiration for the later Gandharan style'.[8] (See Plate 77.) It was discovered in the course of road building in 1951, and was excavated systematically by the French archaeological expedition between 1952 and 1963. The excavations revealed a hilltop complex consisting of the main temple, a secondary temple and a monumental staircase leading down the hill. The main temple stood on a brick platform faced with stone revetment decorated with pilasters. It had strong thick walls, and contained a square central room surrounded by corridors on three sides, with three entrances facing east. In the centre was a stone platform with a huge column in each corner. The bases of these columns are still in situ. The temple building stood in the centre of a large paved courtyard with portico and numerous niches in the walls, where large painted statues once stood. From the outside, the whole complex looked like a fortress, with solid walls, a series of towers and narrow entrances. The secondary temple beyond the outer wall on the north side contained a square fire altar. The 23 feet wide staircase starts from a huge terrace on the east side of the main temple. As the archaeologists followed it downhill, they discovered that it consisted of five flights and five terraces.

In 1957, a large limestone slab, covered with Greek letters in an unknown language was unearthed on the fourth terrace. It has been subsequently found that the twenty-five-line inscription, 'probably the most important single specimen from Surkh Kotal'[9] is in the Eastern Iranian or Bactrian language. It has not yet been fully deciphered, but mentions King Kanishka and refers to the repairs of the sanctuary. There seems to have been a fire during the reign of Kanishka's immediate successor, and it can be assumed that these restorations and repairs were undertaken soon after the fire. This would place the inscription – and the fire – in the second half of the second century A.D. The inscription also includes the word 'Bagolango', Old Iranian for 'temple' or 'sanctuary'. It is easily recognisable in the present-day name of Baghlan. In the Middle Ages, Baghlan was the name of the whole district, thus meaning 'district of the sanctuary'. The original temple of Kanishka extended down to the third terrace; the fourth was the work of the restorers and the fifth was probably added between the third and the fifth centuries A.D. after the Sasanians had succeeded the Kushans. Although Surkh Kotal was built in the peak period of Buddhism, it was certainly not a Buddhist temple. It is assumed that it was a dynastic temple dedicated by king Kanishka to his own divinity. A huge headless statue was found here that could represent Kanishka himself. It is possible that the statue, which is now in the Museum of Kabul, was a cardinal deity in the temple. On the other hand, a stone platform like the one in the central room was typical of the Iranian fire temples and the secondary temple did contain a fire altar. There is little doubt, therefore, that the cult of fire played a leading role in the rites practised here.

Like Ay Khanum, Surkh Kotal is not a Graeco-Buddhist site (or, to use another terminology, Indo-Greek). It is a mixture of Greek and Persian elements, thereby evidencing that the traditions of Achaemenid Persia were still strong several centuries after its disappearance.

To mention only a few examples of the Kushan mixture of Greek and Persian in Surkh Kotal, we may select the following: they wrote their own language in Greek letters; they worshipped their own King Deity with fire; they built a fire altar inside a turreted fortress but surrounded the courtyard with a Greek portico; for decoration they used Iranian motifs such as stepped battlements and arrowheads together with typically Greek motifs such as Corinthian capitals and garlands borne by Amorini; they clothed their figurines in oriental and Central Asian dress and Greek drapery.[10]

Professor Schlumberger preferred to call this distinctive culture Graeco-Iranian.

Samangan, on the road between Tashkurghan and Pul-i Khumri, is a modern town, but some miles from it is the site of Takht-i Rustam or **Haibak**, formerly a Buddhist monastery consisting of a number of caves and a *stupa* dating from the fourth to the fifth centuries A.D. It was visited by several travellers in the nineteenth century, but was first systematically explored by Foucher in 1923, and then by Mizuno in 1959 and 1960.[11]

The monastery stands at the bottom of the hill and has five caves. In the first of these is an anteroom and a large circular room with a huge lotus in full bloom carved in the ceiling. This is a unique form of decoration. The only comparable one, but much smaller, is in one of the monasteries in Taxila. Two niches, one above the other, are in the back wall, but there is no trace of statues. The second cave is a long double corridor with a vaulted ceiling, with two entrances and individual cells for the monks. The third cave, similar to the first, also has an anteroom and a square room with an unadorned ceiling. There is one large niche for a statue, and squinch arches in the corners. The fourth cave, which contains four rooms, was utilitarian. There were benches along three walls in the middle room and a square water tank in the centre. It was most probably used as a bath-house, especially as the fifth cave, next to it, has numerous features indicating that it was a lavatory. On top of the hill, across from this complex, is a *stupa* that again has a unique feature. (See Plate 76.) It looks as if it were sunk into a large pit. In fact it stands in an open-topped cave hewn out of solid rock. The top of the *stupa* shows out of the cave. On it is a *harmika*, a kind of square balcony, also hewn out of the rock. (The *harmika* was originally a support for the pole holding the *chatra*, or umbrella.) Inside the *harmika* is a round and domed room that housed the reliquary. It is possible to enter the cave at the base of the *stupa* through a tunnel, and to walk around it. The passage around the *stupa* is approximately 6 feet wide. The *stupa*, of polished limestone, is 92 feet across and 26 feet high.

The last great archaeological discovery before the curtain dropped on Afghanistan was no doubt V. Sarianidi's excavations at **Tilla-Tepe**, not far from the village of Shibargan, in the years 1977–78. The aptly named Tilla-Tepe (Gold Mound) lies near the site of Yemshi-Tepe, a Bactrian city of the Kushan period, where remains of a temple dating probably from the late second millennium B.C. were first explored. The six tombs excavated at Tilla-Tepe dating from the first century B.C. to the first century A.D., yielded almost 20,000 gold objects, ornaments, jewels etc., as well as important information about the population of that period. Certain aspects of the funerary rites point to Scythian origins: women's jewels prove that women enjoyed a privileged position in the society, a phenomenon typical of the nomads. The artistic quality of the jewels is inferior to the Hellenistic ones of Greek Bactria, and may have been influenced by Parthia. On the other hand, the treatment of animal motifs reflects the Scytho-Sarmatian traditions and an affinity with the Siberian 'animal style'.

There are artefacts pointing to Graeco-Bactrian origin, others may be classified as Graeco-Roman, some are of local Bactrian style, some show a mixture of Graeco-Roman and Siberian Altaic influences; the animal style of Scytho-Sarmatian origin can be found in some. The sixth group is that of objects showing local Eastern Persian or Old Bactrian traditions pointing back to Bronze Age. Here, according to Sarianidi,

> nomad art of the steppes made an important contribution by virtue of its dynamic though conventional lines and its naivete of expression… It may be suggested that nomad art served to catalyze the interaction of the two old – Greek and Bactrian – art trends…[12]

The chronological gap between the Oxus Treasure and Tilla-Tepe has now been filled by the newly found temple treasure at Takht-i Sanghi (Southern Tajikistan), (cf. Litvinski, B. and Pichikian, I., 'Archaeological discoveries in South Tajikistan', *Bulletin of the USSR Academy of Sciences*, 1980).

NOTES ON CHAPTER XVIII
Full details of abbreviations and publications are in the Bibliography

1   Gibb, *Ibn Battuta*, p. 175.
2   Le Strange, *Clavijo*, p. 198.
3   Byron, *Oxiana*, p. 256.
4   Melikian-Shirvani, 'Baba Hatem, un chef-d'oevre inconnu d'époque ghaznévide en Afghanistan', in *VIth International Congress on Iranian Art and Archaeology*, Tehran, 1972.
5   Pugachenkova, G.A., *No Gumbad in Balkh*.
6   Duprée, L., *Afghanistan*, p. 289.
7   Duprée, L., *Afghanistan*, p. 291.
8   Duprée, L., *Afghanistan*, p. 292.
9   Duprée, L., *Afghanistan*, p. 292.
10 Duprée, N.H., *The Road to Balkh*, pp. 18–19.
11 Foucher, A., 'Notes sur les antiquités bouddhiques de Haibak', *JA*, 1924, Mizuno, S., *Haibak and Kashmir-Smast*, 1962.
12 Sarianidi, V., *The Golden Hoard of Bactria*, p. 55.

XIX

THE SOUTH

THE PERIOD OF GLORY OF GHAZNA (Ghazni is a modern spelling) was comparatively short, spanning less than two centuries. In the middle of the tenth century it was a petty town in eastern Afghanistan, theoretically belonging to the Samanids, but in practice control from distant Bukhara was tenuous. Little is known of its history in earlier times, except that after the demise of the Hephthalites (White Huns) some time in the seventh century, it was ruled, together with Kabul, by the Turk-Shahis, a dynasty that introduced a strong Indian influence. The Turk-Shahis were subsequently replaced in the middle of the ninth century by the Hindushahi rajas, a dynasty of Indian origin, and most probably of Brahmin faith. The Arab raids from Sistan, which became frequent from the end of the seventh century onwards, were aimed more at exacting tribute, plunder and slaves than at establishing a permanent military occupation, and in general the local rulers were able to preserve their authority. Connections with India were numerous and there is much evidence of Indian religious and cultural influence until as late as the tenth century.

Samanid control of Ghazna was established when, in 961, their commander-in-chief in Khorassan, Alptigin (*Tigin* – also spelled tegin or tagin – is a Turkish military title) wrested the town from the last Hindushahi ruler and was himself appointed governor. By then the power of the Samanids was already in decline and the administration and defence of their outlying provinces was entrusted, to an ever increasing extent, to Turkish mercenaries and slaves whom the rulers believed to be more reliable that the local landed aristocracy. In this they followed the example of the caliphs of Baghdad, and so via the Samanids the concept of a slave army passed from Baghdad to the Ghaznavids.[1]

Alptigin was followed by a series of other Turkish slave governors until the office fell in 977 to Sabuktagin (Sebüktigin), who held it for twenty years, ruling virtually autonomously.

His eldest son, Mahmud, concentrated the administration of all the provinces in his own hands, and when the Samanid dynasty was extinguished in 999 he found himself undisputed master of Ghazna, Balkh, Bost and Herat, as well as Termez. The rest of Khorassan, namely Merv and Nishapur, was also under his control, but there he had to fend off the claims of the Samanid successors, the Turkish Karakhanids. In 1008, when the Karakhanid rulers were defeated decisively, he ruled over an empire that stretched from western Iran to the gates of India. Over the next years he pursued a systematic policy of bringing under his control the outlying dynasties that had enjoyed loose tributary status under the Samanids. In this way he extended his territories to include Sistan, Khorezm and the principalities on the upper Oxus. Even before he had consolidated his holdings in Khorassan he began to invade India, against which he conducted at least seventeen campaigns. He added north-west India and the Punjab to his empire and enriched his treasury by looting wealthy Hindu temples. Probably more important, his mullahs converted many Hindus to Islam, thus beginning a process that plagues the subcontinent to this day.

The Samanid court in Bukhara served as a model to the Ghaznavid sultans not only in their organisation of administrative offices, but also as a centre of arts and Islamic learning. The Samanids patronised writers, scholars and in particular Persian poets. It was certainly the ambition of Mahmud of Ghazna to emulate his former masters in this respect. Unfortunately, Ghazna was still more like a military camp at his time, and hardly a place to attract a great number of illustrious men. In the course of his campaigns Mahmud brought back entire libraries to Ghazna and used his power quite ruthlessly to bring scholars in – by force, if necessary.

The situation was similar in architecture and the arts. There can be little doubt that artisans and craftsmen were imported from the conquered lands just like the scholars and men of letters. Gradually, during the reign of Mahmud and Masud, 'a certain style of building developed which used marble and carved decoration grafted on to the more sober traditional Persian technique of brick construction and moulded brick decoration'.[2] Little has survived of the buildings of this period, the main reasons being, as listed by Bosworth,

> the effects of an extreme climate; natural catastrophes like earthquakes and floods; the ravages of war; the use of comparatively perishable materials like sun-dried brick, for stone and even fired brick were infrequently used; indifferent workmanship; the theft of building materials by the local population: all these combined to make much building work, however splendid and imposing at the time it was put up, impermanent and short-lived.[3]

Unfortunately, 'no adequate description has come down to us of Ghazna at the time when it was rebuilt and adorned by Mahmud...'

After the defeat of Sultan Masud by the Seljuqs in 1040, Khorassan was lost to the Ghaznavids, thereby changing the cultural orientation of the remaining empire quite considerably. It acquired a 'predominantly Indian outlook',[4] which its heartland had no doubt had before the arrival of Alptigin and Sabuktagin. Overshadowed by the growing importance of Lahore, the city lived on for another century, until the Ghorid sultan Ala-ud-Din surnamed Jahan-suz (World Incendiary), to revenge his brother's death at the hands of Bahramshah the Ghaznavid, took Ghazna by storm in 1149. He then both sacked and burnt the city, which never recovered from the calamity. The tomb of the great Mahmud nevertheless appears to have been spared, unless it was restored, for Ibn Battuta saw it there in the fourteenth century.

The mausoleum of **Sultan Mahmud** is in the village of Rauza, about half a mile outside the town, on the right-hand side of the road when coming from Kabul. It is a modern building constructed on the site of a palace in a garden that was once called Bagh-i Firuzi (Emerald Garden), and was one of Mahmud's favourite resting places.

The tomb inside was in all probability erected by Mahmud's son Masud, and can be dated to the first half of the eleventh century. It is a marble-faced sarcophagus with a triangular prismatic slab on top. The slab is decorated on one side with a carved two-line inscription band in superb calligraphy, and a smaller band running along the base. On the other side is a three-lobed medallion with six lines of Naskhi script. In the middle of each side of the sarcophagus is an ornamental medallion framed with a flat Kufic inscription. The tomb shows the first traces of Indian influence in Islamic art. The bulbous arches in the medallions, as well as the naturalism of its floral decoration, already show certain tendencies which crystallised under the later Ghaznavids into what became known as Indo-Muslim art.

Next to it, in the same village, is an undecorated Timurid building, the mausoleum of **Sultan Abdul Razzak**, built at the beginning of the sixteenth century and recently restored by an Italian archaeological expedition. Abdul Razzak was a one-time rival and challenger of Babur. The mausoleum is an interesting example of a central domed chamber in the middle of a square, flanked by four massive *iwans*, which are linked with fortress-like bastions and round towers.

Excavations of the palace of **Masud III** nearby are the work of Italian archaeologists. **Tepe Sardar** is a mound hiding the remnants of a large *stupa* on a square base where a huge statue of a reclining Buddha was found. The building material was diaper masonry of the Taxila type. Rows of votive and commemorative *stupas* surrounded the main one.

The medieval city of **Ghazna** once stood on the desolate plain between the village and the modern town. (See Plate 90.) In the middle of the plain, accessible by a dusty road running westwards from the main road towards the town, stand two decorated towers, the most famous monuments of Ghazna and two of the very few surviving examples of Ghaznavid architecture and decoration. A sketch made in 1836 shows that originally they were more than twice as high. Above the lower octagonal part rose a circular shaft, which still existed when some early photographs were taken.

The larger tower was built by Masud III, and should be dated between 1099 and 1114, but the smaller tower, with a much simpler decoration, is not older but younger and must be attributed to one of the last Ghaznavids, Bahramshah (1118–52). (See Plates 93 and 94.) A detailed epigraphic analysis of the tower of Bahramshah was made by J. Sourdel-Thomine.[5] This places it firmly under the reign of that last member of the dynasty who still resided in Ghazna. Architecturally, it belongs to the end of the eleventh century and should be compared, for example, with the minaret of Uzgen (Uzkend) in Kirghizstan. The decoration lacks the richness of the arabesque and floral ornament of the older tower, but its geometrical patterns in brick are, like the script, too sophisticated for the building to belong to an earlier period. Views still differ as to whether the towers were built as minarets or some kind of 'towers of victory'.

Two prehistoric sites in the Kandahar province are of interest. **Mundigak**, northwest of the city, and **Deh Morasi Ghundai**, south-west of it. Both were probably, in their earliest period, some 4–5000 years ago, peasant settlements the economy of which was a mixture of farming and animal husbandry. But whereas Deh Morasi Ghundai seems to have remained a small semi-sedentary village growing wheat and barley and breeding sheep, goats and cattle until the end of its existence some time after 1500 B.C., Mundigak developed into an urban centre comparable to the cities of the Indus valley civilisation. In fact, it is highly probable that both sites had connections with that civilisation. Mundigak ceased to be the urban centre in south-east Afghanistan when Kandahar became urban in pre-Achaemenid times.

The site of Deh Morasi is some 20 feet high and 165 feet long; Mundigak is 66 feet high and 495 feet long.[6] Seven successive layers of habitation were uncovered at Mundigak, of which the fourth already shows signs of a fully-fledged town, with a granary and a massive complex, probably a temple and a palace. It seems to have been destroyed at least twice, in its fourth and fifth layer, but has been rebuilt each time. The sixth and seventh layer, which correspond to the periods around and after 1500 B.C., appear to have been occupied only sporadically by nomads or semi-nomads.

The Old City of **Kandahar** – Shahr-i Kuhna – lies about 3 miles west of the modern town, and is dominated by the tall mound of the citadel, the Kasr-i Naranj.

The site was excavated by the British Institute of Afghan Studies in 1974 and 1975. In the first year a trench was cut in the city wall, which revealed layers of five periods, of which the first roughly corresponds to that of Mundigak VI and may be as early as the first half of the first millennium B.C. The pottery finds in its later two seem to belong to the Achaemenid period, and it is possible that the *pakhsa* wall of Period II defended the Achaemenid city of Harakuwatis.

Period III is characterised by unbaked bricks and was, most probably, Greek, while the defences of Period IV which consisted of a solid brick wall, are believed to be Kushan. The layer of Period V is Islamic.[7]

The excavations of the second year concentrated on the high ground within the walled enclosure and had as one of their objectives to seek the solution of the problem of Alexandria of the Arachosians, or Alexandropolis, which might have been the Greek city of Old Kandahar. The layers revealed corresponded to the Periods II to V as identified in the earlier dig. Although no evidence of the Alexander period was recovered, the finds of coins, pottery and some architectural remains would suggest that a Greek colony, or quarter, was added to the pre-existing settlement. This evidence of Greek presence at Kandahar certainly strengthens the hypothesis that Alexandria of the Arachosians was located at Shahr-i Kuhna.[8]

South of the road from Kandahar to Herat, at the confluence of the Rivers Helmand and Arghandab, a vast area of ruins stretching for more than 4 miles along the Helmand marks the ancient city of **Bost** (Kala-i Bost) and the winter residence of the Ghaznavid sultans, the palaces of **Lashkar-i Bazar**. Like Ghazna, Bost was first devastated by the Ghorid Sultan Ala-ud Din in 1151, rebuilt and then destroyed again by the Mongols of Chingiz-Khan. At the close of the fourteenth century the site and its environs were yet again devastated by Timur, who destroyed one of the great dams across the Helmand that contained the head of water that served to irrigate all the western lands of Sistan.

The citadel of Bost commands an impressive view over the neighbouring countryside, littered far into the steppe with remnants of clay walls and ruined buildings. At the foot of the citadel mound, an elegant arch with an 82 feet span was probably constructed as a triumphal entrance to the city. Built originally in the late Ghaznavid period, it was heavily restored in the 1950s; when, despite this, it began to show conspicuous cracks, the Afghan authorities decided to wall it up (1978). It is, or rather was, a graceful, slightly pointed structure of baked bricks, decorated on the inside with geometrical ornaments and on the outside, both on the arch and on the supporting columns, with inscription bands in flowering Kufic. On either side, a horseshoe-shaped blind arch is filled with a imple geometrical ornament in baked brick. Although some sources place it to he eleventh century, the character of its decor points to a somewhat later date. The horseshoe arches were probably inspired by India.

The Arabic Al-Askar (Camp) has become the Persian Lashkargah (Soldiers' Place) or Lashkar-i Bazar (Soldiers' Bazaar). It is a group of three palaces at the north end of the site, on the bank of the Helmand, with courtyards, gardens and a number of auxiliary structures inside a walled enclosure. It was discovered in 1948 by the French archaeological mission, and excavated in five successive campaigns concentrating mainly on the southern palace, the largest of the three. Parts of this palace can be dated to the end of the tenth century, but it seems to have been completed by about 1036. If this is correct, the construction was begun by Mahmud and finished by his son Masud I.

A straight avenue about a third of a mile long provided access to the palace from the south. It was obviously the main shopping street, for it was lined on both sides with shops and stalls, of which about a hundred have been uncovered. The site of the palace is over 1650 feet long. The southern part of it was occupied by a vast rectangular forecourt surrounded by a wall. On one side was a large mosque with a 284 feet frontage and a portal of 35 feet, built probably in the time of Mahmud and Masud I. On the north side of this forecourt was the entrance to the palace, an *iwan* leading to a spacious vestibule in the form of a cross, through which the centre of the palace was reached. This centre was a vast rectangular courtyard, 208 by 162 feet, with an *iwan* in the middle of each side. The northern *iwan* was larger and higher than all the others, and gave access to the audience hall and other public buildings. Private apartments were in the corners, each grouped around a smaller private courtyard. A canal passed through the audience hall and the adjacent rooms carrying running water across the entire width of the palace. Toilets and bathrooms, as well as water tanks, were fed from it. The water was lifted into it by some kind of mechanism, but the source of the water has not been found. A small mosque richly decorated with stucco ornaments was discovered in 1950 inside the great audience hall.[9]

The facade facing the forecourt was decorated in carved stucco. The entrance *iwan* had a terracotta decoration, panels with geometrical ornaments and bands of inscriptions, dating from the middle or late twelfth century. The walls of the audience hall were lavishly decorated, in the lower parts with wall-paintings, higher up with geometrical ornaments in baked brick. On the wall facing the entrance were two large panels framed with inscriptions and filled with carved stucco ornament in the same style as the arch of Bost. On the inside of the entrance *iwan* were hexagonal ornaments and calligraphic bands in elongated Kufic.

The wall-paintings have been removed and placed in the Kabul Museum. Remnants have been found of some forty-four figures, out of a total of perhaps sixty, all clad in ceremonial robes in lively colours and carrying insignia of rank. It is assumed that they depicted the sultan's guard of Turkish slaves. Schlumberger[10] finds traces of Buddhist and Sasanian traditions in this decoration. The costumes indicate Chinese Turkestan, with a marked influence of the steppe nomads. The depiction on the walls of a procession of palace guards was an ancient habit of Oriental rulers which can be traced back to Persepolis and Susa.

NOTES ON CHAPTER XIX
Full details of abbreviations and publications are in the Bibliography

1   Bosworth, C.K., *The Ghaznavids*, p. 33.
2   Bosworth, *The Ghaznavids*, p. 134.
3   Bosworth, *The Ghaznavids*, p. 139.
4   Bosworth, *The Ghaznavids*, p. 135.
5   Sourdel-Thomine, *Deux minarets*, p. 108.
6   Duprée, L., *Afghanistan*, p. 268.
7   Whitehouse, D., 'Excavations at Kandahar, 1974', *Afghan Studies*, I, 1978.
8   McNicoll, A., 'Excavations at Kandahar, 1975', *Afghan Studies*, I, 1978.
9   Schlumberger, D., 'Le palais ghaznévide de Lashkari Bazar', *Syria*, XXX, 1952.
10 Schlumberger, 'Le palais', *Syria*, XXX, 1952.

APPENDIX

AFTERMATH OF DESTRUCTION

FOR TWENTY YEARS the outside world knew next to nothing of the state and preservation of the sites and monuments in Afghanistan. It was only in March 2000 that two articles published simultaneously in the French magazine *Archeologia* shed some light on the state of at least a limited number of them.

The National Museum of Kabul seems to have survived rather well the Soviet occupation but had the misfortune to find itself in the firing line between the warring factions in the civil war. It was hit by an anti-tank rocket, caught fire and partially burned down. Some 80 percent of its collections were either destroyed or subsequently looted. Disappeared, among other things, some 30,000 coins, the famous ivories of Begram and other priceless treasures, including the gold artefacts from Tilla-Tepe.

At Bamiyan, some caves at the base of the Great Buddha were used as storage for arms and ammunition. The concrete supports of the statue were demolished to retrieve the metal bracing. Frescoes above the head were destroyed or looted during fighting between the Taliban and the Hazara. One large fresco covered with soot was spattered with shoe-prints in white paint. The Small Buddha had its head blown off in 1999, and its head and neck were turned into rubble. Half of the draperies on the upper part of the body have disappeared, the lower part is a gaping hole visible from afar. Explosions damaged the right knee as well as the galleries, caves and staircases around the statue. Almost all the frescoes behind the head disappeared between 1995 and 1999. The legs and supports of the Kakrak Buddha were destroyed in 1996.

The minaret of Jam is in danger of collapsing because of the water of the Hari Rud lapping at its base. Rescue operations decided on by UNESCO in 1974 have not been carried out. Some work may have started at the end of 1999 in much more difficult conditions.

In Herat, the western part of the city was almost completely destroyed at the beginning of the Russo-Afghan fighting. The mausoleum of Gawhar Shad was hit by Soviet artillery in 1984 and 1985, and of the two minarets of the *madrasa* only one survived in a rather poor condition.

At Hadda, the Buddhist monastery of Tapa-i Shotor (third to fourth centuries), which was one of the best monuments of Graeco-Buddhist art, was established before the occupation as the first museum in situ in Afghanistan. In 1982 it was destroyed.

Among other sites that were damaged, the sites of Tela-i Tepe and Ay Khanum have undergone extensive pillage, and were even dug up by bulldozers. The twelfth-century *madrasa* Shah-i Mashad, a masterpiece of Ghorid architecture and decoration, was completely destroyed. The Buddhist column, Minar-i Chakri, south-east of Kabul, collapsed in 1998 for lack of maintenance. More than half of the city of Kabul has been turned into 'a lunar landscape' in the factional fighting of 1994–5.

BIBLIOGRAPHY

bbreviations

FJ	*Afghanistan Journal,* Graz
SOAS	*Bulletin of the School of Oriental and African Studies,* London
AR	*Central Asian Review,* London
ESB	*Indo-European Studies Bulletin,* Berkeley
Iém. DAFA	*Mémoires de la Délegation Archéologique Française en Afghanistan,* Paris
A	*Journal Asiatique,* Paris

(Titles marked with an asterisk * are quoted in the text)

HISTORY

arthold, V.V., *Turkestan v epokhu mongol'skogo nashestviya,* Moscow, 1900.

—— *Turkestan down to the Mongol Invasion* (translation), London, 1928, 1958.*

—— *Istoriya orosheniya Turkestana* (History of Irrigation in Turkestan), Moscow, n.d.

l-Biruni, Abu Rayhan, I*zbrannye proizvedeniya* (Selected Works) (Russian translation), Tashkent, 1957.

rockelmann, K., *Geschichte der islamischen Völker und Staaten,* Munich, 1939.

rye, R.N., *The Golden Age of Persia,* London, 1975, 1993.

Gibb, H.A.R., *Arab Conquest in Central Asia,* London, 1923.

Grousset, R., *L'Empire des steppes,* Paris, 1939, 1960.*

Haenisch, E. (tr.), *Die geheime Geschichte der Mongolen,* Leipzig, 1948.

Hookham, H., *Tamburlaine the Conqueror,* London, 1962.*

esný, V., *Buddhismus,* Prague, 1948.

e Strange, G., *The Lands of the Eastern Caliphate,* Cambridge, 1905.

ukonin, V.G., 'Sasanian Conquest in the East of Iran and the Problem of Kushan Chronology', *Abstracts of Papers by Soviet Scholars,* International Conference on the History, Archaeology and Culture of Central Asia in the Kushan Period, Dushanbe, 1968.*

Masson, V.M., *Srednyaya Azia i drevniy vostok* (Central Asia and the Ancient East), Moscow and Leningrad, 1964.

Narain, A.K., *The Indo-Greeks,* Oxford, 1957.

Poucha, P. (tr.), *Tajná Kronika Mongolů* (The Secret History of the Mongols), Prague, n.d.*

Sanders, J.H. (tr.), *Tamerlane,* by Ibn Arabshah, London, 1936.

Stavisky, Bongard and Levin, 'Central Asia in the Kushan Period', *Abstracts of Papers*.*

Sykes, P., *History of Persia*, 2 vols, London, 1915, 1930.

Talbot-Rice, T., *The Scythians*, London 1961.

Tauer, F., *Dějiny a Kultura Islámu* (History and Civilisation of Islam), Prague, 1940.

Tolstov, S.P., *Drevnyaya Kultura Uzbekistana* (Ancient Civilisation of Uzbekistan), Tashkent, 1940.

Vernadsky, G., *The Mongols and Russia*, London, 1953.

Watson, B., *Ssu-Ma Chien, Grand Historian of China*, London, 1958.

Wheeler, G., *The Peoples of Soviet Central Asia*, London, 1966.

Zeymal, E.V., '278 AD – The Date of Kanishka', *Abstracts of Papers*.*

ART

Allan, J.W., *Islamic Ceramics*, Oxford, 1991.

Ashrafi, M.M., *Persian-Tajik Poetry in XIV–XVII centuries miniatures*, Dushanbe, 1974.

Bachinsky, N.M., *Reznoye derevo v arkhitekture Srednei Azii* (Carved Wood in Central Asian Architecture), Moscow, 1947.

Belenitsky, A., *The Ancient Civilization of Central Asia*, Geneva and London, 1969.*

Borovka, G.I., *Scythian Art*, London, 1928.

Bosworth, C.E., *The Development of Persian Culture*, London, 1977.

Canby, S.R., *Persian Painting*, London, 1993.

Cohn-Wiener, E., *Turan*, Berlin, 1930.*

Contenau, G., *Manuel d'archéologie orientale*, 4 vols, Paris, 1927–47.

Creswell, K.A.C., *Early Muslim Architecture*, 2 vols, London and New York, 1932, 1940.

Critchlow, K., *Islamic Patterns*, London, 1976.

Denike, B.P., *Arkhitekturnyi Ornament Srednei Azii* (Architectural Ornament in Central Asia), Moscow and Leningrad, 1939.

——— *Iskusstvo Srednei Azii* (The Art of Central Asia), Moscow, 1927.

Diez, E., *Iranische Kunst*, Vienna, 1944.

Ettinghausen, R., 'The Man-made Setting', *The World of Islam*, London, 1976.

Fischer, K., *Schöpfungen der indischen Kunst*, Köln, 1959.

Frumkin, G., 'Archaeology in Soviet Central Asia', I–VII (*Central Asian Review*, X/4; XI/I; XII/I; XII/3; XIII/I; XIII/3; XIV/I), 1963–66.

Ghirshman, R., *The Art of Ancient Persia*, Paris and New York, 1964.

——— *Iran*, Paris, 1951, London, 1954.*

Grabar, O., *Islamic Architecture and its Decoration*, Chicago, 1964.

Griaznov, M.P. and Bulgakov, A., *L'Art ancien de l'Altai*, Moscow, 1958.

Hillenbrand, R., *Islamic Architecture*, 1994.

Hoag, J.D., *Islamic Architecture*, London, 1979.

Hrbas, M. and Knobloch, E., *The Art of Central Asia*, Prague and London, 1965.*

Kühnel, E., 'Arabesque' (*Encyclopedie de l'Islam*, nouvelle édition, I, Paris, 1957).

—— *Islamische Schriftkunst*, Berlin and Leipzig, 1942.

Lavrov, V.A., *Gradostroitel'naya Kultura Srednei Azii* (Urban Civilisation in Central Asia), Moscow, 1960.

Melikian-Chirvani, 'Eastern Iranian Architecture', *BSOAS*, 1970.

Mongait, A.L., *Archaeology in the USSR*, Moscow, 1959; Baltimore, 1961.

Myrdal, J., *La route de la soie*, Paris, 1980.

Nilsen, V.A., *Stanovlenie feodal'noi arkhitektury Srednei Azii, V–VIII v.* (Principles of Feudal Architecture in Central Asia, Fifth to Eighth Centuries A.D.), Tashkent, 1966.

Pope, A.U., *A Survey of Persian Art*, 6 vols, London and New York, 1938–39, 1964.

—— *Persian Architecture*, London, 1965.*

Pugachenkova, G.A., *Pamyatniki arkhitektury Srednei Azii epokhi Navoyi* (Architectural Monuments in Central Asia from the Nawa'i era), Tashkent, 1957.

—— and Galerkina, O., *Miniatury Srednei Azii* (Central Asian Miniatures), Moscow, 1979.

—— and Rempel, L.I., *Istoriya iskusstva Uzbekistana* (A History of the Art of Uzbekistan), Moscow, 1965.

—— and Rempel, L.I., *Vydayushchiye pamyatniki arkhitektury Uzbekistana* (Important Architectural Monuments in Uzbekistan), Tashkent, 1958.

Rempel, L.I., *Arkhitekturnyi ornament Uzbekistana* (Architectural Ornament in Uzbekistan), Tashkent, 1961.*

Renz, A., *Geschichte und Stätten des Islam*, München, 1977.

Rostovtzev, M.I., *The Animal Style in South Russia and China*, Princeton, 1929.

Safadi, Hamid Y., *Islamic Calligraphy*, London, 1978.

Shishkin, V.A., *Goroda Uzbekistana* (The Cities of Uzbekistan [Tashkent, Samarkand, Bukhara]), Tashkent, 1943.*

Speltz, A., *Der Ornamentstil*, Leipzig, 1912.

Stein, M.A., *Archaeological Reconnaissances*, London, 1937.

Tadgell, C., *The History of Architecture in India*, London, 1990.

Talbot-Rice, T., *Ancient Art of Central Asia*, London, 1965.*

Trever, K.V., *Pamyatniki Greko-baktriyskogo iskusstva* (Monuments of Graeco-Bactrian Art), Moscow and Leningrad, 1940.

Umnyakov, I.I., *Arkhitekturnyie pamyatniki Srednei Azii: Issledovaniye, remont, restavratsiya* (Architectural Monuments of Central Asia: Exploration, Repairs, Restoration), Tashkent, 1929.

Veymarn, B.V., *Iskusstvo Srednei Azii* (The Art of Central Asia), Moscow, 1940.

Vogt-Göknil, U., *Les grands courants de l'architecture Islamique*, Paris, 1975.

von Wersin, Müller, Grah, *Das elementare Ormanet*, Ravensburg, 1940.

Welch, S.C., *Persische Buchmalerei*, München, 1976.

—— *King's Book of Kings*, New York, 1972.

Wilber, D.N., *The Architecture of Islamic Iran*, Princeton, 1955.

Woolley, L.C., *The Art of the Middle East*, New York, 1961.

Zasypkin, V.N., *Arkhitektura Srednei Azii* (The Architecture of Central Asia), Moscow, 1948.

—— *Architekturnyie pamyatniki Srednei Azii* (The Architectural Monuments of Central Asia), Moscow, 1928.

Zodchestvo Uzbekistana (Architecture of Uzbekistan), Tashkent, 1959.

TRAVEL

Beal, S. (tr.), *Travels of Fa-Hsien* [400] *and Sung Yun* [518], London, 1869.

Beazley, C.R., *Texts and Versions of Carpini and Rubruck*, London, 1903.

Burnes, A., *Travels into Bokhara*, London, 1834.

d'Avezac, M., *Recueil de voyages et de mémoires* (Latin text of J.P. Carpini), Paris, 1839.

Fleming, P., *News from Tartary*, London, 1935.

Gibb, H.A.R. (tr.), *The Travels of Ibn Battuta*, London, 1929.*

Giles, H.A. (ed.), *Fa-Sien, Travels 399–414 A.D.* or *Record of Buddhist Kingdoms*, Cambridge, 1923.

Jenkinson, A., *Early Voyages and Travels to Russia and Persia*, 2 vols, London, 1886.*

Julien, S. (tr.), *Hiuan-Tsiang: Mémoires sur les contrées occidentales*, Paris, 1857.

Knobloch, E. (tr.), *Putování k Mongolům* (*Carpini, Rubruck, Clavijo*), Prague, 1964.

Komroff, M., *Contemporaries of Marco Polo*, London, 1928.

Latham, R.E. (tr.), *The Travels of Marco Polo*, London, 1958.

Le Strange, G. (tr.), *Clavijo, Ruy Gonzales de: Embassy to Tamerlane*, London, 1928.*

Lunt, J., *Bokhara Burnes*, London, 1969.

Michel-Wright, *Recueil de voyages et de mémoires* (Latin text of W. Rubruck), Paris, 1839.

Nikitin, A., *Journeys across the Three Seas* (ed. by V.P. Adrianova-Perets, in Russian), Moscow, 1958.

Risch, G., *Johann de Plano Carpini*, Leipzig, 1930.

Rockhill, W., *The Journey of William of Rubruck*, London, 1900.

Telfer, J.B. (tr.), *Schiltberger, J.: Travels and Bondage*, London, 1879.

OTHER GENERAL SOURCES

'Art and Mankind', *Larousse Encyclopaedia*, I, Chapter 7; II, Chapters 1–3, Paris, 1957; London, 1962.

Bol'shaya Sovietskaya Entsiklopediia (Great Soviet Encyclopaedia), 2nd ed., Moscow, 1956.

ntral Asian Research Centre, *Bibliography of Recent Soviet Source Material*, 2 vols, London, 1959.

ntral Asian Review (CAR), 1963–66.

cyclopédie de l'Islam, nouvelle edition, Paris, 1957.

rt de l'Islam des origines à 1700 (catalogue), Paris, 1971.

wis, B., ed. *The World of Islam*, London, 1976.

KHOREZM

ılyamov, Y.G., *Pamyatniki goroda Khivy* (Monuments of Khiva), Tashkent, 1941.

aterialy Khorezmskoy ekspeditsii (Papers of the Khorezmian Expedition), nos 1–7, Moscow, 1959–63.

lyavsky, V.I., *Urgench i Mizdakhkan*, Moscow, 1948.

ılstov, S.P., 'Drevniy Khorezm' (Ancient Khorezm), *Po sledam drevnikh kultur* (Retracing Ancient Civilisations), Moscow, 1948.

—— *Po sledam drevnie-khorezmiiskoy tsivilizatsii* (Retracing the Civilisation of Ancient Khorezm), Moscow, 1948.*

—— *Po drevnim deltam Oksa i Yaksarta* (The Ancient Deltas of the Oxus and the Jaxartes), Moscow, 1962.

ainberg, B.I., 'Archaeological Material from Khorezm and the Problem of Kushan Chronology', *Abstracts of Papers*.

akubovsky, A.Y., *Razvaliny Urgencha* (The Ruins of Urgench), Leningrad, 1930.

ZARAFSHAN

iulyamov, Y.G., Islamov, U. and Askarov, A., *Pervobytnaya kultura i voznikoveniye oroshaemogo zemledeliya v nizovyakh Zerafshana* (Primitive Culture and the Appearance of Irrigated Agriculture in the Lower Zarafshan Region), Tashkent, 1966.

storiya Uzbekskoy S.S.R. (The History of the Uzbek S.S.R.), I, Tashkent, 1955.

Masson, M.E., *Sobornaya Mechet' Timura* (Timur's Cathedral mosque), Tashkent, 1926.

—— *Mavzoley Gur Emir* (The Mausoleum of Gur Emir), Tashkent, 1926.

—— *Registan i ego medresse* (Registan and its Madrasas), Tashkent, 1926.

Nilsen, V.A., *Monumental'naya arkhitektura bukharskogo oazisa, XI–XII. v.* (Monumental Architecture in the Bukhara Oasis, Eleventh to Twelfth Centuries), Tashkent, 1956.

Polupanov, S.N., *Arkhitekturnyie pamyatniki Samarkanda* (Architectural Monuments of Samarkand), Moscow, 1948.

Pugachenkova, G.A., *Po drevnim pamyatnikam Samarkanda i Bukhary* (Ancient Monuments of Samarkand and Bukhara), 2nd ed., Moscow, 1968.*

—— and Rempel, L.I., *Bukhara – Sokrovishche arkhitektury Uzbekistana* (Bukhara – Treasures of Uzbekistan Architecture), Tashkent, 1949.

—— 'Mazar Arab-Ata v Time' (Mausoleum Arab Ata in Tim), *Sov. Arkheologiya*, 1961.

Shishkin, V.A., *Arkhitekturnyie pamyatniki Bukhary* (Architectural Monuments of Bukhara), Tashkent, 1936.

—— *Varakhsha* (in Russian), Moscow, 1963.

Yakubovsky, A.Y., 'Drevnii Pyandzhikent' (Ancient Pendzhikent), in *Po sledam drevnikh kultur* (Retracing Ancient Civilisations), Moscow, 1961.

—— *Samarkand pri Timure i Timuridakh* (Samarkand under Timur and the Timurids), Leningrad, 1933.

—— and others, *Zhivopis drevnego Pyandzhikenta* (Paintings of Ancient Pendzhikent), Moscow, 1954.

Zhivopis i skulptura drevnego Pyandzhikenta (Paintings and Sculpture of Ancient Pendzhikent).

TURKMENISTAN

Dyakonov, I.M. and Livshits, V.A., *Documenty iz Nisy, I v. do n.e.* (Documents from Nisa, First Century B.C.), Moscow, 1960.

Freykin, Z.G., *Turkmenskaya S.S.R.*, Moscow, 1954.

Lecomte, O., 'Le complex culturel de Geoktchik Depe', *Archéologia* 352/99.

Masson, M.E. and Pugachenkova, G.A., *Parfyanskiye ritony Nisy*, Moscow, 1956. English tr. *The Parthian Rhytons from Nissa*, Ashkhabad, 1959.

Masson, V.M., *Neoliticheskiye poseleniya i srednevekovyie goroda* (Neolithic Settlements and Medieval Towns), 1971.

—— and Sarianidi, V.I., *Central Asia, Turkmenia before the Achaemenids*, 1972.

Pilipko, V.N., *Pozdneparfiiskiye pamiatniki Akhala* (Late-Parthian Monuments of Akhal), 1990.

Pribytkova, A.M., *Pamyatniki XI veka v Turkmenii* (Eleventh-century Monuments in Turkmenia), Moscow, 1955.

Pugachenkova, G.A. and Rempel, L.I., *Puti razvitiya arkhitektury yuzhnogo Turkmenistana* (Development of Architecture in South Turkmenistan), Moscow, 1958.

Pugachenkova, G.A. and Yelkovich, L.Y., *Ocherki po istorii iskusstva Turkmenistana* (Outline of History of Art of Turkmenistan), Ashkhabad, 1956.

Pumpelly, R., *Explorations in Turkestan, Expedition of 1904*, 1–2, Washington, 1908.

Shishkin, I.B., *U sten velikoi Namazgi* (At the Walls of the Great Namazga), 1977.

The Ancient Cities of Merv, International Merv Project, London 1996.

Trudy yuzhno-turkmenskoy arkheologicheskoy kompleksnoy ekspeditsii (Papers of the South Turkmenian Complex Archaeological Expedition – Yutake), I–XII, Ashkhabad, 1949–64.

hukovsky, V., 'Razvaliny starogo Merva' (The Ruins of Ancient Merv), *Materialy po arkheologii Rossiyi* (Papers on Russian Archaeology), no. 16, St. Petersburg, 1894.

THE AMU DARYA VALLEY AND SOUTHERN TAJIKISTAN

Ibaum, L.I., *Balalyk-Tepe*, Tashkent, 1960.

nnaev, T.D., *Rannesrednevekoyie poseleniya Severnogo Tokharistana* (Early Medieval Settlements in Northern Tokharistan), 1988.

alton, O.M., *The Treasure of the Oxus*, London, 1926, 3rd ed., 1964.

toriya tadzhikskogo naroda (The History of the Tajik People), I, Moscow, 1963.

iferev, O.V., Samusenko, V.E., *Kyrgyzstan, Tadzhikistan, Turkmenistan*, 1992.

uknitsky, P., *Tadzhikistan*, Moscow, 1951.

Iukhtarov, A., *Epigraficheskiye pamiatniki Kukhistana XI–XIX vekov* (Epigraphic Monuments in Kuhistan), 1978.

itchikjan, I.R., *Oxos-Schatz und Oxos-Tempel: Achämenidische Kunst in Mittelasien*, 1992.

'ugachenkova, G.A., *Khalchayan*, Tashkent, 1965.

—— and Rtveladze, E.V., *Severnaia Bakriia-Tokharistan* (Northern Bactria and Tokharistan), 1990.

'ermezskaya arkheologicheskaya ekspeditisiya' (The Termez Archaeological Expedition), *Publications of the Uzbek Academy of Sciences*, 1/2, Tashkent, 1945.

'urgunov, B.A., 'Ayrtam Town Site', *Abstracts of Papers*.

/ertogradova, V.V., *Indiiskaia epigrafika iz Kara-tepe v starom Termeze* (Indian Epigraphy from Kara-Tepe in Old Termez), 1995.

'asypkin, V.N., 'Pamyatniki arkhitektury termezskogo rayona' (Architectural Monuments in the Termez Region), *Kultura Vostoka* (Civilisation of the East), Moscow and Leningrad, 1928.

THE SYR DARYA AND FERGHANA VALLEYS

Azimdzhanova, S.A., *Istoriya Fergany v XV. veke* (History of Ferghana in the Fifteenth Century), Tashkent, 1957.

Bernshtam, A.N., *Po sledam drevnikh kultur* (Traces of Ancient Civilisations), 1954 (Tien-Shan).

Litvinsky, B.A., Okladnikov, A.P. and Ranov, V.A., *Drevnosti Kayrak-kumov* (The Ancient Past of the Kayrak Kum Desert), Dushanbe, 1962.

Tolstov, S.P., *Po drevnim deltam Oksa i Yaksarta*, Moscow, 1962.

Zasypkin, V.N., 'Pamyatniki Kasana i Safid Bulenda' (The Monuments of Kasan and Safid Bulend), *Skhidnii Svit*, 1929.

KAZAKHSTAN AND KIRGHIZSTAN

Akishev, K.A., *Proshloe Kazakhstana po arkheologicheskim istochnikam* (Archaelogical Sources of Kazakhstan's History), 1976.

Baipakov, K.M., *Po sledam drevnikh gorodov Kazakhstana* (Traces of Kazakhstan's Ancient Cities), 1990.

Dzhamgerchinov, B.D., *Stranitsy istorii i materialnoi kultury Kirghizstana* (Pages on History and Material Culture of Kirghizstan), 1975.

Davidovich, E.A., *Kirgiziia pri Karakhanidakh* (Kirghizia under the Karakhanids), 1983.

Mariashev, A.N., Rogozhinskii A.E., *Naskalnye izobrazheniya v gorakh Eskiolmes* (Rock-engravings in the Eskiolmes Mountains), 1991.

Tulepbaev, B.A., *Srednevekovaia gorodskaia kultura Kazakhstana i Srednei Azii* (Medieval Urban Civilisation in Kazakhstan and Central Asia), Alma Ata, 1983.

XINJIANG

Bussagli, M., *Paintings of Central Asia*, Geneva, 1963.

Dabbs, J.A., *The History of the Discovery and Exploration of Chinese Turkestan*, The Hague, 1963.

Davis-Kimball, J., 'The Kangjiashimenzi Petroglyphs in Xinjiang, Western China', *IESB* 7/2, 1999.

—— *Examples of Uyghur Architectural Art*, Kashgar, 1984.

Gray, B., *Buddhist Paintings of Tun-huang*, London, 1959.

Grünwedel, A., *Alt-Kutscha*, Berlin, 1920.

Le Coq, A. von, *Buried Treasures of Chinese Turkestan*, London, 1928.

—— and Waldschmidt, E., *Die Buddhistische Spätantike in Mittelasien*, 7 vols, Berlin, 1923–33.

Maillart, E., *Oasis interdites*, Paris, 1937, 1989.

Pelliot, P., 'Les Influences iraniennes en Asie Centrale et à L'Extrême Orient', *Revue d'histoire et de littérature réligieuse*, Fey, 1912.

—— *Les Grottes de Touen-houang*, 6 vols, Paris, 1920–24.

Poucha, P., *Do nitra Asie* (Innermost Asia), Prague, 1962.*

Stein, M.A., *Ancient Khotan*, Oxford, 1907.

—— *Ruins of Desert Cathay*, 2 vols, London, 1912.

—— *Sand-buried Ruins of Khotan*, London, 1903.

—— *Serindia*, Oxford, 1921.

—— *Innermost Asia*, Oxford, 1921.

—— *The Thousand Buddhas, Ancient Buddhist paintings from the Cave-temples of Tun-huang*, London, 1921–22.

—— *On Ancient Central Asian Tracks*, London, 1933.*

Wayland-Barber, E., *The Mummies of Urümchi*, London, 1999.

Yaldiz, M., *Archäologie und Kunstgeschichte Chinesisch-Zentralasiens (Xinjiang)*, Leiden-Köln, 1987.

AFGHANISTAN

Auboyer, J., *Afghanistan et son art*, Paris, 1968.*

Ball, W., Gardin, J.-C., *Archaeological gazeteer of Afghanistan*, 1982.

Baker, P.H.B., Allchin, F.R., *Shahr-i Zohak and the History of the Bamiyan Valley*, 1991.

Bernard, P., Francfort, H.P., *Etudes de géographie historique sur la plaine d'Aï-Khanoum*, 1978.

Byron, R., *The Road to Oxiana*, London, 1937.*

—— Timurid Monuments in Afghanistan', *IIIe Congres Int. d'art et d'archéologie iraniens*, 1935.

Bosworth, C.E., *The Ghaznavids*, Edinburgh, 1963.

—— *The Later Ghaznavids*, Edinburgh, 1978.

Barthoux, J.J., 'Les fouilles de Hadda', *Mém. DAFA* IV, 1933.

Dagens, E., Le Berre, M. and Schlumberger, D., *Monuments préislamiques d'Afghanistan*, Paris, 1964.

Diez, E. and Niedermeyer, O., *Afghanistan*, Leipzig, 1924.

Duprée, L., *Afghanistan*, Princeton, 1973.*

Duprée, N.H., *The National Museum of Afghanistan*, Kabul, 1974.

—— *The Road to Balkh*, Kabul, 1967.

—— *Herat*, Kabul, 1966.

Dyakonov, M.M., 'Drevnyaya Baktria' (Ancient Bactria) in *Po sledam drevnikh kultur* (Retracing Ancient Civilisations), Moscow, 1954.

Flury, S., 'Le décor épigraphique des monuments de Ghazna', *Syria*, VI, 1925.

Foucher, A., *L'Art gréco-bouddhique du Gandara*, 2 vols, Paris, 1905, 1951.

—— 'Notes sur les antiquités bouddhiques de Haïbak', *JA*, 1924.

Franz, G.H., 'Der buddhistische Stupa in Afghanistan', *AFJ* 4/4/1977.

Ghirshman, R. and T., *Bégram, Recherches archéologiques et historiques sur les Kouchans*, Cairo, 1946.

Gilles, R., 'L'Afghanistan, cinquante ans d'archéologie, vingt ans de guerre', *Archéologia*, 365/2000.

Godard, A., Godard, J. and Hackin, J., 'Les antiquités bouddhiques de Bamyian', *Mém. DAFA* II, 1928.

Golombek, L., *The Timurid Shrine at Gazur Gah*, Toronto, 1968.*

Hackin, J., *Recherches archéologiques en Asie Centrale*, Paris, 1936.

—— L'Oeuvre de la délégation archéologique française en Afghanistan, Paris, 1922–32.

—— L'Art bouddhique de la Bactriane et les orignes de l'art gréco-bouddhique, Kabul, 1937.

—— Buddhist Art in Central Asia, India Society, 1938.

Helms, S.W., Excavations at Old Kandahar in Afghanistan, 1976–8, London, 1997.

Knobloch, E., 'Survey of Archaeology and Architecture in Afghanistan' (Part I, The South), AFJ 1/8/1981.

Kruglikova, I.T., Dilberdzhin, khram Dioskurov, 1986.

LeBerre, M., Lashkar-i Bazar, Paris, 1978.

Lewis, J., 'Pillage d'une culture. Le patrimoine afghan en péril', Archéologia, 365/2000.

Marshall, Sir J., The Buddhist Art of Gandhara, Cambridge, 1960.

—— Taxila, 3 vols, Cambridge, 1951.

Masson, M.E., Termezskaya arkheologicheskaya ekspeditsiya, 1936–38 (The Termez Archaeological Expedition), 2 vols, Tashkent, 1941–43.

Melikian, S., 'Baba Hatem, un chef d'oeuvre inconnu d'époque ghaznévide en Afghanistan', in VIth Int. Congress on Iranian Art and Archaeology, Tehran, 1972.

Mizuno, S., Haibak and Kashmir-Smast, 1962.

McNicoll, A., 'Excavations at Kandahar, 1974', Afghan Studies, 1978.

Mukhtarov, A.M., Balkh in the late Middle Ages, Bloomington, 1993.

Papin, C., 'Fouilles d'Aï Khanoum', Mém. DAFA VIII, Paris, 1992.

Pugachenkova, G.A., Iskusstvo Afghanistana (The Art of Afghanistan), Moscow, 1963.

—— 'Mechet Nu Gumbad v Balkhe' (The No Gumbad Mosque in Balkh), Sov. Arkheologiya, 3, 1970.

Rowland, B., Ancient Art of Afghanistan, Treasures of the Kabul Museum, New York, 1966.

Sarianidi, V.I., The golden hoard of Bactria, New York, 1985.

Schlumberger, D., 'Aï-Khanoum, ville hellénistique du nord de l'Afghanistan', Revue Archéologique, II, 1964, pp. 196–7.

—— 'Aï-Khanoum, une ville hellénistique en Afghanistan', Comptes rendus de l'Académie des Inscriptions et Belles Lettres, I, 1965, p. 36.

—— 'Le palais ghaznévide de Lashkar-i Bazar', Syria, XXIX, 1952.

—— and Bernard, P., 'Aï-Khanoum', Bulletin de correspondance hellénique, LXXXIX, 1965, II, p. 590.

Sourdel-Thomine, J., 'Deux minarets de l'époque seljoukide en Afghanistan', Syria, XXX, 1953.

Sykes, P., History of Afghanistan, London, 1940.

Taizi Zemaryalai: Architecture et décor rupestre des grottes de Bamiyan, Paris, 1977.

Tarn, W.W., The Greeks in Bactria and India, 2nd ed., Cambridge, 1951.

Toynbee, A., Between Oxus and Jumna, London, 1961.

Waldschmidt, W., Gandara, Kutscha, Turfan, Leipzig, 1925.

Whitehouse, D., 'Excavations at Kandahar, 1974', Afghan Studies, 1978.

INDEX

Bold page numbers indicate main references in the text. Italic page numbers indicate map, plan or figure references.